Best Practices in
Data
Cleaning

This book is dedicated to my parents, James and Susan Osborne. They have always encouraged the delusions of grandeur that led me to write this book. Through all the bumps life placed in my path, they have been the constant support needed to persevere. Thank you, thank you, thank you.

I also dedicate this book to my children, Collin, Andrew, and Olivia, who inspire me to be the best I can be, in the vague hope that at some distant point in the future they will be proud of the work their father has done. It is their future we are shaping through our research, and I hope that in some small way I contribute to it being a bright one.

My wife deserves special mention in this dedication as she is the one who patiently attempts to keep me grounded in the real world while I immerse myself in whatever methodological esoterica I am fascinated with at the moment. Thank you for everything.

Best Practices in
Data
Cleaning

A Complete Guide to Everything You Need to Do Before and After Collecting Your Data

Jason W. Osborne
Old Dominion University

Los Angeles | London | New Delhi
Singapore | Washington DC

Los Angeles | London | New Delhi
Singapore | Washington DC

FOR INFORMATION:

SAGE Publications, Inc.
2455 Teller Road
Thousand Oaks, California 91320
E-mail: order@sagepub.com

SAGE Publications Ltd.
1 Oliver's Yard
55 City Road
London EC1Y 1SP
United Kingdom

SAGE Publications India Pvt. Ltd.
B 1/I 1 Mohan Cooperative Industrial Area
Mathura Road, New Delhi 110 044
India

SAGE Publications Asia-Pacific Pte. Ltd.
33 Pekin Street #02-01
Far East Square
Singapore 048763

Acquisitions Editor: Vicki Knight
Associate Editor: Lauren Habib
Editorial Assistant: Kalie Koscielak
Production Editor: Eric Garner
Copy Editor: Trey Thoelcke
Typesetter: C&M Digitals (P) Ltd.
Proofreader: Laura Webb
Indexer: Sheila Bodell
Cover Designer: Anupama Krishnan
Marketing Manager: Helen Salmon
Permissions Editor: Adele Hutchinson

Copyright © 2013 by SAGE Publications, Inc.

Printed in the United States of America

Library of Congress Cataloging-in-Publication Data

Osborne, Jason W.

Best practices in data cleaning : a complete guide to everything you need to do before and after collecting your data / Jason W. Osborne.

p. cm.
Includes bibliographical references and index.

ISBN 978-1-4129-8801-8 (pbk.)

1. Quantitative research. 2. Social sciences— Methodology. I. Title.

H62.O82 2013
001.4'2—dc23   2011045607

This book is printed on acid-free paper.

12 13 14 15 16 10 9 8 7 6 5 4 3 2 1

CONTENTS

PREFACE

If I am honest with myself, the writing of this book is primarily a therapeutic exercise to help me exorcize 20 or more years of frustration with certain issues in quantitative research. Few concepts in this book are new—many are the better part of a century old. So why should you read it? Because there are important steps every quantitative researcher should take prior to collecting their data to ensure the data meet their goals. Because after collecting data, and before conducting the critical analyses to test hypotheses, other important steps should be taken to ensure the ultimate high quality of the results of those analyses. I refer to all of these steps as *data cleaning*, though in the strictest sense of the concept, planning for data collection does not traditionally fall under that label.

Yet careful planning for data collection is critically important to the overall success of the project. As I wrote this book, it became increasingly evident to me that without some discussion on these points, the discussion on the more traditional aspects of data cleaning were moot. Thus, my inclusion of the content of the first few chapters.

But why the need for the book at all? The need for data cleaning and testing of assumptions is just blatantly obvious, right? My goal with this book is to convince you that several critical steps should be taken prior to testing hypotheses, and that your research will benefit from taking them. Furthermore, I am not convinced that most modern researchers perform these steps (at the least, they are failing to report having performed these actions). Failing to do the things I recommend in this book leaves you with potential limitations and biases that are avoidable. If your goal is to do the best research you can do, to draw conclusions that are most likely to be accurate representations of the population(s) you wish to speak about, to report results that are most likely to be replicated by other researchers, then this is a basic guidebook to helping accomplish these goals. They are not difficult, they do not take a long time to master, they are mostly not novel, and in the grand scheme of things, I am frankly baffled as to why anyone would *not* do them. I demonstrate the benefits in detail throughout the book, using real data.

Scientists in other fields often dismiss social scientists as unsophisticated. Yet in the social sciences, we study objects (frequently human beings) that are uniquely challenging. Unlike the physical and biological sciences, the objects we study are often studying us as well and may not be motivated to provide us with accurate or useful data. Our objects vary tremendously from individual to individual, and thus our data are uniquely challenging. Having spent much of my life focusing on research in the social sciences, I obviously value this type of research. Is the research that led me to write this book proof that many researchers in the social sciences are lazy, ill-prepared, or unsophisticated? Not at all. Most quantitative researchers in the social sciences have been exposed to these concepts, and most value rigor and robustness in their results. So why do so few report having performed these tasks I discuss when they publish their results?

My theory is that we have created a mythology in quantitative research in recent decades. We have developed traditions of doing certain things a certain way, trusting that our forebears examined all these practices in detail and decided on the best way forward. I contend that most social scientists are trained implicitly to focus on the hypotheses to be tested because we believe that modern research methods somehow overcome the concerns our forebears focused on—data cleaning and testing of assumptions.

Over the course of this book, I attempt to debunk some of the myths I see evident in our research practices, at the same time highlighting (and demonstrating) the best way to prepare data for hypothesis testing.

The myths I talk about in this book, and do my best to convincingly debunk, include the following.

- The *myth of robustness* describes the general feeling most researchers have that most quantitative methods are "robust" to violations of assumptions, and therefore testing assumptions is anachronistic and a waste of time.
- The *myth of perfect measurement* describes the tendency of many researchers, particularly in the social sciences, to assume that "pretty good" measurement is good enough to accurately describe the effects being researched.
- The *myth of categorization* describes many researchers' belief that dichotomizing continuous variables can legitimately enhance effect sizes, power, and the reliability of their variables.

- The *myth of distributional irrelevance* describes the apparent belief that there is no benefit to improving the normality of variables being analyzed through parametric (and often nonparametric) analyses.
- The *myth of equality* describes many researchers' lack of interest in examining unusually influential data points, often called *extreme scores* or *outliers,* perhaps because of a mistaken belief that all data points contribute equally to the results of the analysis.
- The *myth of the motivated participant* describes the apparent belief that all participants in a study are motivated to give us their total concentration, strong effort, and honest answers.

In each chapter I introduce a new myth or idea and explore the empirical or theoretical evidence relating to that myth or idea. Also in each chapter, I attempt to demonstrate in a convincing fashion the truth about a particular practice and why you, as a researcher using quantitative methods, should consider a particular strategy a best practice (or shun a particular practice as it does not fall into that category of best practices).

I cannot guarantee that, if you follow the simple recommendations contained in this book, all your studies will give you the results you seek or expect. But I can promise that your results are more likely to reflect the *actual state of affairs in the population of interest* than if you do not. It is similar to when your mother told you to eat your vegetables. Eating healthy does not guarantee you will live a long, healthy, satisfying life, but it probably increases the odds. And in the end, increasing the odds of getting what we want is all we can hope for.

I wrote this book for a broad audience of students, professors teaching research methods, and scholars involved in quantitative research. I attempt to use common language to explore concepts rather than formulas, although they do appear from time to time. It is not an exhaustive list of every possible situation you, as a social scientist, might experience. Rather, it is an attempt to foment some modest discontent with current practice and guide you toward improving your research practices.

The field of statistics and quantitative methodology is so vast and constantly filled with innovation that most of us remain merely partially confused fellow travelers attempting to make sense out of things. My motivation for writing this book is at least partly to satisfy my own curiosity about things I have believed for a long while, but have not, to this point, systematically tested and collected.

I can tell you that despite more than 20 years as a practicing statistician and 13 years of teaching statistics at various levels, I still learned new things in the process of writing this book. I have improved my practices and have debunked some of the myths I have held as a result. I invite you to search for one way you can improve your practice right now.

This book (along with my many articles on best practices in quantitative methods) was inspired by all the students and colleagues who asked what they assumed was a simple question. My goal is to provide clear, evidence-based answers to those questions. Thank you for asking, and continue to wonder. Perhaps I will figure out a few more answers as a result.

If you disagree with something I assert in this book, and can demonstrate that I am incorrect or at least incomplete in my treatment of a topic, let me know. I genuinely want to discover the best way to do this stuff, and I am happy to borrow ideas from anyone willing to share. I invite you to visit my webpage at http://best-practices-online.com/ where I provide data sets and other information to enhance your exploration of quantitative methods. I also invite your comments, suggestions, complaints, constructive criticisms, rants, and adulation via e-mail at jasonwosborne@gmail.com.

ABOUT THE AUTHOR

Jason W. Osborne is currently an Associate Professor of Educational Psychology at Old Dominion University. He teaches and publishes on best practices in quantitative and applied research methods. He has served as evaluator or consultant on projects in public education (K–12), instructional technology, higher education, nursing and health care, medicine and medical training, epidemiology, business and marketing, and jury selection. He is chief editor of *Frontiers in Quantitative Psychology and Measurement* as well as being involved in several other journals. Jason also publishes on identification with academics (how a student's self-concept impacts motivation to succeed in academics) and on issues related to social justice and diversity (such as stereotype threat). He is the very proud father of three and, along with his two sons, is currently a second degree black belt in American tae kwon do.

⚜ ONE ⚜

WHY DATA CLEANING IS IMPORTANT

Debunking the Myth of Robustness

You must understand fully what your assumptions say and what they imply. You must not claim that the "usual assumptions" are acceptable due to the robustness of your technique unless you really understand the implications and limits of this assertion in the context of your application. And you must absolutely never use any statistical method without realizing that you are implicitly making assumptions, and that the validity of your results can never be greater than that of the most questionable of these.

(Vardeman & Morris, 2003, p. 26)

The applied researcher who routinely adopts a traditional procedure without giving thought to its associated assumptions may unwittingly be filling the literature with nonreplicable results.

(Keselman et al., 1998, p. 351)

Scientifically unsound studies are unethical.

(Rutstein, 1969, p. 524)

Many modern scientific studies use sophisticated statistical analyses that rely upon numerous important assumptions to ensure the validity of the results and protection from undesirable outcomes (such as Type I or

Type II errors or substantial misestimation of effects). Yet casual inspection of respected journals in various fields shows a marked absence of discussion of the mundane, basic staples of quantitative methodology such as data cleaning or testing of assumptions. As the quotes above state, this may leave us in a troubling position: not knowing the validity of the quantitative results presented in a large portion of the knowledge base of our field.

My goal in writing this book is to collect, in one place, a systematic overview of what I consider to be *best practices* in data cleaning—things I can demonstrate as making a difference in your data analyses. I seek to change the status quo, the current state of affairs in quantitative research in the social sciences (and beyond).

I think one reason why researchers might not use best practices is a lack of clarity in exactly *how* to implement them. Textbooks seem to skim over important details, leaving many of us either to avoid doing those things or having to spend substantial time figuring out how to implement them effectively. Through clear guidance and real-world examples, I hope to provide researchers with the technical information necessary to successfully and easily perform these tasks.

I think another reason why researchers might not use best practices is the difficulty of changing ingrained habits. It is not easy for us to change the way we do things, especially when we feel we might already be doing a pretty good job. I hope to motivate practice change through demonstrating the benefits of particular practices (or the potential risks of failing to do so) in an accessible, practitioner-oriented format, I hope to reengage students and researchers in the importance of becoming familiar with data *prior* to performing the important analyses that serve to test our most cherished ideas and theories. Attending to these issues will help ensure the validity, generalizability, and replicability of published results, as well as ensure that researchers get the power and effect sizes that are appropriate and reflective of the population they seek to study. In short, I hope to help make our science more valid and useful.

ORIGINS OF DATA CLEANING

Researchers have discussed the importance of assumptions from the introduction of our early modern statistical tests (e.g., Pearson, 1931; Pearson, 1901; Student, 1908). Even the most recently developed statistical tests are developed in a context of certain important assumptions about the data.

Mathematicians and statisticians developing the tests we take for granted today had to make certain explicit assumptions about the data in order to formulate the operations that occur "under the hood" when we perform statistical analyses. A common example is that the data are normally distributed, or that all groups have roughly equal variance. Without these assumptions the formulae and conclusions are not valid.

Early in the 20th century, these assumptions were the focus of much debate and discussion; for example, since data rarely are perfectly normally distributed, how much of a deviation from normality is acceptable? Similarly, it is rare that two groups would have exactly identical variances, so how close to equal is good enough to maintain the goodness of the results?

By the middle of the 20th century, researchers had assembled some evidence that some minimal violations of some assumptions had minimal effects on error rates under certain circumstances—in other words, if your variances are not identical across all groups, but are relatively close, it is probably acceptable to interpret the results of that test despite this technical violation of assumptions. Box (1953) is credited with coining the term *robust* (Boneau, 1960), which usually indicates that violation of an assumption does not substantially influence the Type I error rate of the test. Thus, many authors published studies showing that analyses such as simple one-factor analysis of variance (ANOVA) analyses are "robust" to nonnormality of the populations (Pearson, 1931) and to variance inequality (Box, 1953) when group sizes are equal. This means that they concluded that modest (practical) violations of these assumptions would not increase the probability of Type I errors (although even Pearson, 1931, notes that strong nonnormality can bias results toward increased Type II errors).

Remember, much of this research arose from a debate as to whether even minor (but practically insignificant) deviations from absolute normality or exactly equal variance would bias the results. Today, it seems almost silly to think of researchers worrying if a skew of 0.01 or 0.05 would make results unreliable, but our field, as a science, needed to explore these basic, important questions to understand how our new tools, these analyses, worked.

Despite being relatively narrow in scope (e.g., primarily concerned with Type I error rates) and focused on what then was then the norm (equal sample sizes and relatively simple one-factor ANOVA analyses), these early studies appear to have given social scientists the impression that these basic assumptions are unimportant. Remember, these early studies were exploring, and they were concluding that under certain circumstances minor (again, practically insignificant) deviations from meeting the exact letter of the assumption (such as exact equality of variances) did not appreciably increase Type I error rates. These early studies do not mean, however, that all analyses are robust to dramatic violations of these assumptions, or to violations of these assumptions without meeting the other conditions (e.g., exactly equal cell sizes).

Despite all our progress, almost all our analyses are founded on important, basic assumptions. Without attending to these foundations, researchers may be unwittingly reporting erroneous or inaccurate results.

Note also that the original conclusion (that Type I error rates were probably not increased dramatically through modest violation of these assumptions under certain specific conditions) is a very specific finding and does not necessarily generalize to broad violations of any assumption under any condition. It is only focused on Type I error rates and does not deal with Type II error rates, as well as misestimation of effect sizes and confidence intervals.

Unfortunately, the latter points seem to have been lost on many modern researchers. Recall that these early researchers on "robustness" were often applied statisticians working in places such as chemical and agricultural companies as well as research labs such as Bell Telephone Labs, not in the social sciences where data may be more likely to be messy. Thus, these authors are viewing "modest deviations" as exactly that—minor deviations from mathematical models of perfect normality and perfect equality of variance that are practically unimportant. It is likely that social scientists rarely see data that are as clean as those produced in those environments.

Further, important caveats came with conclusions around robustness, such as adequate sample sizes, equal group sizes, and relatively simple analyses such as one-factor ANOVA.

This mythology of robustness, however, appears to have taken root in the social sciences and may have been accepted as broad fact rather than narrowly, as intended. Through the latter half of the 20th century, the term came to be used more often as researchers

---

Some Relevant Vocabulary

Type I Error Rate: the probability of rejecting the null hypothesis when in fact the null hypothesis is true in the population.

Type II Error Rate: the probability of failing to reject the null hypothesis when in fact the null hypothesis is false in the population.

Misestimation of Effect Size: failure to accurately estimate the true population parameters and effects.

Robust: generally refers to a test that maintains the correct Type I error rate when one or more assumptions is violated. In this chapter, I argue that robustness is largely a myth in modern statistical analysis.

published narrowly focused studies that appeared to reinforce the mythology of robustness, perhaps inadvertently indicating that robustness was the rule rather than the exception.

In one example of this type of research, studies reported that simple statistical procedures such as the Pearson product-moment correlation and the one-way ANOVA (e.g., Feir-Walsh & Toothaker, 1974; Havlicek & Peterson, 1977) were robust to even "substantial violations" of assumptions.[1] It is perhaps not surprising that robustness appears to have become unquestioned canon among quantitative social scientists, despite the caveats to these latter assertions, and the important point that these assertions of robustness usually relate only to Type I error rates, yet other aspects of analyses (such as Type II error rates or the accuracy of the estimates of effects) might still be strongly influenced by violation of assumptions.

However, the finding that simple correlations might be robust to certain violations is not to say that similar but more complex procedures (e.g., multiple regression) are equally robust to these same violations. Similarly, should one-way ANOVA be robust to violations of assumptions,[2] it is not clear that similar but more complex procedures (e.g., factorial ANOVA or analysis of covariance—ANCOVA) would be equally robust to these violations. Yet as social scientists adopted increasingly complex procedures, there is no indication that the issue of data cleaning and testing of assumptions was revisited by the broad scientific community. Recent surveys of quantitative research in the social sciences affirms that a relatively low percentage of authors in recent years report basic information such as having checked for extreme scores or normality of the data, or having tested assumptions of the statistical procedures being used (Keselman, et al., 1998; Osborne, 2008b; Osborne, Kocher, & Tillman, 2011). It seems, then, that this mythology of robustness has led a substantial percentage of social science researchers to believe it unnecessary to check the goodness of their data and the assumptions that their tests are based on (or to report having done so).

With this book, I aim to change that. I will show how to perform these basic procedures effectively, and perhaps more importantly, show you why it is important to engage in these mundane activities.

ARE THINGS REALLY THAT BAD?

Recent surveys of top research journals in the social sciences confirm that authors (as well as reviewers and editors) are disconcertingly casual about data cleaning and reporting of tests of assumptions. One prominent review of education and psychology research by Keselman and colleagues (1998) provided a thorough review of empirical social science during the 1990s. The authors reviewed studies from 17 prominent journals spanning different areas of education and psychology, focusing on empirical articles with ANOVA-type designs.

In looking at 61 studies utilizing univariate ANOVA between-subjects designs, the authors found that only 11.48% of authors reported anything related to assessing normality, almost uniformly assessing normality through descriptive rather than inferential methods.[3] Further, only 8.20% reported assessing homogeneity of variance, and only 4.92% assessed both distributional assumptions and homogeneity of variance. While some earlier studies asserted ANOVA to be robust to violations of these assumptions (Feir-Walsh & Toothaker, 1974), more recent work contradicts this long-held belief, particularly where designs extend beyond simple one-way ANOVA and where cell sizes are unbalanced, which seems fairly common in modern ANOVA analyses within the social sciences (Lix, Keselman, & Keselman, 1996; Wilcox, 1987).

In examining articles reporting multivariate analyses, Keselman and colleagues (1998) describe a more dire situation. None of the 79 studies utilizing multivariate ANOVA procedures reported examining relevant assumptions of variance homogeneity, and in only 6.33% of the articles was there any evidence of examining of distributional assumptions (such as normality).

Similarly, in their examination of 226 articles that used some type of repeated-measures analysis, only 15.50% made reference to some aspect of assumptions, but none appeared to report assessing sphericity, an important assumption in these designs that when violated can lead to substantial inflation of error rates and misestimation of effects (Maxwell & Delaney, 1990, p. 474).

Finally, their assessment of articles utilizing covariance designs ($N = 45$) was equally disappointing—75.56% of the studies reviewed made no mention of any assumptions or sample distributions, and most (82.22%) failed to report any information about the assumption of homogeneity of regression slope, an assumption critical to the validity of ANCOVA designs.

Another survey of articles published in 1998 and 1999 volumes of well-respected educational psychology journals (Osborne, 2008b) showed that indicators of high-quality data cleaning in those articles were sorely lacking. Specifically, authors in these top educational psychology journals almost never reported testing any assumptions of the analyses used (only 8.30%

reported having tested any assumption). Only 26.0% reported reliability of data being analyzed, and none reported any significant data cleaning (e.g., examination of data for outliers, normality, analysis of missing data, random responding).

Finally, a recent survey of recent articles published in prominent American Psychological Association (APA) journals' 2009 volumes (Osborne, et al., 2011) found improved, but uninspiring results (see Figure 1.1). For example, the percentage of authors reporting data cleaning ranged from 22% to 38% across journals. This represents a marked improvement from previous surveys, but still leaves a majority of authors failing to report any type of data cleaning or testing of assumptions, a troubling state of affairs.

Similarly, between 16% and 18% reported examining data for extreme scores (outliers), 10% and 32% reported checking for distributional assumptions (i.e., normality), and 32% and 45% reported dealing with missing data in

Figure 1.1   Percentage of Papers Reporting Having Checked for Each Data Cleaning Aspect

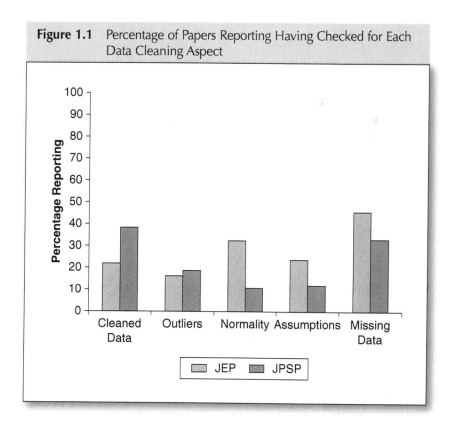

some way. Clearly, even in the 21st century, the majority of authors in highly respected scholarly journals fail to report information about these basic issues of quantitative methods.

WHY CARE ABOUT TESTING ASSUMPTIONS AND CLEANING DATA?

Contrary to earlier studies, it is not clear that most statistical tests are robust to most violations of assumptions, at least not in the way many researchers seem to think. For example, research such as that by Havlicek and Peterson (1977) shows one-factor ANOVA to be more robust to violations of distributional assumptions than violations of the assumption of homogeneity of variance, but primarily when cell sizes are equal. One-way ANOVA appears to be less robust to violations of distributional assumptions when cell sizes are unequal, or to violations of variance homogeneity under equal or unequal cell sizes (e.g., Lix, et al., 1996; Wilcox, 1987). Yet this information about the robustness of simple one-way ANOVA, a relatively rare procedure in modern times, does little to inform us as to the relative robustness of more complex ANOVA-type analyses. In fact, recent arguments by research ethicists such as Vardeman and Morris (2003) state that statistical assumptions must be routinely assessed in order to ensure the validity of the results, and researchers such as Rand Wilcox (e.g., 2003, 2008) have made contributions by providing strong alternatives to traditional procedures for use when typical parametric assumptions fail the researcher.

One of the primary goals of this book is to convince researchers that, despite a seemingly ingrained mythology of robustness, it is in the best interests of everyone concerned to screen and clean data and test assumptions. While robustness research often focuses on Type I error rates (which are important), cleaning data and attending to assumptions also can have important beneficial effects on power, effect size, and accuracy of population estimates (and hence, replicability of results), as well as minimizing the probability of Type II error rates.

HOW CAN THIS STATE OF AFFAIRS BE TRUE?

So how is it that we have come to this place in the social sciences? In the beginning of the 20th century, researchers explicitly discussed the importance of testing assumptions. Yet contemporary researchers publishing in prominent empirical journals seem not to pay attention to these issues. Is it possible that authors, editors, reviewers, and readers are unaware of the importance of data screening and cleaning? Perhaps. It is true that most modern statistical textbooks seem to provide little concrete guidance in data cleaning and testing of assumptions, and it is also true that many modern statistical packages do not always provide these tests automatically (or provide guidance on how to interpret them). I have taught graduate statistics classes for many years now, and having surveyed many textbooks, I am troubled at how few seem to motivate students (and researchers) to focus on these issues. Even when texts do discuss these issues, it is often abstractly and briefly, giving the reader little concrete guidance on how to perform these tests and how to think about the results of the tests of assumptions. It is possible that many students complete their doctoral training in the social sciences without focusing on these seemingly mundane issues.

It also is possible that some portion of researchers are faithfully testing assumptions and not reporting having done so. I would encourage all researchers to both *perform and report the results of* data cleaning and testing assumptions, even if no action is necessary. It gives the reader confidence in the results.

Data cleaning and testing of assumptions remain as relevant and important today as a century ago, and perhaps even more so. Data cleaning is critical to the validity of quantitative methods. Not only can problematic data points lead to violation of other assumptions (e.g., normality, variance homogeneity) but can lead to misestimation of parameters and effects without causing severe violation of assumptions. For example, in Chapter 7 I demonstrate that effectively dealing with extreme scores can improve the accuracy of population parameter estimates, decrease Type I and Type II errors, and enhance effect sizes and power.

There is good evidence that two of the most basic assumptions in many statistical procedures (that data come from populations that conform to the normal density function with homogenous variances) appear rarely met in practice (Micceri, 1989). This raises important concerns about the validity of conclusions based on these assumptions in the absence of overt information about whether they are met. Further, I will demonstrate how paying attention to basic issues such as distributional assumptions may protect researchers from errors of inference, as well as lead to strengthened effect sizes (and hence, power and significance levels). These are not only relevant to parametric statistical procedures, coincidentally. Meeting these distributional assumptions also can positively influence the results of nonparametric analyses (e.g., Zimmerman, 1994, 1995, 1998).

Additionally, I will review issues such as the importance of dealing with missing data effectively, response sets and how they can bias your results, the basic mechanics of identifying and dealing with extreme or influential scores, performing data transformations, issues around data cleaning when the data consist of repeated measures, and using data sets that involve complex sampling. In each chapter, my goal is to use empirical evidence and theory to guide the quantitative researcher toward best practices in applied quantitative methods.

THE BEST PRACTICES ORIENTATION OF THIS BOOK

It is my belief that quantitative researchers should be able to defend their practices as being the best available, much like medical doctors are encouraged to use the best practices available. In this spirit, I attempt to empirically demonstrate each major point in this book. For example, many authors have argued that removal of outliers (or influential scores) does harm to the data and the results, while others have argued that failure to do so damages the replicability of the results.[4] In my mind, it is less interesting to debate the philosophical aspects than to examine the evidence supporting each side. We, as quantitative researchers, should be able to definitively test which perspective is right and find evidence supporting a course of action. In the chapter on extreme scores (Chapter 7), I attempt to assemble a compelling empirical argument showing that it is a best practice to examine your data for influential data points, and to thoughtfully consider the benefits and costs of different courses of action. Similarly, there has been debate about whether it is appropriate to transform data to improve normality and homogeneity of variance. Again, I think that is something we can test empirically, and thus in Chapter 8 I attempt to persuade the reader through evidence that there are good reasons for considering data transformations. Further, in that chapter I present evidence that there are ways to perform transformations that will improve the outcomes.

Thus, the spirit of the book is evidence based. If I cannot demonstrate the benefit or importance of doing something a particular way, I will not recommend it as a best practice. Further, if I cannot clearly show you how to incorporate a practice into your statistical routine, I will not recommend it as a best practice. In other words, I propose that we as a field move toward a "survival of the fittest" mentality in our statistical practices. If we can show that, under certain circumstances, one practice is better than another, we should adopt it as a best practice, and shun others as less effective, at least in those situations where we have demonstrated a clear advantage of one technique over another.

As we move toward increasing specialization in the sciences, I believe it is unrealistic for scholars to remain current and expert in all areas. Thus, we need a cadre of statistical scholars who push the envelopes of innovation, who blaze the trail practitioners use, but we can no longer expect all researchers to be scholars of statistical methods. We must create clear, practitioner-oriented guidelines that help researchers get the best outcomes possible without assuming they are masters of matrix algebra and statistical theory. In this vein, my goal in each chapter is to make procedures explicit so that practitioners can successfully apply them. I encourage my colleagues to do the same. Just as practicing nurses and doctors need explicit, research-based guidelines on implementing best practices, practicing researchers need clear guidance in order to do the greatest good.

DATA CLEANING IS A SIMPLE PROCESS; HOWEVER . . .

In conceptualizing this book, I intended to produce a simple series of procedures that researchers could follow. Yet the more deeply I delved into this world, the more I realized that this is often not a simple, linear process. There is an art to data cleaning and statistical analysis that involves application of years of wisdom and experience. Not all readers at this time have extensive wisdom and experience with quantitative data analysis. Thus, the best you can do is to use your best professional judgment at all times. Every data set presents unique opportunities and challenges, and statistical analysis cannot be reduced to a simple formulaic approach. To do so ignores the complexities of the processes we deal with in the research enterprise and opens the researcher to miscarriages of scientific justice. This book is a beginning, not an end, to your exploration of these concepts. I cannot anticipate every eventuality, so all researchers must take the advice contained within as a set of guidelines that (I hope) generally work in most cases, but may not be appropriate in your particular case. This is where the art of data analysis meets the science of statistics. Intimate familiarity with your own data, experience, and solid training in best practices will prepare you to be optimally successful in most cases, but only you can determine when it is appropriate to deviate from recommended best practices. The only thing I would suggest is that whatever decisions you make in a particular analysis, you should be able to justify your course of action to a disinterested party (e.g., a qualified peer reviewer or dissertation committee member).

ONE PATH TO SOLVING THE PROBLEM

As my students (Brady Kocher and David Tillman) and I explored the mysteries surrounding statistical practice this past year, it has become increasingly clear that the peer review and publishing process itself can be part of the solution to the issue of data cleaning.

It may be the case that some portion of researchers publishing in the journals we examined did faithfully screen and clean their data and faithfully ensure that important assumptions were met prior to submitting the research for peer review. Perhaps these aspects of data analysis are viewed as too mundane or unimportant to report. Alternatively, some portion of researchers may be aware of the tradition of screening and cleaning data but for some reason may be under the impression that when using modern statistical methods and modern statistical software it is unnecessary to screen and clean data. In a perfect world, editors and peer reviewers would serve as a methodological safety net, ensuring that these important issues are paid attention to.[5]

Regrettably, the usual peer-review process implemented by most scholarly journals seems ill-prepared to remedy this situation. Elazar Pedhazur, in Chapter 1 of *Multiple Regression in Behavioral Research* (Pedhazur, 1997), is even stronger in indicting current research quality in the social sciences, and the failure of the peer review process:

> Many errors I draw attention to are so elementary as to require little or no expertise to detect. . . . Failure by editors and referees to detect such errors makes one wonder whether they even read the manuscripts. (p. 10).

Unfortunately, Pedhazur is not the only prominent scholar to question the quality of the traditional peer-review process (see also Kassirer & Campion, 1994; Mahoney, 1977; Peters & Ceci, 1982; Weller, 2001). Reviews of the literature (e.g., Hall, Ward, & Comer, 1988) going back decades find that a disturbingly large portion of published educational research appears to contain serious methodological flaws. Many of these errors are unnecessary and largely the result of poor methodological training (e.g., Thompson, 1999).

Yet as problematic as peer review might be, in at least one specific instance it appears that the system may have worked as a powerful agent of positive change in statistical practice. In 1999 the APA released guidelines for statistical methods in psychology journals (Wilkinson & Task Force on Statistical Inference, 1999) that specified that effect sizes should be routinely reported. In response, many journals now include effect size reporting in their author guidelines and review criteria, and as a result, we have seen a substantial increase in the reporting of effect size, at least partly because journal gatekeepers were mandating it. In the same spirit, it would be simple for professional organizations such as the APA to mandate authors report on data screening, cleaning, and testing of assumptions.

Until that day, I hope this book encourages you, the reader, to change your practice to incorporate these easily-to-use techniques that can have unexpected payoffs. This book continues the spirit of best practices begun in my first edited volume (Osborne, 2008a) by presenting researchers with clear, easily implemented suggestions that are research based and will motivate change in practice by empirically demonstrating, for each topic, the benefits of following best practices and the potential consequences of *not* following these guidelines.

FOR FURTHER ENRICHMENT

1. Review the author instructions for journals generally considered to be top tier or most respected in your field. See if any of them explicitly instruct authors to report testing assumptions, data cleaning, or any of the other issues we raise.

2. On our book's website (http://best-practices-online.com/), I provide links to author instructions from journals in various fields. Which journals or fields have the most explicit author instructions? Which have the least explicit instructions? Can you see any differences in the articles contained in journals that have more explicit directions for authors?

3. Review a recent study of yours (or your advisor) where statistical assumptions were not tested and where the data are still available (we all have

them, and I am as guilty as everyone else). As you work through this book, apply the various data cleaning techniques and test all assumptions for all statistical tests used in the study. Perhaps all the assumptions are met and your results now have even more validity than you imagined. Congratulations! Perhaps after cleaning the data and testing assumptions, your results are changed. Sometimes that can be a positive outcome, or sometimes that can be disappointing.

4. If you have an interesting example of results and conclusions that changed after revisiting a data set and testing assumptions, I would love to hear from you at jasonwosborne@gmail.com. Send me a summary of what you found, and how things changed.

NOTES

1. Yet again, it is important to point out that these studies are often focused narrowly on probability of Type I error rather than accuracy of parameter estimates or effect sizes. These latter aspects of analyses are often as important in modern research as the probability of making a Type I error.

2. To be clear, it is debatable as to whether these relatively simple procedures are as robust as previously asserted.

3. For more information on best practices in assessing normality, see Chapter 5.

4. These arguments are covered in greater depth in Chapter 7, and therefore are not reproduced here.

5. I must thank one of my doctoral committee members from years ago, Scott Meier, who gently reminded me to make sure I had done due diligence in cleaning my data and paying attention to extreme scores. Dr. Meier's gentle reminder salvaged what was turning out to be rather dismal results, allowing me to identify a very small number of inappropriately influential scores that were substantially biasing my results. Removal of these few scores led to strong support for my original hypotheses, as well as a two-decade-long appreciation of the power of "sweating the small stuff."

REFERENCES

Boneau, C. A. (1960). The effects of violations of assumptions underlying the t test. *Psychological Bulletin, 57*(1), 49-64. doi: 10.1037/h0041412

Box, G. (1953). Non-normality and tests on variances. *Biometrika, 40*(3–4), 318–335.

Feir-Walsh, B., & Toothaker, L. (1974). An empirical comparison of the ANOVA F-test, normal scores test and Kruskal-Wallis test under violation of assumptions. *Educational and Psychological Measurement, 34*(4), 789–799.

Hall, B. W., Ward, A. W., & Comer, C. B. (1988). Published educational research: An empirical study of its quality. *The Journal of Educational Research, 81*(3), 182–189.

Havlicek, L. L., & Peterson, N. L. (1977). Effect of the violation of assumptions upon significance levels of the Pearson r. *Psychological Bulletin, 84*(2), 373–377. doi: 10.1037/0033-2909.84.2.373

Kassirer, J., & Campion, E. (1994). Peer review: Crude and understudied, but indispensable. *JAMA, 272*(2), 96–97.

Keselman, H. J., Huberty, C. J., Lix, L. M., Olejnik, S., Cribbie, R. A., Donahue, B., Levin, J. R. (1998). Statistical practices of educational researchers: An analysis of their ANOVA, MANOVA, and ANCOVA analyses. *Review of Educational Research, 68*(3), 350–386.

Lix, L., Keselman, J., & Keselman, H. (1996). Consequences of assumption violations revisited: A quantitative review of alternatives to the one-way analysis of variance F test. *Review of Educational Research, 66*(4), 579–619.

Mahoney, M. (1977). Publication prejudices: An experimental study of confirmatory bias in the peer review system. *Cognitive Therapy and Research, 1*(2), 161–175.

Maxwell, S., & Delaney, H. (1990). Designing experiments and analyzing data: A model comparison perspective. Pacific Grove, CA: Brooks/Cole.

Micceri, T. (1989). The unicorn, the normal curve, and other improbable creatures. *Psychological Bulletin, 105*(1), 156–166. doi: 10.1037/0033-2909.105.1.156

Osborne, J. W. (2008a). *Best practices in quantitative methods.* Thousand Oaks, CA: Sage.

Osborne, J. W. (2008b). Sweating the small stuff in educational psychology: How effect size and power reporting failed to change from 1969 to 1999, and what that means for the future of changing practices. *Educational Psychology, 28*(2), 1–10.

Osborne, J. W., Kocher, B., & Tillman, D. (2011). *Sweating the small stuff: Do authors in APA journals clean data or test assumptions (and should anyone care if they do)?* Unpublished Manuscript, North Carolina State University.

Pearson, E. (1931). The analysis of variance in cases of non-normal variation. *Biometrika, 23*(1–2), 114–133.

Pearson, K. (1901). Mathematical contribution to the theory of evolution. VII: On the correlation of characters not quantitatively measurable. *Philosophical Transactions of the Royal Society of London, A 195*, 1–47.

Pedhazur, E. J. (1997). *Multiple regression in behavioral research: Explanation and prediction* (3rd. ed.). Fort Worth, TX: Harcourt Brace College.

Peters, D., & Ceci, S. (1982). Peer-review practices of psychological journals: The fate of published articles, submitted again. *Behavioral and Brain Sciences, 5*(2), 187–195.

Rutstein, D. D. (1969). The ethical design of human experiments. *Daedalus, 98*(2), 523–541.

Student. (1908). The probable error of a mean. *Biometrika, 6*(1), 1–25.

Thompson, B. (1999). Five methodology errors in educational research: The pantheon of statistical significance and other faux pas. In B. Thompson (Ed.), *Advances in social science methodology* (pp. 23–86). Stamford, CT: JAI Press.

Vardeman, S., & Morris, M. (2003). Statistics and ethics. *The American Statistician, 57*(1), 21–26.

Weller, A. (2001). *Editorial peer review: Its strengths and weaknesses.* Medford, N.J.: *Information Today.*

Wilcox, R. (1987). New designs in analysis of variance. *Annual Review of Psychology, 38*(1), 29–60.

Wilcox, R. (2003). *Applying contemporary statistical techniques.* San Diego: Academic Press.

Wilcox, R. (2008). Robust methods for detecting and describing associations. In J. W. Osborne (Ed.), *Best practices in quantitative methods* (pp. 266–280). Thousand Oaks, CA: Sage.

Wilkinson, L., & Task Force on Statistical Inference, APA Board of Scientific Affairs. (1999). Statistical methods in psychology journals: Guidelines and explanations. *American Psychologist, 54*(8), 594–604.

Zimmerman, D. W. (1994). A note on the influence of outliers on parametric and non-parametric tests. *Journal of General Psychology, 121*(4), 391–401.

Zimmerman, D. W. (1995). Increasing the power of nonparametric tests by detecting and downweighting outliers. *Journal of Experimental Education, 64*(1), 71–78.

Zimmerman, D. W. (1998). Invalidation of parametric and nonparamteric statistical tests by concurrent violation of two assumptions. *Journal of Experimental Education, 67*(1), 55–68.

❧ SECTION I ❧

BEST PRACTICES AS YOU
PREPARE FOR DATA COLLECTION

⚜ TWO ⚜

POWER AND PLANNING FOR DATA COLLECTION

Debunking the Myth of Adequate Power

A good friend and colleague recently came to me for help with data analysis for a study she was completing. In this study, teachers participated in professional development for new instructional technology and then received follow-up technical support as they attempted to incorporate the new technology into lesson plans. The 30 teachers were randomly assigned to receive support either traditionally (e.g., face-to-face, in person) or via video conferencing. This is a particularly interesting and important issue for teachers in rural and underserved areas where access to technical support may be scarce relative to teachers in suburban and relatively wealthy areas. The goal of the study was to explore whether there were any differences in teacher outcomes as a function of which type of technical support they received. The hope was that there were no differences between the two groups. In hypothesis testing terminology, my friend wanted to *retain the null hypothesis*, allowing her to assert that the two groups fared equally well regardless of which type of technical support they received.

Unfortunately, only 9 of 15 in one group and only 4 of 15 in another group returned follow-up surveys. Thus, when the data were analyzed, almost every statistical test was nonsignificant. My friend was initially delighted, believing this was evidence supporting her notion that teachers fare equally well with both types of technical support.

As is often the case, my friend's mood became more somber after talking to me.[1] She had the misfortune of approaching me for help with this study at the same time I was writing this chapter. From what little you know of her

19

study thus far, do you see any potential issues with drawing conclusions about the groups' equivalence?

POWER AND BEST PRACTICES IN STATISTICAL ANALYSIS OF DATA

"It may be accepted as a maxim that a poorly or improperly designed study involving human subjects—one that could not possibly yield scientific facts (that is, reproducible observations) . . . is by definition unethical." (Rutstein, 1969, p. 524)

Imagine you are planning a study. You have spent a great deal of time reviewing literature, figuring out how to measure the variables you need, planning your analyses, and probably imagining how the final published article will be received. How do you decide how many participants you need to include in your sample? Do you simply use as many as you can get to participate? That can be costly, but can definitely have benefits (e.g., more power, more representative sample). Do you go with the old[2] rule of thumb of 10 participants per variable (or group)? Do you choose a number that seems reasonable? Fortunately, there is a relatively simple, empirically valid method to estimate how large a sample you might need for any particular study using power analysis.

Statistical power is the ability to correctly reject a false null hypothesis (in other words, to detect effects when indeed effects are present) and is calculated based on a particular effect size, alpha level, and sample size as well as in the context of a particular analytic

Defining Some Key Terms

Statistical Power: is the ability to correctly reject a false null hypothesis. Power is conceptualized as the probability of rejecting a false null hypothesis. There are two types of power discussed in this chapter.

A Priori Power: is an estimate of power that is calculated prior to beginning a study that estimates how many data points a researcher needs, given a Type I error rate and estimated effect size.

A Posteriori Power: is power that is calculated after data are collected and analyzed. Similar to a priori power, this type of power tells a researcher the probability of correctly rejecting a false null hypothesis at a particular effect size, given the size of the sample in the data set.

strategy. Jacob Cohen (1962, 1988, 1992) spent many years encouraging the use of power analysis in planning research, reporting research, and interpreting results (particularly where null hypotheses are not rejected). Indeed authors were discussing the issue of power more than half a century ago (e.g., Deemer, 1947).

Though it is unclear how many researchers actually calculate power and sample size *before* conducting a study, when I reviewed some literature recently, few seemed to report having done so (in educational psychology journals, only 2% of articles in the 1998–99 volumes reported calculating power of any kind; see Osborne, 2008). This raises interesting questions about the science we rely on. Further, recent surveys of the literature generally indicate that a relatively low percentage of studies meet Cohen's criterion for "acceptable" power. I also reported that, although power in the field of psychology has increased from the 1960s to the 1990s, only 29% of randomized experimental studies, and only 44% of nonexperimental (or quasi-experimental) studies in prominent psychology journals met the criterion of having calculated power of .80 or higher (Osborne, 2008).

In this chapter I discuss how power is important in two different aspects of quantitative research: planning research sampling strategies and interpreting null results.

First, Cohen and others (see Cohen, 1962, 1988, 1992) have argued that no prudent researcher would conduct research without first making a priori analyses to determine the optimal sample size to maximize the probability of correctly rejecting the null hypothesis. Researchers who fail to do this risk having either (a) an insufficient sample size to detect the anticipated effect, thus wasting resources and effort, or (b) a sample that is far larger than needed to reliably detect an anticipated effect, thus wasting resources and effort on gathering substantially more data than is needed. As you might imagine, if you were planning for your dissertation this might be important information, particularly if it is difficult to gather data (or if you want to complete your degree in a reasonable timespan). You want to ensure you have enough power to adequately test your hypotheses, but do not want to waste extra months or years collecting unneeded data.

Second, a posteriori analyses of power are useful in shedding light on null results (i.e., the finding that there was no significant relationship between two variables or no significant differences between two or more groups). For example, in a study that fails to reject the null hypothesis, a power analysis can inform the researcher and reader about how to interpret the results. Failure to reject the null hypothesis when there was low power to detect effects of reasonable magnitudes (such as in my friend's case) is much less informative than when there was substantial power to detect effects of reasonable magnitude and still none are detected. In the latter case, one can be more certain that there truly are minimal differences between groups, whereas in the former case it is difficult to draw any clear conclusions about the data.

HOW NULL-HYPOTHESIS STATISTICAL TESTING RELATES TO POWER

Null-hypothesis statistical testing (NHST) has been reviled in the literature by many as counterproductive and misunderstood (for an excellent overview of the issues, see Fidler & Cumming, 2008; Killeen, 2008; Schmidt, 1996). Many authors have acknowledged the significant issues with NHST and some (Killeen, 2008; Schmidt, 1996) have proposed alternatives such as the probability of replication as a more interesting or useful replacement.

NHST is the classic procedure used in many areas of science where a scientist proposes two hypotheses. The first, a null hypothesis (H_o), is generally a hypothesis that there is no effect (e.g., no relationship, no difference between groups) and can be stated in very simple forms as:

$$H_o: r_{xy} = 0; \text{ or}$$

$$H_o: \bar{x}_1 = \bar{x}_2$$

Conversely, alternative hypotheses are generally what the researcher expects or hopes to find, and is often stated as a "significant effect" (e.g., a relationship between two or more variables, a significant difference between two or more groups).

$$H_a: r_{xy} \neq 0; \text{ or}$$

$$H_a: \bar{x}_1 \neq \bar{x}_2$$

One could imagine that it is often the case that few group averages are exactly identical and that few correlations between two variables are exactly

.00000. So in an absolute sense, it is almost always the case that null hypotheses are false if taken to enough decimal places (Cohen, 1988). In other words, group means of 50.000001 and 50.000002 are not equal in the strictest mathematical sense, but for practical purposes probably are functionally equal. Likewise, a correlation of .00001 is technically not equal to 0, but in a practical sense it is a little different. Further, it is possible to have two means that differ by hundreds (e.g., $\bar{x}_1 = 42,500.00$ and $\bar{x}_2 = 42,756.00$) and that look very different, yet one could imagine a scenario where those two means are not statistically or practically different (e.g., average yearly salaries, estimated number of years until a country's debt is paid off).

Thus, while it is often informative to look descriptively at what the data tells us, examples like this should make it clear that we need a better way of making decisions about our data. Inferential tests such as null-hypothesis statistical testing were developed to guide researchers in determining whether they could conclude that there was a significant effect (Fisher, 1925).

WHAT DO STATISTICAL TESTS TELL US?

Statistical tests tell us the probability of obtaining the observed results (the pattern of group means and standard deviations, or the observed correlation coefficient, F, odds ratio, r^2, and so on) if the null hypothesis were true in the population. In other words, the p value answers the following question: "What is the probability of getting the results observed in the data if in fact there are no group differences or no relationships in the population?" This concept is a little confusing at first, as we often are told that the p value is the probability of obtaining the results "by chance" or some similar, but technically inaccurate, interpretation.

Thus, we establish two different possible decisions we can make regarding our hypotheses and two different (yet unknowable) states of "reality." Take, for example, a simple comparison of two groups. It is possible that the two groups are either identical or different in some way. It is also possible that I, as a researcher, can draw one of two different conclusions about those groups based on data I collect: that the groups are significantly different or that the groups are not significantly different. As Table 2.1 shows, this gives us four possible outcomes, two of which are potential errors.

Table 2.1 Hypothesis Testing and Errors of Inference

		Population or Unknowable "Reality"	
		Groups are Not Different	**Groups are Different**
Decision Based on Data Gathered	**Groups are not Significantly Different**	Correct Decision	Type II Error
	Groups are Different	Type I Error	Correct Decision

Thus, we hope that our data lead to a correct decision, but it is possible that we make either a Type I error (concluding there is a significant effect when none exists in the population) or Type II error (failing to conclude a significant effect exists when there is in fact an effect in the population). Understandably, as our field evolved, a primary focus was on minimizing the probability of making a Type I error. For example, if I am testing a new drug on patients and comparing them to placebo or control groups, I want to be very sure that new drug is actually producing significant differences before recommending doctors prescribe it. Likewise, we want to be relatively certain that a psychological or educational intervention will produce the desired differences over existing interventions prior to recommending implementation. In the earlier decades of the 20th century this decision rule ($\alpha = .05$) was more flexible. At this point it is routinely assumed that we fix alpha at .05, meaning that we give ourselves only a 5% chance of making a Type I error in our decision making.

Thus, when performing statistical tests that give us probabilities (p values), we accepted the rule that if $p < .05$ (in other words, that there is less than a 5% chance that we would get the observed data from a population where the null hypothesis was true), then we reject the null hypothesis and conclude that significant differences exist between groups. Why, might you ask, are we happy to institutionalize a 5% chance of making such an important error? Why not set the bar at 1% or 0.01% so that we are very certain of not making an error of this type? We very well could do that, but in doing so, we would drastically increase the odds of making the other type of error, a Type II error. Thus, the scholars settled on 5% as small enough to avoid significant harm to the body of knowledge but large enough to avoid causing a high rate of the other type of error, which as you soon will see, can be equally problematic.

Significance tests *do not* tell us several critical things about our results. First, *p* values do not tell us the probability that the results would be replicated in a subsequent sample or study. In fact, it is power that gives us insight into the probability of replication given identical circumstances (Schmidt, 1996). Second, and most importantly, significance tests *do not* tell us the importance of a particular effect. We often see researchers use terms like *marginally significant, significant,* and *highly significant* to indicate ever smaller *p* values. Yet *p* values are determined by various factors, including sample size and effect size. Thus, a very small effect in a very large sample can have a very small *p* value, but be practically unimportant. Likewise, a large effect in a small sample (like my friend's study) may have a relatively large *p* value (i.e., *p* in excess of .05). And in neither case do we know anything about the probability of replicating the result unless we know the power of each test. Finally, *p* values do not tell us anything about the probability of making a Type II error (failing to reject a null hypothesis when there is a significant effect in the population). Only power can tell us the probability of making this type of error.

So what does failure to reject the null hypothesis mean? It is not clear that in the seminal works by Fisher (e.g., Fisher, 1925) he intended that failure to reject the null hypothesis to mean the *acceptance* of the null (Schmidt, 1996) as we often think today. In other words, if you fail to reject the null hypothesis, two different possibilities exist: (a) that you have no clear information about the nature of the effect, or (b) that you have sufficient information about the nature of the effect and you can conclude that the null is accurate. A similar issue exists within our U.S. criminal justice system. Failing to convict someone accused of a crime can mean: (a) that there is not sufficient evidence to convict, or (b) there is clear evidence of innocence.

This is an important distinction (in both the legal and scientific communities). Imagine the situation where you are evaluating two educational interventions, one that is very simple, traditional, and inexpensive, and one that uses expensive instructional technology in an attempt to improve student outcomes. Failure to reject the null could mean that you have insufficient information to draw any inferences or it could mean that the two interventions are not producing significantly different outcomes. The ability to conclude the null is valid is important from a policy perspective. It means school districts could save millions of dollars every year by implementing the "traditional" intervention in lieu of the high-technology intervention, as outcomes are identical. In contrast, not having enough information means just that: no conclusion is possible.

The difference between being unable to draw conclusions and being able to conclude the null hypothesis is valid is related to the power of the study. If the study had sufficient power to detect appropriate sized effects and failed to, that allows us to be more confident in concluding the null is supported. If the study did not have sufficient power to reliably detect appropriate sized effects, then no conclusion is possible. This is a common misconception in the scientific literature (Schmidt, 1996), and yet another reason to ensure you have the appropriate power in your research.

HOW DOES POWER RELATE TO ERROR RATES?

Power comes into play in this discussion in two different ways. First, power is the power to reject a false null hypothesis. In other words, if there really are differences between two groups in the unknowable "reality," a study with greater power will be more likely to reject the null hypothesis, leading the researcher to the correct conclusion—that there are differences between the groups (when in fact, differences between the groups exist). So, following our examples thus far, if you are testing a new drug and the drug is really having a beneficial effect on patients, power is the probability you will detect that effect and correctly reject the null hypothesis. Theoretically, if your power is .80, you will correctly reject the null hypothesis on average 80% of the time (given a particular effect size, sample size, and alpha level). Conversely, even in situations where there is a real effect in the population, and there are real group differences, with a power level of .80, 20% of the time you will *fail to detect that effect.* In other words, you may have a wonderfully effective drug that can save people from misery, disease, and death, but under this hypothetical scenario, 20% of the time you will not realize it. This is a Type II error—the failure to reject a null hypothesis when in the unknowable "reality" there is an effect.

As you can imagine, this is an undesirable outcome. While we want to be sure to avoid Type I errors (e.g., asserting an intervention is effective when in fact it is not), it seems to me equally troubling to fail to see effects when they are present. Fortunately, there is a simple way to minimize the probability of Type II errors—ensure you have sufficient a priori power to detect the expected effects. Researchers who fail to do a priori power analyses risk gathering too little or too much data to test their hypotheses. If a power analysis indicates that $N = 100$ subjects would be sufficient to reliably detect a particular effect,[3] gathering a sample of $N = 400$ is a substantial waste of resources.

Second, a posteriori analyses of power are useful in shedding light on null results. For example, if a study that fails to reject the null hypothesis had power of .90 to detect anticipated or reasonable effect sizes, one can be more confident that failing to reject the null was the correct decision, as well as more confident in asserting that the null hypothesis is an accurate description of the population effect. However, in the context of poor power, failure to detect a null hypothesis gives little information about whether a Type II error has occurred. Taking my friend's research on professional development for teachers, under the scenario described (four teachers in one group and nine teachers in another group who returned surveys), the power to detect a *moderately large* (e.g., $d = 0.50$) is only about .30 (see Figure 2.1). In other words, 70% of the time that analysis will miss an obvious effect just because there is not enough power to see it. Even if all teachers had returned their surveys, in the best case that study only had power of .45, meaning that more than half of the time a moderately sized effect will be missed solely due to lack of power. Given this, is it legitimate to conclude from her null results that the two groups were really equal? Or is it the case that we should be very cautious in concluding *anything* about the groups?

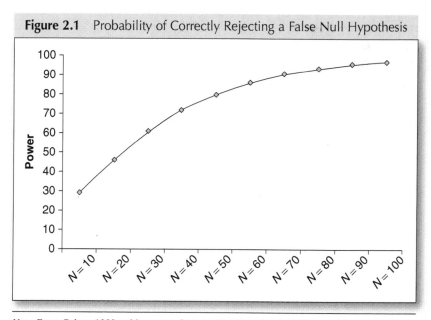

Figure 2.1   Probability of Correctly Rejecting a False Null Hypothesis

Note. From Cohen, 1988, p.30: power of t-test with effect size $d = 0.50$, $\alpha = .05$

LOW POWER AND TYPE I ERROR RATES IN A LITERATURE

Aside from Type II error rates, low power has implications for Type I error rates in the overall body of research. The social sciences have been accused of having low power as a field for many decades, despite the fact that some recent reviews of the literature, like mine (Osborne, 2008), find good power to detect effects in most studies. Rossi (1990) argued that the power of a group of studies can influence their reliability and usefulness as a whole. The argument Rossi proposed was that low power in a large group of studies can increase the proportion of Type I errors in a field, which can influence consistency in replication of results across studies.

To understand this novel perspective on the importance of power to Type I error rates, let us assume that there is a strong bias toward journal editors publishing only studies that report statistically significant findings (Dickersin & Min, 1993). Let us further imagine a field where there is very poor power, such that the average study in the field had a power of .20. Thus, out of 100 studies performed within this field, we assume that 5% will end up with Type I errors and get published with erroneous results. With power of .20, 20 out of 100 will detect real effects that exist, while 80% will miss existing effects and be discarded or remain unpublished. Thus, taking this extreme situation, 20 studies with true effects will be published for every five that are published with false effects (Type I errors). Following Rossi's argument, that leads us to a 20% Type I error rate (five out of 25 total articles published in the field) rather than the 5% we assume from setting alpha at .05.

This example represents an extreme and unrealistic situation. Or does it? Cohen's 1962 survey of the top-tier psychological literature concluded power of .48 to detect medium-sized effects. While that is substantially better than the .20 in the example above, it does produce inflated Type I error rates for the field. Again, assuming a very strong publication bias, we would have approximately 50 true effects published for every five false effects, which leads to a 10% Type I error rate in the field—double the rate we think it is. While this might not sound like a serious problem, if you were being tested for cancer, would you rather have a test that has a 5% chance of a false positive or 10% chance?

Further, we often have controversies in fields that lead to confusion and tremendous expenditure of resources when in fact the conflicting results may be more methodological than substantive—marginal power producing conflicting results, noncomparable samples or methods, and so on. When power is low in a field, there can be wide variation in the replicability of a real, moderately strong effect in the population. In a simulation presented later in this chapter, small, low-power samples taken of a "population" produced wildly fluctuating estimates of the effect, leading to a Type II error almost half the time. Imagine this was the study of the effect of homework on student achievement (or exercise on lifespan). If there was a real relationship between the two variables in the population, but researchers repeatedly used convenience samples that had poor power, one could easily see how controversy could develop. Half the researchers would assert there is no significant relationship between the two variables, and half would find powerful, significant effects, leaving practitioners at a loss to draw valid conclusions.

Thus we are left with a situation where statistical power is a very important concept, but reviews of power in many disciplines are discouraging. Cohen's (1962) initial survey of the *Journal of Applied and Social Psychology*, a top-tier psychology journal at the time, found that power to detect a small effect in this literature was .18, medium effect was .48, and a large effect was .83. In other words, unless researchers in psychology were studying phenomena with large effect sizes (which is assumed to be relatively rare in the social sciences), researchers generally had less than a 50:50 chance of detecting effects that existed—the exact situation described in the previous paragraph. Reviews of other areas (Rossi, 1990; Sedlmeier & Gigerenzer, 1989) paint a similarly bleak picture for more recent research. These reviews indicate that, by the end of the 1980s, little had changed from the early 1960s regarding power.[4]

HOW TO CALCULATE POWER

Each statistical test has different methods for computing power. Thus, this is not a simple issue to address. Authors such as Cohen (1988) have published books that collect this information, and software is freely available to compute power for many different common analyses, such as G*Power (Faul, Erdfelder, Buchner, & Lang, 2009).[5] There are also commercial power analysis programs that often handle more complex analyses. If you are performing a particular type of analysis, many webpages provide calculators (the Department of Epidemiology and Biostatistics at the University of California, San Francisco have attempted to catalogue some of these.)[6]

Using G*Power to do some simple calculations, you can see in Table 2.2 that it is often not a large increase in sample size to increase power from .80 to .95, although it is evident that power to detect small effects is difficult to come by.

Table 2.2   Sample Sizes Needed to Achieve Power of .80 and .95
Given Small, Medium, and Large Effect Sizes

	Sample Size Needed to Achieve Power = 0.80	Sample Size Needed to Achieve Power = 0.95
Simple Correlation[1]		
$\rho = .10$	779	1,289
$\rho = .30$	82	134
$\rho = .50$	26	42
Independent Groups t-Test[2]		
$d = 0.20$	788	1,302
$d = 0.50$	128	210
$d = 0.80$	52	84
Repeated Measures ANOVA[3]		
$f = 0.10$	138	216
$f = 0.25$	24	36
$f = 0.40$	12	16
Logistic Regression[4]		
Odds ratio = 1.50	308	503
Odds ratio = 3.00	53	80
Odds ratio = 8.00	26	35

Note. Effect size conventions taken from Cohen (1988).

1. Calculated at $\alpha = .05$, two-tailed test

2. Calculated at $\alpha = .05$, two-tailed test, equal cell sizes, total sample reported

3. Calculated at $\alpha = .05$, two groups, four measurements each, correlation among repeated measures = .50, no nonsphericity correction

4. Odds ratios of 3.00 are considered important in epidemiological literature (Kraemer, 1992), thus this was selected as a medium effect size. Odds ratios inflate quickly (and not linearly) and thus 8.00 was selected as a large effect (Hsieh, Bloch, & Larsen, 1998), and 1.50 was selected as a small effect size. Unfortunately, there is not agreement about what constitutes large, medium, and small effects in odds ratio. Two-tailed tests, no other IVs were included in the analysis; the IV was assumed to be normal.

THE EFFECT OF POWER ON THE
REPLICABILITY OF STUDY RESULTS

To demonstrate the effect of power on the potential quality of results, I used data from the base year of the Education Longitudinal Study of 2002 (Bozick, Lauff, & Wirt, 2007). The 15,244 students with complete data on both 10th grade family socioeconomic status (BYSES1) and 10th grade Math IRT score (BYTXMIRR) were used as the example population for the purposes of this demonstration. In this population, the correlation between those two variables is $\rho = .43$.[7] Given this effect size in the population, G*Power estimated that a sample of $N = 60$ would produce power of .95, and $N = 37$ would produce power of .80. However, to demonstrate the effects of reduced power, I will begin the demonstration with samples of $N = 20$, which should give power of .50, which is only slightly less than that estimated to detect a medium effect size of the average psychological study published in the latter part of the 20th century (Rossi, 1990). To simulate the effect of relatively inadequate power on research and error rates, I randomly drew 100 samples from this population, each with a sample size of $N = 20$,[8] and calculated the correlation described above. If the argument presented in this chapter is correct, a substantial number of the samples should lead to Type II errors (failure to reject the null hypothesis). Further, there should be substantial variability in the ability to replicate the population parameter. The data generated is presented in full in the appendix of this chapter and is summarized in Figure 2.2.

As expected, the average correlation over the 100 samples was close to the population parameter of .43 (average $r = .44$) but due to the low sample size the range of outcomes was somewhat alarming—ranging from $r_{20} = .02$ to .88. In this example, 44.0% of the correlations produced Type II errors (failing to reject a false null hypothesis), producing an observed power that is similar to the theoretical power calculated (.56). Thus, had I been a researcher with a limited, representative sample from this population, the odds are almost 50:50 that I would have committed a Type II error, incorrectly failing to reject the null hypothesis. Perhaps more disturbing, it is likely I would have seriously misestimated the effect size.

By converting the correlation coefficients to effect sizes (r^2), we can evaluate the extent of the misestimation of effect size attributable to having an

Figure 2.2 Results of 100 Correlation Coefficients (N=20)

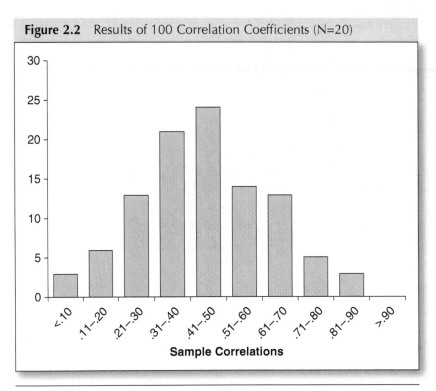

Note. Calculated from samples of $N = 20$ where the population coefficient is $\rho = .43$

inappropriately small sample size. I squared each calculated correlation coefficient, subtracted it from the square of .43 ($\rho^2 = .1849$, the population effect size) and then divided by the population effect size (.1849) to calculate the percentage by which each calculated correlation coefficient was misestimated. This ranged from 0.00% to 319.00%, with an average of 66.76% (and a standard deviation of 56.88%). To explore the effect of low power on the precision of the population estimate ($\rho = .43$) I calculated a 95% confidence interval for the correlation coefficient from the 100 samples of $N = 20$. This calculation (mean $\pm 1.96\ SD$) yields a 95% confidence interval that ranges from .10 to .78, hardly a strong point estimate.

In contrast, when samples are appropriately powered at .95 power ($N = 60$), the results are markedly different. As Figure 2.3 shows, in this case, the average correlation coefficient was .44 with a standard deviation of 0.10, ranging from .13 to .64. Furthermore, as expected, only 4.0% of the samples produced Type II errors, and the magnitude of the misestimation was markedly

Figure 2.3 Results of 100 Correlation Coefficients (N=60)

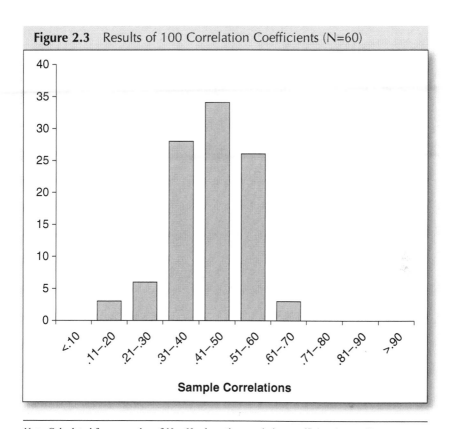

Sample Correlations

Note. Calculated from samples of $N = 60$ where the population coefficient is $\rho = .43$

reduced (37.28% with a standard deviation of 29.01%, significant at $F_{(1, 198)} =$ 21.32, $p < .0001$, $\eta^2 = .10$).

In other words, the odds that a Type II error in the $N = 20$ samples would be made were 18.86 times that of the $N = 60$ samples (the odds ratio is significant at $p < .0001$). Furthermore, the samples of $N = 60$ create a more precise population estimate. When once again figuring the 95% confidence interval, we get a range of .24 to .64, a narrower range than the $N = 20$ sample.

CAN DATA CLEANING FIX THESE SAMPLING PROBLEMS?

Unfortunately, in many cases poor sampling cannot be corrected by data cleaning. In subsequent chapters, we will explore the benefits of screening for extreme scores and normality of variables prior to analyses such as this. Thus, it is probably natural to wonder if those techniques would help offset the issues raised in this chapter from poor sampling, and to my knowledge no research addresses this issue definitively.

However, taking a few of the $N = 20$ samples that produced substantial misestimation, it does not appear to be the case that an oddly skewed sample or the presence of extreme scores is responsible for the misestimation. For example, taking one sample that produced a seriously misestimated correlation of $r_{(20)} = .69$ (Sample07), there is no evidence of extreme scores[9] (no score more than 2 standard deviations from the mean on either variable, nor is the normality of either variable tremendously out of line (skew was −0.60 for BYSES1 and -0.03 for BYTXMIRR). Further, when a transformation was applied to BYSES1 to correct normality that misestimation actually *increased*, subsequently calculating a $r_{(20)} = .72$. Finally, screening the data for bivariate outliers using standardized residuals failed to show any evidence of extreme biavariate scores (outliers) that were substantially skewing the estimation of the correlation (standardized residuals ranged from $z = −1.56$ to 1.83, well within normal range). Similar effects were found on other substantially misestimated samples, both those that overestimate the population correlation and those that substantially underestimate the population correlation (e.g., Sample10). Both of these sample data files will be available online.

CONCLUSIONS

I hope at this point it is obvious that calculating a priori power is in your best interest as a researcher to help maximize the probability that your study will be a success and that your data gathering will be maximally efficient. I also hope that the discussions concerning a posteriori power helps clarify best practices when dealing with interpretation of null findings. Specifically, I would suggest calculating a posteriori power given a sample size and alpha = .05 for small, medium, and large effects (Cohen and others have published guidelines for this, such as $d = 0.20$, 0.50, and 0.80) to establish the probability of detecting a small, medium, or large effect in a particular sample. If power was good, and your study did not detect an effect (or did not detect an important sized effect), you can be more confident accepting the null hypothesis than if your sample did not have sufficient power to detect even moderate or large effects.

The unfortunate truth that I had to share with my friend is that little can be done with a study such as hers when there is such poor power. Because she failed to do a power analysis and gather appropriate amounts of data, she may have wasted a good deal of her time without being able to clearly answer the question she was posing. This is an avoidable problem. I encourage you to always calculate power *prior to* engaging in data collection so that your research can be maximally productive and successful.

FOR FURTHER ENRICHMENT

1. Explore the data sets sampled at $N = 20$ from the population posted online (http://best-practices-online.com) to see if any of the samples that produced seriously misestimated effects can be salvaged through conventional data cleaning methods.

2. Download the "population" data set and take a sample of your own. Calculate the correlation coefficient and see how close you are to the "true" population estimate of $\rho = .43$. Take a smaller or larger sample and see whether your results change.

3. Take a recent study that you were involved in (or one from a good journal in your field, preferably a study your advisor published recently). Using the freely available software G*Power, calculate how much power that study had to detect a small, medium, or large effect (for example, using t-tests, $d = 0.20, 0.50,$ and 0.80 for small, medium, and large effect sizes). Are you satisfied with that level of power? If not, calculate what sample size you (or your advisor) would have needed to gather in order to have sufficient power.

4. Review articles in a top journal in your field. Note how many articles mention the term *power* and in what context. What percentage appear to have performed an a priori power analysis?

5. Find an article in your field that concludes null findings (e.g., no relationship, no difference between groups). Do the authors discuss whether they had sufficient power to detect effects of reasonable magnitude? If not, perform your own test to see if their conclusions are warranted. If

power to detect reasonable effects is not high, their conclusions might be suspect.

APPENDIX

Data from first simulation: $\rho = .43$, $N = 20$, and power $= .50$, or $N = 60$ and power $= .95$

Table 2.3   Results of 100 Correlation Coefficients

Sample	cale_r_N20	$p <$	cale_r_N60	$p <$
1	0.34	.15	0.36	.005
2	0.4	.08	0.51	.0001
3	0.57	.009	0.33	.01
4	0.5	.03	0.4	.002
5	0.28	.24	0.28	.03
6	0.26	.28	0.51	.0001
7	0.57	.008	0.57	.0001
8	0.07	.77	0.49	.0001
9	0.34	.14	0.4	.001
10	0.3	.2	0.44	.0001
11	0.44	.05	0.4	.001
12	0.56	.01	0.44	.0001
13	0.11	.63	0.53	.0001
14	0.19	.42	0.44	.0001
15	0.5	.02	0.6	.0001
16	0.51	.02	0.5	.0001
17	0.43	.05	0.13	.32
18	0.33	.16	0.36	.005
19	0.59	.006	0.41	.001
20	0.31	.187	0.31	.02

	Observed *r*, N=20		Observed *r*, N=60	
21	0.36	.12	0.38	.003
22	0.62	.004	0.44	.001
23	0.73	.0001	0.42	.001
24	0.44	.05	0.5	.0001
25	0.29	.21	0.38	.003
26	0.28	.24	0.57	.0001
27	0.37	.11	0.54	.0001
28	0.4	.08	0.59	.0001
29	0.39	.09	0.43	.001
30	0.78	.0001	0.46	.0001
31	0.33	.16	0.59	.0001
32	0.25	.29	0.48	.0001
33	0.66	.002	0.52	.0001
34	0.61	.004	0.53	.0001
35	0.35	.126	0.52	.0001
36	0.67	.001	0.53	.0001
37	0.52	.018	0.42	.001
38	0.5	.027	0.52	.0001
39	0.46	.04	0.56	.0001
40	0.46	.044	0.53	.0001
41	0.52	.019	0.36	.005
42	0.58	.008	0.4	.002
43	0.47	.036	0.33	.011
44	0.76	.0001	0.55	.0001
45	0.3	.21	0.43	.001
46	0.52	.019	0.56	.0001

(Continued)

(Continued)

Sample	Calculated *r* (N=20)	ρ <	Calculated *r* (N=60)	ρ <
47	0.31	.19	0.32	.012
48	0.47	.038	0.45	.0001
49	0.3	.2	0.36	.005
50	0.43	.05	0.34	.008
51	0.88	.0001	0.49	.0001
52	0.36	.12	0.45	.0001
53	0.26	.26	0.55	.0001
54	0.48	.03	0.44	.0001
55	0.45	.046	0.39	.002
56	0.47	.035	0.51	.0001
57	0.54	.015	0.56	.0001
58	0.61	.004	0.29	.024
59	0.41	.07	0.29	.023
60	0.24	.3	0.45	.0001
61	0.48	.03	0.35	.006
62	0.67	.001	0.14	.29
63	0.19	.42	0.53	.0001
64	0.27	.25	0.41	.001
65	0.23	.32	0.46	.0001
66	0.37	.11	0.42	.001
67	0.59	.007	0.37	.003
68	0.64	.003	0.43	.001
69	0.69	.001	0.56	.0001
70	0.45	.05	0.45	.0001
71	0.4	.09	0.18	.18
72	0.34	.14	0.64	.0001

Sample	Calculated r (N=20)	$\rho <$	Calculated r (N=60)	$\rho <$
73	0.7	.001	0.4	.002
74	0.18	.45	0.29	.03
75	0.37	.11	0.44	.0001
76	0.19	.43	0.58	.0001
77	0.45	.047	0.62	.0001
78	0.57	.009	0.5	.0001
79	0.46	.04	0.64	.0001
80	0.68	.001	0.38	.003
81	0.45	.05	0.48	.0001
82	0.45	.05	0.25	.05
83	0.35	.14	0.4	.002
84	0.49	.03	0.37	.004
85	0.02	.93	0.21	.11
86	0.35	.14	0.41	.001
87	0.59	.006	0.53	.0001
88	0.72	.0001	0.4	.001
89	0.67	.001	0.37	.004
90	0.7	.001	0.4	.002
91	0.03	.9	0.34	.009
92	0.37	.11	0.43	.001
93	0.72	.0001	0.44	.001
94	0.59	.006	0.45	.0001
95	0.48	.03	0.5	.0001
96	0.27	.25	0.47s	.0001
97	0.65	.002	0.33	.009
98	0.34	.14	0.38	.003
99	0.19	.42	0.45	.0001
100	0.5	.025	0.53	.0001

NOTES

1. A statistician with a strong conscience must often deliver disappointing news to friends and colleagues. This is apparently our lot in life.

2. Antiquated might be a better term for this "rule of thumb."

3. I am often troubled by what authors consider "acceptable" or "sufficient" in terms of power. Many, including Cohen, have suggested .80 as a reasonable level of power, and I have seen papers published in reputable journals with much less. However, I doubt that doctoral students would be happy with only an 80% chance of successfully defending a dissertation, or a parent would be satisfied with an 80% chance a child's school bus will safely deliver the child to school and home again. Why are we satisfied with failing to detect effects 20% of the time, when it is often possible to easily increase power to .90 or higher? Again referring to Figure 2.1, increasing sample size from $N = 50$ to $N = 70$ increases power from .80 to .90.

4. However, my review of the educational psychology literature (Osborne, 2008) indicated that observed power in some branches of the social sciences may be much better than generally assumed.

5. Available from http://www.psycho.uni-duesseldorf.de/abteilungen/aap/gpower3/.

6. See http://www.epibiostat.ucsf.edu/biostat/sampsize.html.

7. In this case, no transformations were done as both variables were close to normal (skew = −0.02, kurtosis = −0.65 for BYSES1 and skew = −0.03 and kurtosis = −0.85 for MYTXMIRR).

8. Sampling was done with replacement, meaning that after each correlation coefficient was calculated, all individuals were returned to the pool of 15,244 before the next sample was taken. This is important to prevent the samples from becoming increasingly nonrepresentative of the population.

9. See later chapters for information on extreme scores, standardized residuals, and transformation to improve normality. Unfortunately, at this point you have to trust me.

REFERENCES

Bozick, R., Lauff, E., & Wirt, J. (2007). *Education Longitudinal Study of 2002 (ELS: 2002): A first look at the initial postsecondary experiences of the sophomore class of 2002* (NCES 2008-308). Washington, DC: National Center for Education Statistics, Institute of Education Sciences, U.S. Department of Education.

Cohen, J. (1962). The statistical power of abnormal-social psychological research: A review. *Journal of Abnormal and Social Psychology, 65*(3), 145–153.

Cohen, J. (1988). *Statistical power analysis for the behavioral sciences* (2nd ed.). Hillsdale, NJ: Lawrence Erlbaum.

Cohen, J. (1992). A power primer. *Psychological Bulletin, 112*(1), 155.

Deemer, W. L. (1947). The power of the t test and the estimation of required sample size. *Journal of Educational Psychology, 38*(6), 329–342.

Dickersin, K., & Min, Y.-I. (1993). Publication bias: The problem that won't go away. *Annals of the New York Academy of Sciences, 703*(1), 135–148.

Faul, F., Erdfelder, E., Buchner, A., & Lang, A. (2009). Statistical power analyses using G* Power 3.1: Tests for correlation and regression analyses. *Behavior Research Methods, 41*(4), 1149.

Fidler, F., & Cumming, G. (2008). The new stats: Attitudes for the 21st century. In J. W. Osborne (Ed.), *Best practices in quantitative methods* (pp. 1–14). Thousand Oaks, CA: Sage.

Fisher, R. A. (1925). *Statistical methods for research workers.* Edinburgh: Oliver & Boyd.

Hsieh, F., Bloch, D., & Larsen, M. (1998). A simple method of sample size calculation for linear and logistic regression. *Statistics in Medicine, 17*(14), 1623–1634.

Killeen, P. R. (2008). Replication statistics. In J. W. Osborne (Ed.), *Best practices in quantitative methods* (pp. 103–124). Thousand Oaks CA: Sage.

Kraemer, H. C. (1992). *Evaluating medical tests.* Newbury Park, CA: Sage.

Osborne, J. W. (2008). Sweating the small stuff in educational psychology: How effect size and power reporting failed to change from 1969 to 1999, and what that means for the future of changing practices. *Educational Psychology, 28*(2), 1–10.

Rossi, J. S. (1990). Statistical power of psychological research: What have we gained in 20 years? *Journal of Counseling and Clinical Psychology, 58*(5), 646–656.

Rutstein, D. D. (1969). The ethical design of human experiments. *Daedalus, 98*(2), 523–541.

Schmidt, F. (1996). Statistical significance testing and cumulative knowledge in psychology: Implications for training of researchers. *Psychological Methods, 1*(2), 115–129.

Sedlmeier, P., & Gigerenzer, G. (1989). Do studies of statistical power have an effect on the power of studies? *Psychological Bulletin, 105*(2), 309–316.

❧ THREE ❧

BEING TRUE TO THE
TARGET POPULATION

Debunking the Myth of Representativeness

Often ours seems to be a science of just those sophomores who volunteer to participate in our research and who also keep their appointment with the investigator.

(Rosenthal & Rosnow, 2009, p. 87)

The social sciences have long been heavily dependent on undergraduates at research universities for their data, particularly in recent decades (e.g., Sears, 1986). I have nothing in particular against college-age students (in fact, I think quite highly of several). But when research depends on convenience samples of students who volunteer for a study and then remember to show up, I often have questions as to whether the results from that study tell us anything useful about the population we were originally trying to understand. It is arguable that students taking introduction to psychology classes (where many professors in the social sciences get their participants) are hardly representative of the undergraduate population as a whole, and once we start talking about differences between undergraduates who volunteer for experiments and those who do not (Rosnow, Rosenthal, McConochie, & Arms, 1969), things can get more tenuous. Yet at the same time, one has to be careful to think about the goal of the research. It is possible that a group of undergraduates are *on the surface* unrelated to the group you wish to generalize to, but if the psychological, physiological, or biological processes in that group are the same as the

43

Sampling 101

I remember reading an article (I will decline to cite the article to protect anonymity of the authors) on commitment to work in the industrial-organizational psychology literature a few years back. It was a survey looking at how invested individuals are (or how committed to their work they are) as a function of various aspects of the work environment. The researchers' goal was to make important statements about how companies can help their employees become more psychologically invested in their work, theoretically improving productivity and quality of work, as well as satisfaction and other variables important to the industrial-organizational psychology literature. The study surveyed about 100 undergraduates about their experiences and perceptions working at a job and about their commitment to their job. The authors made broad, important-sounding statements concluding that various factors are important to white-collar professionals in commitment to work.

It seems that it should be common sense that the sample you are studying should bear at least a passing similarity to the population to which you want to generalize. Undergraduates are rarely working full-time in a role related to their ultimate careers of choice (or careers similar to those to which the authors wanted to generalize). A convenience sample of undergraduates in a psychology class might not even be representative of the working undergraduate population. Therefore, although the article was published in a respected journal, it is probably not terribly informative about how real professionals in real jobs feel about the issues that were being surveyed.

If you really want to know what working, white-collar professionals are thinking, I'm afraid you have to actually survey them.

processes of the group you wish to generalize to, then perhaps it is not such a stretch after all, at least when studying processes that are more universal (e.g., Greenberg, 1987).

To take a simple and silly (and probably not approved by the human subjects review board) example, imagine I take a convenience sample of 100 students from my undergraduate psychology class. One by one I bring each student into the research lab and observe what happens when I drop a heavy weight on one of their feet. Let us speculate that not only will there be pain in that foot, but also a healthy range of emotions directed at the experimenter. Is it impossible to generalize those findings to, say a population of executives at an insurance company or a group of firefighters from Mississippi? As Greenberg (1987) and others would argue, the basic processes are similar, and therefore generalizability probably does not suffer as long as we do not range too far from the sample demographics (it probably does not generalize to individuals with neuropathy who cannot feel pain in their feet, for example).

But does memory work in octogenarians in the same way that it does for undergraduates? What about motivation? Does media violence influence males and females in the same way? What about people with differing levels of education or from different racial or ethnic backgrounds? As you can see, the question of generalizability and sampling can get complex.

In this chapter I explore some issues around generalizability and argue that along with calculating power (see Chapter 2) crafting your sampling plan is one of the most important things you, as a researcher, can do to ensure the high quality and usefulness of your work. Specifically, we review here the importance of thinking about the goal of the research and population of interest, as well as making sure the subjects included in the analyses match those goals.

SAMPLING THEORY AND GENERALIZABILITY

It was not terribly long ago in the history of the sciences that males were the overwhelmingly preferred subjects, and most studies used males (usually Caucasian) *exclusively* (Carlson & Carlson, 1960; Dresser, 1992). The assumption in both health and social science was that the normal male pattern of response was the typical *adult* response (McKenna & Kessler, 1977), despite substantial evidence regarding sex differences across many disciplines. Indeed, into the early 1990s medical research seemed to be predominantly based on Caucasian males.[1,2] The implications are obvious—and legendary. Not all groups respond to medications, interventions, education, and social situations identically. Thanks to more progressive, diverse samples, we now have drugs that appear to be effective *primarily* for certain racial groups (Temple & Stockbridge, 2007), psychological theories that take into account differences in males and females (such as moral reasoning development, Gilligan & Attanucci, 1994), and research into information processing across the lifespan (e.g., Cerella, 1985). So diversity itself is a laudable goal and can benefit science through serendipity, but it is not always possible to have broad dimensions of diversity represented in every sample for every research question.

In a nutshell, the goal of sampling is to gather data on whatever phenomenon is being studied in such a way as to make the best case possible for drawing inferences about the population of interest. The idea is that good science depends on drawing the strongest conclusions possible, and that to do that, a sample should represent the group and phenomenon as best possible.[3] However, some authors have argued this is essentially impossible, that all research samples are atypical at some level (Oakes, 1972), and that it is only when many studies comprising many samples can be looked at together that we can begin to examine the generalizability of effects (Lynch, 1999). This last point argues for more use of meta-analysis (studies that statistically summarize the results of many other studies, which few would argue with). Yet meta-analysis is only possible after a good number of original studies of high quality have been performed.

While there is a robust literature on generalizability in the sciences, let us start with some basic assumptions. First, researchers want to do the best job they can in matching a sample to a target population. Second, the match will never be perfect. Third, researchers can do some basic things, particularly in relation to planning and data cleaning, that can make things better. But fourth, everything depends on theory (Lynch, 1999). And that last point is perhaps the one that is most difficult to convey, but most important to grasp. It is the proposed mechanisms, theories, and understandings that help determine what constitutes a good sample for a particular goal.

A sample can be botched in limitless ways. This chapter covers some of the most common issues around sampling. Remember as you develop your own sampling plan that it is only your expertise in the particular area of research that can concretely guide you to good sampling practices.

AGGREGATION OR OMISSION ERRORS

Aggregation errors are errors not of sampling per se, but rather of failing to identify subsamples that may not function identically. When this happens, failing to examine subgroups can lead to errors in inference. Omission errors are the failure to examine a particular subgroup that may have a very different pattern.

A hypothetical example illustrating this effect was presented by Lynch (1982). In this paper, Lynch described a theoretical taste test experiment in which respondents rated their liking for three cola brands on a scale from 1 (worst) to 10 (best) in a traditional marketing experiment. Imagine the researchers performing this study are unfamiliar with the concept of subgroups (more technically, moderator variables that influence responses) and therefore do not separate out college students from stay-at-home mothers, the two most common subgroups in Lynch's example. As presented in Figure 3.1, students rate the three colas as 8, 7, and 4, respectively, and mothers rate the same colas 2, 6, and 7, respectively. These subgroup results indicate the first cola as the preference of students, the third cola the preference for mothers. If students' and housewives' ratings are equally numerous in the population and the researcher somehow achieved a probability sample, the mean ratings of the three colas would be 5.0, 6.5, and 5.5, respectively.

If we failed to separate out the two groups in our sample, we would conclude that all three colas are largely similar in terms of consumer preference, although cola #2 was preferred by a slight margin. This is of course a mischaracterization of the data, in that the third set of findings is representative of *no group in the population* that was sampled. Students preferred cola #1 and mothers preferred cola #3, a fact that would be lost on the researchers who failed to disaggregate their data by group, and no group preferred cola #2. This example reinforces the need for diversity in sampling, either within a single

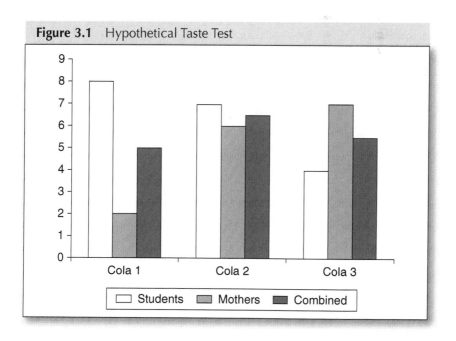

Figure 3.1 Hypothetical Taste Test

study or across multiple studies. If the researchers had only gone to a local high school or university (thus only getting students), their conclusions would probably not have generalized to other nonstudent groups.

A real example with profound implications involves recent studies of the heart medication known as BiDil (isosorbide dinitrate/hydralazine hydrochloride, see Temple & Stockbridge, 2007). This drug combination was initially considered a failure after two trials as it appeared to have no beneficial effect within the majority-Caucasian samples. It was not until the data were analyzed separately by race that strong beneficial effects for African Americans were detected, and a third trial was performed to examine the effectiveness of the drug in a solely African American sample. Because African Americans made up a small portion of the original samples, that effect was lost until separated out. In this case, a null effect in a large portion of the sample threatened to obscure an important effect in a small portion of the sample. I wonder how many other drugs such as this have been overlooked in the testing process due to insufficient diversity or failure to recognize heterogeneous subgroup effects.

I experienced a similar aggregation effect in one of my very first publications (Osborne, 1995) when I was looking at Claude Steele's theory of stereotype threat (e.g., Steele, 1997). The details of the theory, while fascinating (to me, anyway), are irrelevant for this discussion except to say that Steele hypothesized a weaker link between self-esteem and academic outcomes in students from traditionally academically stigmatized groups (e.g., African American students in the United States) than among other students (e.g., Caucasian students). I set out to test that aspect of the theory within the context of a large national database and did the simplest possible test—I looked at the pattern of correlations between the two groups and failed to find significantly different patterns of this relationship across racial subgroups. This was contrary to the theory and was puzzling. Steele was a reviewer on the original manuscript, and suggested examining the trends separately by race and sex, which found some interesting and heretofore masked effects. Figure 3.2 presents the final data that separated out males from females in each racial group.

If you examine the two lines that represent African American males and females and imagine the groups combined, you would see no real change from 8th grade to 10th grade. Likewise, aggregating the Caucasian males and females would yield no discernable pattern, failing to show support for Steele's interesting theory. Yet once disaggregated, the pattern from the African American males lent support to the theory.

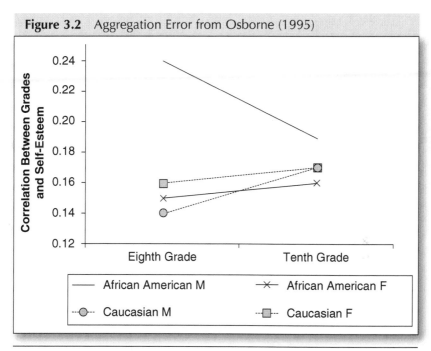

Figure 3.2   Aggregation Error from Osborne (1995)

Data taken from Osborne (1995).

INCLUDING IRRELEVANT GROUPS

In epidemiology and the medical sciences it is often very important to define the "denominator"—the group of individuals in whom the researcher is interested. For example, if you are interested in studying the effects of smoking on a particular outcome, you must define what it means to be a *smoker*, which helps make the research more precise and also defines the population to which the epidemiologist wants to generalize. It sounds simple, right? A smoker is one who smokes, who uses tobacco. But tobacco may be used in many ways. Do you include individuals who use snuff (inhaled tobacco) or chewing tobacco? Do you include those who smoke tobacco in the form of cigars, cigarillos, pipes, and hookahs, or are you only interested in those who smoke cigarettes (the most common way to use tobacco in the United States)? And what about people who just smoke occasionally, such as the "social smoker" who may only have a cigarette once a week or once a month? What about smokers who also smoke other substances, such as marijuana, that might have very different effects than tobacco? What about those smokers who previously used tobacco but have stopped? Do you include them if they stopped a week ago? What about 20 years ago? And what about "passive smokers," people who are exposed to secondhand smoke by virtue of living with a smoker or working in an environment that contains secondhand smoke (e.g., a pub or nightclub where smoking is allowed)? As you can see, it is not always simple to define your population of interest, but it is extremely important. People who smoke cigars, for example, might be at risk for very different sorts of outcomes than cigarette smokers (e.g., Iribarren, Tekawa, Sidney, & Friedman, 1999) and those who previously quit smoking may have different outcomes than current smokers (Critchley & Capewell, 2003). In other words, failing to accurately define your denominator can leave you with a sloppy sample—one filled with error that can mask or undermine your ability to detect an effect that is really present in the population.

In this spirit, political surveys that occur around elections rarely attempt to survey the entire population, but rather "likely voters." In other words, those surveys are only interested in predicting (or understanding) those individuals who are able to, and are likely to, actually vote. This population is not at all representative of the population as a whole, but of course is more germane to answering the question of attempting to predict the outcomes of elections.

I was involved in one recent example of this issue. In an evaluation study, we examined the effects of having all students in a high school use laptops as part of routine instruction. The focus of the study was concerned primarily with the academic effects, or the effects on teachers and student performance in what the Department of Education considered "core" subjects—mathematics, sciences, social studies, and language arts. As part of the study, we administered a survey to teachers in schools implementing a one-to-one laptop program for students. However, teacher assistants, guidance counselors, librarians, assistant principals, and other non–core-teaching faculty (e.g., music, physical education, art teachers) also responded to the survey. The results would have been dramatically skewed or obscured had we not filtered out individuals who were not core content area classroom teachers. Not only would we have not directly addressed the goals of survey—to understand how classroom teachers in core content areas were utilizing an instructional technology environment where every student had a laptop—but it is likely that we would have failed to have observed some important effects due to the "noise" in the data caused by having individuals outside our target population included in the data set. This is an example of where careful thought in terms of sampling (and checking at data cleaning) was critical to the quality of the results.

Despite our instructions to schools that only core content area teachers respond to the survey, some schools invited all faculty/staff to respond to the survey to prevent people from feeling left out.[4]

Another challenge from this study involved the question of what to do with teachers or students who transferred to the school after the pilot project began. Our decision was to exclude anyone not present at the beginning of the 3-year study. This may be a controversial decision, but it was based on the fact that teachers coming to the school after all the training was completed would not show the same benefits or changes as a teacher who experienced a full summer's worth of training. Likewise, if students came to the school mid-year, they would not have benefitted from a full year of laptop usage, and thus did not represent the population we were interested in generalizing to (students and teachers who were in a one-to-one laptop environment a full year with all the benefits of appropriate training).

One final example from a recent collaboration with a colleague (Osborne & Blanchard, 2011) again illustrates the importance of paying attention to how you conceptualize your sample. My colleague, Dr. Blanchard, was analyzing data from a study she conducted evaluating the effects of a progressive teaching method (compared to a more traditional teaching method) on student outcomes, such as test scores. Despite all expectations to the contrary, the data from the student tests were not showing any significant benefit of the new teaching method compared to traditional teaching. One problem with research in the social sciences (and education in particular) is that we often rely on people with little motivation to participate in our research (e.g., middle school students, introduction to psychology undergraduates) to be motivated to try their best, often at difficult tasks. And due to ethical guidelines for the treatment of human subjects (Galliher, 1973; Shalala, 2000), it is often difficult to motivate participants through penalizing those who fail to fully participate. In other words, there is no real incentive for some students to spend a good deal of their time taking a test that has little bearing on their grade or life, just to make a researcher happy.

But Blanchard had the foresight to include some questions toward the end of the lengthy knowledge test that allowed us to identify students who were randomly responding (i.e., just randomly answering rather than thoughtfully answering test items).[5] This turned out to be critical to the study.

Conceptually, Blanchard wanted to evaluate what benefit, if any, students would get from learning particular science topics using a different teaching methodology. Remember, the question to be addressed was the comparative effect of the two teaching strategies on students who are trying to learn the material. She was not interested in the effects of the two teaching strategies on student performance when they randomly respond to test items. Thus, when we screened out students who were randomly answering from the sample, we were focusing our sample to represent the group we were most interested in. As Figure 3.3 shows, it turned out those students engaging in random respond-ing do seem to be qualitatively different than the students who at least appeared to be doing a conscientious job of taking the exam. Furthermore, once these students were removed from the data set, the effects of the interven-tion were statistically significant in the expected direction.

Figure 3.3   Differences in Test Score Growth as a Function of Random Responding Status

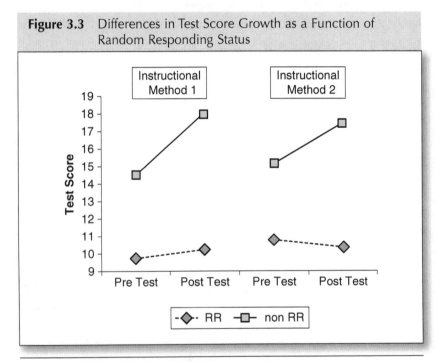

Data taken from Osborne and Blanchard (2011).

NONRESPONSE AND GENERALIZABILITY

As Chapter 6 in this book explores, individuals who choose not to participate in your research or not to respond to particular questions, may substantially bias the results of a study. One example of this insidious effect is found in a now-classic series of studies by Steele and Aronson (1995). In one of their experiments, they found that when individuals belonging to a stigmatized group are uncomfortable (experiencing stereotype threat, in this case), they are less likely to complete questions about the content of racial stereotypes or even answer basic demographic questions such as race of participant. In this one group (African American students) that was critical to the research question, 75% of Ivy League undergraduates chose to skip the question asking them to indicate their race. Luckily, the experimenters had that information without getting it directly from the students, but in other contexts, such as Internet surveys, that data would have been lost, substantially skewing the results.

Thus, researchers must take all ethical steps possible to ensure they protect against creating a situation where nonresponse (particularly disproportional nonresponse from a particular group) could bias the results. This is especially true when researching sensitive topics or topics that have changed in social desirability over the years. As Tourangeau and Yan (2007) report, nonresponse or misreporting is particularly likely when an individual has something embarrassing to report. Thus, women may skip questions on sexual activity or abortion, drug users often misrepresent their actual drug use, and health care workers may skip (or misreport) smoking or health behavior related questions, particularly if they do not conform to the expectations of society. People belonging to socially stigmatized groups (often of particular interest to researchers in the social sciences) may be more likely to refuse to participate in research (or parts of surveys) relating to their group membership, as Steele and Aronson (1995) found.

Furthermore, researchers must be sensitive to how changing societal norms could bias results. To again use smoking as an example, surveys tracking self-reported smoking behavior over the decades might show dramatic decreases in smoking. But researchers must wonder if that is due to one of the following.

- True reductions in smoking as a result of better information about the health risks associated with smoking.
- Smokers being less likely to participate in those sorts of surveys in recent years due to smoking being more socially stigmatized.
- Smokers who participate in surveys misrepresenting their actual behaviors out of social desirability concerns.

Unfortunately, without other data, it is difficult to know which of these three very different conclusions is warranted. Fortunately, there are methods to minimize the biases that these social desirability effects can introduce into samples.

In the case of sensitive questions (e.g., sexual activity or finances), research seems to indicate that answering the questions on a paper questionnaire or computer is preferable to an interviewer asking the questions (Turner et al., 1998), preferably in the absence of significant others (e.g., a spouse or romantic partner). Research also has found that perceived similarity of the participant to the researcher can reduce misrepresentations or nonresponse (Tourangeau & Yan, 2007).That is, a person who has engaged in illicit drug use is more likely to be candid when that person perceives the respondent as similar (ideally, perhaps someone who has likewise engaged in illicit drug use in the past, but alternatively similar in other sociodemographic characteristics such as race, sex, age, income level, and education).

Of course, it is not always easy to know which questions may be sensitive across all potential demographic groups. For example, older individuals, males, individuals on disability, and those with less education were more likely to refuse to respond to a national health survey (Korkeila et al., 2001), indicating health may be a more sensitive topic for some groups than for others (it would be difficult to see health questions being more sensitive to teenagers or young adults unless they involved illicit or high-risk activity, for example). It is also easy to imagine employees of a company being uncomfortable saying negative things about the company or superiors for fear of embarrassment, humiliation, or reprisal (Dalton & Metzger, 1992).

There are, unfortunately, an almost infinite number of possibilities when it comes to sensitive questions, depending on the combination of the target population's demographic characteristics and the type of research. It is impossible to list all the possibilities, so each researcher must think carefully about the topic being researched and the target population to be sampled, perhaps pilot testing procedures and questions with members of that group to identify potential hazards that could bias data or increase the odds of nonresponse.

CONSENT PROCEDURES AND SAMPLING BIAS

It is generally considered a good thing that most researchers must go through rigorous review processes before subjecting human (or animal) participants to research protocols. However, it is possible that the process of obtaining informed consent may bias the sample unintentionally. In some fields, where rigorous informed consent must convey long lists of possible negative outcomes, no matter how minute the odds of experiencing those outcomes (e.g., medical research), informed consent has led to low levels of recruitment through increasing the anxiety of patients who are already in a very anxious state (Tobias & Souhami, 1993). From an ethical point of view, this is entirely necessary, at least given the current state of research ethics. But from a research methodology point of view, these procedures may be doing significant harm to the goal of the research—to generalize to a particular patient population.

Furthermore, in studies with differing levels of intervention (e.g., a radical new cancer therapy versus traditional radiation that is thought to be less effective—or worse, a placebo), it is not beyond reason that patients initially eager to participate in the groundbreaking research would be less enthusiastic in participating in the research that does nothing but give them traditional care—thus opening the door for differential refusal rates or other factors that could lead to biased samples, skewed results, and less-than-ideal generalizability.

In the social sciences (and particularly education) informed consent or assent procedures can be particularly problematic. Parents of minors seem wary, in this information age, of allowing their children to provide information to researchers or participate in studies. Informed consent in educational settings can be particularly problematic, often having to go through multiple stages of school, teacher, student to take home to the parent, the parent to sign or not, and the student to return the signed form to the teacher, who turns it over to the school, who ultimately turns it over to the researcher. As you can imagine, this is a long chain of events fraught with potential for loss of informed consent, even in cases where the student and parent intended to provide informed consent. Thus, again, researchers must be thoughtful about how best to maximize the possibility of receiving informed consent and eliminating the structural and procedural hurdles to obtaining it in order to maximize participation rate and minimize loss of informed consent through unintentional misplacement.

In one study of mine (Osborne & Walker, 2006) that was particularly effective at obtaining informed consent, my research team and I partnered with local high schools to obtain informed consent from parents for the research when parents came into the school to enroll their children as students before the school year began. This eliminated many potential problems with sending home papers with students and achieved a high rate of consent without sacrificing ethics.

In another study of elementary school students, we took advantage of the fact that parents received a folder with student work, forms to be signed, and important information every Monday from the teacher. We worked with teachers to send home informed consent forms with students in their Monday folders, and because parents were used to looking at folders every Monday and students were required to return them every Tuesday morning, we received a good response to our informed consent forms.

Aside from structural and procedural issues, a variety of cultural, psychological, and situational factors can influence individual's decisions to provide informed consent (e.g., volunteering to participate in a study). For example, in applying research on volunteerism, Roberts (2002) suggests that to the extent researchers can help potential participants clarify and enumerate cultural, religious, and personal beliefs and values (e.g., empowerment, charity, being relationship-focused) can highlight to individuals that participation in research may be congruent with their values and beliefs and may help them achieve these ephemeral, yet important goals.

GENERALIZABILITY OF INTERNET SURVEYS

I am sure I could write an entire book on this issue.[6] Let us start by putting this type of research in context of what used to be the "high-technology" survey methodology, phone banks. At the time, calling people's home phones was the best, most efficient way of reaching large numbers of the U.S. population. However, the issue of sampling was a tricky one. First, not every household had a phone (though most did, at least in the United States). So people living in poverty were more likely to be underrepresented in any phone survey. This, by extension, meant that individuals belonging to traditionally disadvantaged minority groups were less likely to be included in a phone sample. Furthermore, at some times and in some communities, women were more likely to be at home during the day than men, so phone calls during normal business hours were more likely to get responses from a female household member. And there was great discussion about how time of day affected sampling. Calling during the dinner hour was traditionally thought to be the ideal time to catch people at home, but also may be the least likely time for someone who answered the phone to want to participate in a phone survey. Yet calling later in the evening had strong disadvantages, and calling during the day may mean oversampling the unemployed, the retired, people with nontraditional jobs, or stay-at-home parents.

And there was the issue of the population (or the denominator). While most people had their phone numbers listed in the phone company database (the phone book), there was a segment of the population who paid extra to have phone numbers "unlisted." Thus, the population being sampled would include only those households with a phone number listed in the directory and who happened to be home at the particular time called. As you can see, this has been a thorny issue for years.

Fast forward to modern times and the situation is much more complex. Up to one-quarter of the U.S. population no longer has household phones (land lines) and instead many rely on cellular phones that have no centralized directory. Those with land lines are less representative of the population now, and those with cellular phones are very difficult to reach for surveys. The Internet is present in many homes, but finding e-mail addresses and getting people to respond to Internet surveys, even from large respected research universities, can be challenging. People do not seem to want to share information in this new information age. Thus researchers are left in a more challenging environment than ever.

Internet surveys are problematic from a sampling perspective for several reasons. First, it is probably not ever a best practice to simply post a survey that is open for anyone to access and invite the world to respond. On the Internet, it is difficult to know who is responding, what country they are in, whether they are legitimate or providing poor information, and even whether the same person might fill out the survey dozens of times.

So finding a database that contains the population of interest is important. The database must be relatively up-to-date (as e-mail addresses can change rapidly relative to home phone numbers, which used to remain more stable), representative of the population of interest, and must include e-mail addresses (which is not as common as one might think). Then you are sampling those individuals who have access to the Internet and e-mail and who check it, as well as who choose to respond to your survey. Fortunately, some databases contain enough information to do a minimal check comparing respondents to nonrespondents for representativeness (which I discuss in more detail and recommend as a best practice in Chapter 6).

Recent research still shows a large generational gap in access to (and interest in using) the Internet. Participants in a prominent, large-scale survey on health and retirement found that among adults in the United States aged 50 or older, only 30% reported using the Internet, and of those, only 73% indicated willingness to do a Web-based survey (Couper, Kapteyn, Schonlau, & Winter, 2007). Furthermore, there were significant demographic, socioeconomic, and health status differences between those who can be surveyed through the Internet and those who cannot.

Other researchers have found similar biases in Internet research. For example, a group of researchers looking at sampling bias in sexual health research (Ross, Månsson, Daneback, Cooper, & Tikkanen, 2005) found that, compared with a "gold standard" random selection population based sexual health survey, an Internet survey targeting the same population diverged substantially from the traditional sampling methodology. Internet samples were more likely to be urban, better educated, and younger. In line with the previous discussion of nonresponse and sensitivity issues: individuals responding to the Internet survey were more likely to admit to being attracted to individuals of the same sex or to report higher numbers of sex partners in the past year.

Thus, even in the 21st century, surveys through the Internet have the likelihood of being substantially biased, even given the best database to start with, unless great care is taken to compile a large, unbiased sample. On the positive side, recent psychological research (Gosling, Vazire, Srivastava, & John, 2004) showed that large Internet surveys *can* provide results similar to traditionally administered surveys published in psychological journals[7] in some basic ways (e.g., the Big Five personality traits). Given the efficiencies of Web-based research, this is a desirable methodology to continue to explore, albeit with care to protect samples from becoming biased.

RESTRICTION OF RANGE

When I began graduate school two decades and more in the past, one of my first advisors was interested in self-esteem. In this research lab, we often split university students who had responded to a common self-esteem inventory (the Rosenberg Self-View Inventory) at the median into "high" and "low" self-esteem groups for research purposes (I will defer the discussion of the drawbacks of median-splits on continuous variables to Chapter 11, where I delve into this issue in more detail). Let us focus on the sampling issue—in a research university, are students that score below the median on a measure of global self-esteem (or depression, or many other constructs) truly *low* in self-esteem? Are we generalizing to the population we want to?

Consider a more representative sample than university students: eighth graders from the National Education Longitudinal Study of 1988 (Ingels, 1994). This nationally representative sample asked secondary school students seven of the original 10 questions from the Rosenberg SVI[8] measured on a scale of 1 (strongly disagree) to 4 (strongly agree). The mean for this nationally representative sample was 3.10 and the median was 3.14. Thus, splitting people into low and high self-esteem through a median split would allow us to compare those students who seem to be *very high* (above 3.14 on a 1-to-4 scale) and only moderately high (in fact, only 2.7% averaged a 2.0 or lower, and only 10.1% averaged 2.5 or lower, the conceptual middle for a 1-to-4 scale). Though I no longer have the data from those original studies of university students with my first advisor, my recollection at the time was that university students tended to have even higher self-esteem, on average, and thus, "low" self-esteem in that sample was still moderately high. In other words, from either of these two sources of data, it would be difficult to generalize to the population of individuals with truly low self-esteem.

Conceptually, this is a restriction of range issue, in that the observed range in a variable is restricted in some way from varying in the same way that one would expect in the population. As my comment at the beginning of the chapter indicates, university students also have very restricted ranges of employment, and thus generalizing their experiences to employees in the overall population is risky. Socioeconomic status (SES) and of course age, as well as depression, romantic relationship experiences, and many other variables, are similarly restricted in university samples (which again make up a large majority of the research in the social sciences). Likewise, in the general (noninstitutionalized) population it is likely that researchers looking at mental disorders are likely to find only mild degrees of severity, limiting generalizability of findings. Similarly, studies of combat veterans or rape survivors suffering from post-traumatic stress disorder (PTSD) may not generalize to members of the population with less severe traumatic stress experiences. The list of potential issues could go on indefinitely, but researchers again must use judgment and care when examining their sampling frameworks or generalizing their conclusions. To the extent that range was restricted in the sample, it is important to include that as a caveat when discussing the findings.[9]

The issues of ceiling and floor effects are similar to restriction of range. In the case of a ceiling or floor effect, the restriction of range is due to a mismatch between the sample and the measure used. Continuing the discussion from the previous paragraph: it should make sense that one has to use a

Ceiling Effect: Caused by a mismatch of an instrument that is too sensitive with a sample that is relatively extreme on the trait being assessed. This causes too many to score at the uppermost end of the scale, where they "find the ceiling." This is the measurement equivalent of shouting into a highly sensitive stethoscope.

Floor Effect: Caused by a mismatch of an instrument that is not sensitive enough with a sample that shows relatively low levels of the trait being assessed. This causes too many to score at the lowest end of the scale, where they "find the floor." This is the measurement equivalent of someone who has very poor hearing attempting to hear a quiet whisper.

measure appropriate for the expected range of the variable in the population of interest. So, looking at individuals who recently experienced a traumatic event, one needs to select a measure of stress, anxiety, or depression that is sensitive to the range commonly seen in the population. If I were to give measures intended for the general population to these groups, they would probably cluster at the upper end of the scale—finding the ceiling—indicating that there might be more severe symptoms than this scale can measure. This restriction of range likely will skew any results from this study in that the variables of interest are not accurately being measured.

Conversely, if we were to give measures of anxiety, depression, or stress designed for individuals experiencing PTSD to samples from the general population, it is likely they would cluster at the bottom end of the scale—finding the floor. In other words, a measure designed to be sensitive in the range of people experiencing PTSD likely will not be sensitive to the range of variation found in a general population. Again, this floor effect will result in restriction of range that will harm the fidelity of the results.

All this is to say that restriction of range can be caused by many different issues, from unfortunate sampling decisions to unfortunate choices in measures and operationalizations, and in all cases this restriction can cause undesirable outcomes for the results. They are best avoided by thoughtful matching of measures to the intended sample of a study prior to collecting any data. Examples of these effects are presented in Figures 3.4 through 3.7.

As an example of these effects, I utilized data from the Education Longitudinal Study of 2002 (ELS 2002) available from the National Center for Educational Statistics.[10] Those of us in education know that family socioeconomic status can dramatically affect student outcomes. For example, in this data set, we see a relatively strong relationship between SES and reading

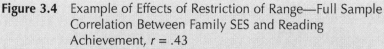

Figure 3.4   Example of Effects of Restriction of Range—Full Sample
Correlation Between Family SES and Reading
Achievement, $r = .43$

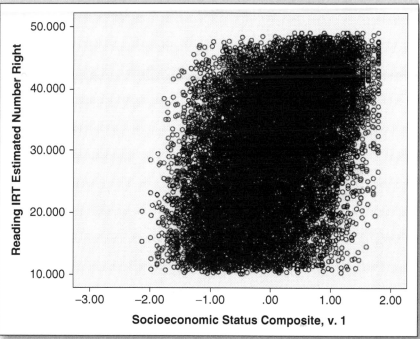

achievement scores for 10th graders ($r = .43$, $p < .0001$) for the general population. However, let us imagine that we were studying low-performing students only (defined for this example by students who perform below the 5th
percentile on a 10th grade math achievement test). Theory tells us that restriction of range can lead to substantial misestimation of effects, and indeed that
is the case for this sample. As Figure 3.5 shows, in this subgroup there is no
significant relationship ($r = .03$, not significant). The scatterplot in Figure 3.5
also shows what might be a floor effect, wherein students who are among the
lowest-performing students cluster at the minimum value of the achievement
scale. This might indicate that this test, aimed at average 10th grade students,
might not be sensitive to diversity amongst those who are lowest performing.

A more extreme example of misestimation amongst special populations is
evident in Figure 3.6 on page 63. In this case, we selected only students identified by their parents as mentally retarded. Using this extreme population, we

Figure 3.5   Example of Effects of Restriction of Range Correlation
Between Family SES and Reading Achievement, ONLY
Students Identified as Performing Below 5th Percentile
on Math Achievement, $r = .03$

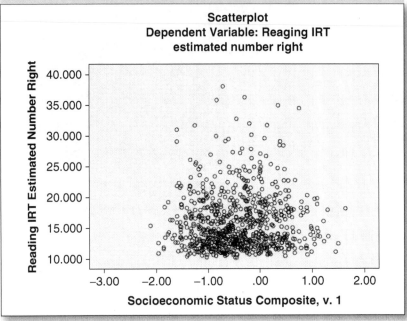

see an even more serious misestimation of this relationship, which is this case
was $r = -.33$ (not significant due to low numbers).

Finally, we can see that this restriction of range effect is evident when
looking at the other end of the spectrum, students scoring above the 95th percentile on a math achievement test. As Figure 3.7 on page 64 shows, the effect
is again misestimated ($r = .24$, $p < .0001$). It is also evident that in this sub-
population, there appears to be a ceiling effect, where the achievement test
normed to the average student population of 10th graders appears not to be
sensitive to the performance of highly accomplished students.

EXTREME GROUPS ANALYSIS

A less common issue related to restriction of range is that of extreme groups
analysis (EGA) (Preacher, Rucker, MacCallum, & Nicewander, 2005),

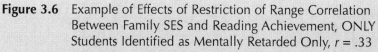

Figure 3.6   Example of Effects of Restriction of Range Correlation Between Family SES and Reading Achievement, ONLY Students Identified as Mentally Retarded Only, $r = .33$

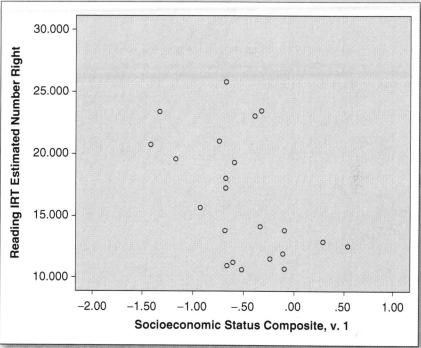

wherein researchers may choose individuals that represent extremes of a distribution. For example, we could choose people who score above or below a certain IQ cutoff, or my advisor and I could have choosen the 25 individuals with the lowest self-esteem and the 25 individuals with the highest self-esteem for comparison or intervention. The latter approach, called *post hoc* subgrouping, is generally to be avoided.

There are some benefits to this approach, properly applied, in terms of efficiency where resources prohibit use of large numbers of participants, and enhance power and effect size. There are, however, serious problems with this approach. First, when using this approach without strong justification, it appears that a researcher is merely attempting to artificially (unethically) inflate apparent effect sizes. I label this as unethical as the effect size from this sort of analysis is rarely representative of the effect size in the general population, because the comparison is between two groups at different extremes of a

Figure 3.7   Example of Effects of Restriction of Range Correlation
Between Family SES and Reading Achievement, ONLY
Students Identified as High Performing Via Math
Achievement > 95th Percentile $r = .24$

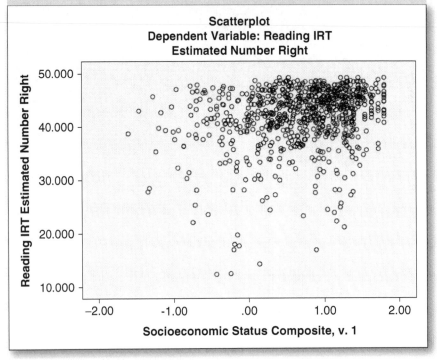

distribution. As mentioned previously, EGA is more acceptable in some specific instances, but those tend to be relatively rare.

Another drawback to EGA is that researchers are assuming a linear relationship between the variable being subjected to EGA and the outcome variable of
interest. It is not always clear that perfectly linear relationships exist, however,
and where curvilinearity exists, this approach could create significant problems.
For example, if we assume there is a strong curvilinear effect between student
anxiety and academic performance, comparing students at the extremely low
and high ends of anxiety would dramatically misestimate the overall nature of
the relationship. Therefore EGA should always be strongly justified prior to
being used. Furthermore, data should *not* be dichotomized, but rather original
scores should be maintained to prevent loss of power or effect size—for more
on the issue of dichotomizing, see Chapter 11 or (Preacher et al., 2005).

CONCLUSION

Truly excellent research is often as much an art as a science. This issue of sampling is particularly vexing in that it is difficult to create clear guidelines for researchers that will always constitute best practices given the range of issues researched, methodologies used, and populations targeted. In general, the best research must start with the best sample, and the best sampling frame begins with a thoughtful and careful reflection on the goals of the research and how best to accomplish those goals given the practical limitations a researcher is working within.

FOR FURTHER ENRICHMENT

1. Experiment with how ceiling and floor effects can distort results of analyses. Download the data set from the website for this book. In it you will find several variables that have generally strong correlations, such as family socioeconomic status and student achievement. While neither variable suffers from restriction of range, we can simulate a restriction of range issue.

   a. Explore how the correlation between reading achievement (BYTXRIRR) and socioeconomic status (BYSES1) is influenced by restricting analyses to students whose parents have less than a high school education or more than a graduate school education.

2. Review articles from a respected journal in your field (or from a list of recent articles published by your advisor). See if you can identify any of the following issues raised in this chapter.

   a. Use of extreme groups analysis.
   b. Mismatch between measures used and sample (possible floor or ceiling effect).
   c. Whether there is potential restriction of range (almost any convenience sample, such as college students, will have strong possibilities of this).
   d. Whether there might be aggregation errors (i.e., groups that were combined that might have been analyzed separately).
   e. Whether the purpose of the article is met through the sample. If not, can you describe a sampling methodology that would have better met the goals of the study?

3. Examine data you have collected for a research project (or one your advisor or colleague has collected if you do not have data on-hand) for evidence of ceiling or floor effects, restriction of range, combining of groups that may not be homogenous, and so on. If you do not find evidence of such effects, simulate them as I did for the examples in this chapter and explore how your conclusions would change with less ideal sampling.

NOTES

1. Dresser (1992) highlights the astounding finding that until very recently studies on the impact of obesity and uterine cancer were *conducted solely on men.*

2. The historical reasons for this male-only bias are varied. They include the fact that, for much of the earlier part of the 20th century in the United States, Caucasian males were the majority of students at research universities where much of the research was taking place. It is also my impression that a perception existed that it was easier to get studies approved by institutional review boards when they included only males because women of child-bearing age constituted a population more at risk for harm (and thus, legal liability). I am sure there are other reasons as well, but rarely would reason lead us to assert "we exhaustively researched this issue and conclude that Caucasian males are the best sample to represent the groups to which we wish to generalize."

3. Note that I am not arguing that all samples should include representative aspects of *all possible groups*, but rather of all groups one is interested in researching. Yet where possible, examining diversity in responses often leads to valuable insights, such as the heart medication that seemed to be a dismal failure at first (Temple & Stockbridge, 2007), discussed later in the chapter.

4. A laudable and important goal, but one that can create challenges in data cleaning for statisticians and researchers.

5. The details of how this happened and recommendations for dealing with this issue are contained in Chapter 10 of this book.

6. But Dillman (2007) already did. Those interested in web-based surveys, or survey methodology in general, are strongly encouraged to get his book and refer to it often.

7. One note of caution: these authors are essentially saying that a very large Internet survey of more than 360,000 participants essentially generated some similarities to the body of 510 samples published in the *Journal of Personality and Social Psychology* in 2002. In this journal, 85% were student samples, 80% were Caucasian, and the mean age was 22.9 years of age, compared to 24.3 for the Internet sample. These findings reinforce the admonition to use Internet samples with caution if not seeking adolescent, primarily Caucasian, college student samples.

8. From a technical point of view, the SVI has such high internal consistency (often exceeding alpha of .90) that the National Center for Educational Statistics, the

governmental organization responsible for this data set, decided it was acceptable to eliminate several items in the interest of space. I have mixed feelings about this, but that is a discussion for another time (such as in Chapter 9, where we explore issues concerning reliability of measurement). In general, losing those three items does not significantly alter the internal consistency of the scale.

9. There are corrections for restriction of range, particularly in relation to correlation coefficients, but there appears to be some debate over whether the corrected relationships are more or less accurate than the uncorrected correlations (and little is done with other techniques outside simple correlations). This is an issue best handled from a sampling methodology framework.

10. More information on this public data set is available at http://nces.ed.gov/surveys/els2002/.

REFERENCES

Carlson, E. R., & Carlson, R. (1960). Male and female subjects in personality research. *Journal of Abnormal and Social Psychology, 61*(3), 482–483.

Cerella, J. (1985). Information processing rates in the elderly. *Psychological Bulletin, 98*(1), 67–83.

Couper, M. P., Kapteyn, A., Schonlau, M., & Winter, J. (2007). Noncoverage and non-response in an internet survey. *Social Science Research, 36*(1), 131–148.

Critchley, J., & Capewell, S. (2003). Mortality risk reduction associated with smoking cessation in patients with coronary heart disease: A systematic review. *Jama, 290*(1), 86–97.

Dalton, D., & Metzger, M. (1992). Towards candor, cooperation, & privacy in applied business ethics research: The randomized response technique (RRT). *Business Ethics Quarterly, 2*(2), 207–221.

Dillman, D. (2007). *Mail and internet surveys: The tailored design method.* New York: John Wiley.

Dresser, R. (1992). Wanted: Single, white male for medical research. *The Hastings Center Report, 22*(1), 24–29.

Galliher, J. (1973). The protection of human subjects: A reexamination of the professional code of ethics. *The American Sociologist, 8*(3), 93–100.

Gilligan, C., & Attanucci, J. (1994). Two moral orientations: Gender differences and similarities. In B. Puka (Ed.), *Caring Voices and Women's Moral Frames: Gilligan's View* (pp. 123–137). New York: Garland.

Gosling, S., Vazire, S., Srivastava, S., & John, O. (2004). Should we trust web-based studies. *American Psychologist, 59*(2), 93–104.

Greenberg, J. (1987). The college sophomore as guinea pig: Setting the record straight. *The Academy of Management Review, 12*(1), 157–159.

Ingels, S. (1994). *National Education Longitudinal Study of 1988: Second follow-up: Student component data file user's manual.* Washington, DC: U.S. Deptartment of

Education, Office of Educational Research and Improvement, National Center for Education Statistics.

Iribarren, C., Tekawa, I. S., Sidney, S., & Friedman, G. D. (1999). Effect of cigar smoking on the risk of cardiovascular disease, chronic obstructive pulmonary disease, and cancer in men. *New England Journal of Medicine, 340*(23), 1773–1780.

Korkeila, K., Suominen, S., Ahvenainen, J., Ojanlatva, A., Rautava, P., Helenius, H., & Koskenvuo, M. (2001). Non-response and related factors in a nation-wide health survey. *European Journal of Epidemiology, 17*(11), 991–999.

Lynch, J. (1982). On the external validity of experiments in consumer research. *Journal of Consumer Research, 9*(3), 225–239.

Lynch, J. (1999). Theory and external validity. *Journal of the Academy of Marketing Science, 27*(3), 367–376.

McKenna, W., & Kessler, S. J. (1977). Experimental design as a source of sex bias in social psychology. *Sex Roles, 3*(2), 117–128.

Oakes, W. (1972). External validity and the use of real people as subjects. *American Psychologist, 27*(10), 959–962.

Osborne, J. W. (1995). Academics, self-esteem, and race: A look at the assumptions underlying the disidentification hypothesis. *Personality and Social Psychology Bulletin, 21*(5), 449–455.

Osborne, J. W., & Blanchard, M. R. (2011). Random responding from participants is a threat to the validity of social science research results. *Frontiers in Psychology, 1*, 1–7.

Osborne, J. W., & Walker, C. (2006). Stereotype threat, identification with academics, and withdrawal from school: Why the most successful students of colour might be most likely to withdraw. *Educational Psychology, 26*(4), 563–577.

Preacher, K., Rucker, D., MacCallum, R., & Nicewander, W. (2005). Use of the extreme groups approach: A critical reexamination and new recommendations. *Psychological Methods, 10*(2), 178–192.

Roberts, L. W. (2002). Informed consent and the capacity for voluntarism. *American Journal of Psychiatry, 159*(5), 705–712.

Rosenthal, R., & Rosnow, R. (2009). *Artifacts in behavioral research: Robert Rosenthal and Ralph L. Rosnow's classic books* (pp. 48–92). New York: Oxford University Press.

Rosnow, R., Rosenthal, R., McConochie, R., & Arms, R. (1969). Volunteer effects on experimental outcomes. *Educational and Psychological Measurement, 29*(4), 825–846.

Ross, M. W., Månsson, S.-A., Daneback, K., Cooper, A., & Tikkanen, R. (2005). Biases in internet sexual health samples: Comparison of an internet sexuality survey and a national sexual health survey in Sweden. *Social Science & Medicine, 61*(1), 245–252.

Sears, D. (1986). College sophomores in the laboratory: Influences of a narrow data base on social psychology's view of human nature. *Journal of Personality and Social Psychology, 51*(3), 515–530.

Shalala, D. (2000). Protecting research subjects—what must be done. *New England Journal of Medicine, 343*(11), 808–810.

Steele, C. M. (1997). A threat in the air: How stereotypes shape intellectual identity and performance. *American Psychologist, 52*(6), 613–629.

Steele, C. M., & Aronson, J. (1995). Stereotype threat and the intellectual test performance of African Americans. *Journal of Personality and Social Psychology, 69*(5), 797–811.

Temple, R., & Stockbridge, N. (2007). BiDil for heart failure in black patients: The U.S. Food and Drug Administration perspective. *Annals of Internal Medicine, 146*(1), 57–62.

Tobias, J., & Souhami, R. (1993). Fully informed consent can be needlessly cruel. *British Medical Journal, 307*(6913), 1199–1201.

Tourangeau, R., & Yan, T. (2007). Sensitive questions in surveys. *Psychological Bulletin, 133*(5), 859–883.

Turner, C., Ku, L., Rogers, S., Lindberg, L., Pleck, J., & Sonenstein, F. (1998). Adolescent sexual behavior, drug use, and violence: Increased reporting with computer survey technology. *Science, 280*(5365), 867–873.

⊰ FOUR ⊱

USING LARGE DATA SETS WITH PROBABILITY SAMPLING FRAMEWORKS

Debunking the Myth of Equality

Large, governmental or international data sets are important resources for researchers in the social sciences. They present researchers with the opportunity to examine trends and hypotheses within nationally (or internationally) representative data sets that are difficult to acquire without the resources of a large research institution or governmental agency. In Chapter 3 I introduced you to the Education Longitudinal Study of 2002 from the National Center for Educational Statistics, and in coming chapters I again refer to this and other large data sets for examples and demonstrations. Students in my research classes often use at least one of these publicly available data sets each semester. They are valuable tools for exploring policy questions, important trends, historical changes, and testing new theories (as I did with Claude Steele's stereotype threat theories a decade or more ago).[1]

Yet all too often, students and researchers jump into using one of these publicly accessible data sets without fully understanding some of the technical issues around using them. In this chapter, I try to present some of the larger issues so that if you are considering using them, you understand the importance of accounting for complex sampling methodologies even before you begin cleaning the data for analysis.

While these data sets are valuable, there are drawbacks to using them. For example, individual researchers must take the data as given—in other words, we have no control over the types of questions asked, how they are asked, to whom they are asked, and when they are asked. Variables might not be measured in an ideal way, or they might not be ideally suited to answering the particular questions you, as an individual researcher, might wish to ask.

The one cost of using these types of data is the expectation that researchers will utilize best practices in using these samples. Specifically, researchers must take the time to understand the sampling methodology used and appropriately make use of weighting and design effects, which to a novice can be potentially confusing and intimidating. There is mixed evidence on researchers' use of appropriate methodology (e.g., Johnson & Elliott, 1998), which highlights the need for more conversation around this important issue. Specifically, there is some question as to whether even studies using these types of data sets published in top-tier, peer reviewed journals are utilizing appropriate methodology for dealing with the complexities introduced with the types of sampling these data sets employ.

WHAT TYPES OF STUDIES USE COMPLEX SAMPLING?

Many large, interesting databases available to researchers use complex sampling, such as data from the following.

- National Center for Educational Statistics (NCES) in the United States. For example, the Education Longitudinal Study 2002 (ELS 2002), National Education Longitudinal Study of 1988 (NELS 88), and Third International Mathematics and Science Study (TIMSS).[2]
- Centers for Disease Control and Prevention (CDC), such as the National Health Interview Survey (NHIS) and the National Health and Nutrition Examination Survey (NHANES).[3]
- The Bureau of Justice Statistics, including the National Crime Victimization Survey (NCVS).[4]

Almost any survey seeking a representative sample from a large population probably will have a complex multistage probability sampling methodology, as it is relatively efficient and allows for estimation of representative samples.

WHY DOES COMPLEX SAMPLING MATTER?

In most of the examples cited above, the samples are not simple random samples of a population of interest, but rather complex samples with multiple goals. For example, in NELS 88, students in certain underrepresented racial groups and in private schools were *oversampled* (i.e., more respondents selected than would typically be the case for a representative sample), meaning that the sample is not, in its initial form, necessarily representative (Ingels, 1994; Johnson & Elliott, 1998). Furthermore, in any survey like the ones discussed above there is a certain amount of nonresponse that may or may not be random (see Chapter 6 on missing data), making unweighted samples potentially still less representative.

In contrast to simple random sampling, multistage probability sampling often utilizes cluster sampling (especially where personal interviews are required), in which clusters of individuals within primary sampling units are selected for convenience. For example, in ELS 2002, approximately 20,000 students were sampled from 752 schools, rather than simply random sampling from the approximately 27,000 schools that met criteria within the United States (Bozick, Lauff, & Wirt, 2007). In the case of educational research, there are multiple possible strategies a researcher could use to get a large sample. One way, involving a simple random sample, would be to get a list of all students in all schools within the United States and randomly select a certain number of them, which would produce a nationally representative sample, but at huge cost. One reason institutions use probability sampling is that when they have to interview students and parents, it is inefficient to go to a school to only interview one student and parent. In theory, this approach could leave researchers crisscrossing the country going to thousands of different schools.

Another drawback of simple random sampling is that small groups of interest may be completely missed by simple random sampling. For example, in earlier national studies such as High School and Beyond, there was an interest in making sure certain underrepresented minority groups (e.g., Alaskan natives, Native Americans) were represented in large enough numbers to be analyzable. With simple random sampling it is possible that even large samples would not have enough members of these groups to analyze effectively. Further, special interest groups (e.g., African American students at private schools) are likely to suffer a similar fate under a simple random sampling technique.

Another possibility would be convenience sampling, wherein a researcher goes around the country to selected schools and samples. This has obvious drawbacks in terms of representativeness, but obvious appeal in terms of efficiency. Multistage probability sampling attempts to combine the advantages of convenience sampling with the advantages of random sampling to produce an efficient way to create a truly representative sample. This sampling methodology identifies groups of institutions, for example, and then randomly selects a certain number of individuals within that institution. By knowing the number of institutions and the number of students within each institution, researchers can create weights that, when appropriately applied, allow the sample to be representative of the population of interest.

But because this is not a simple random sample, individuals within clusters are more similar than individuals randomly sampled from the population as a whole. This allows organizations to assemble nationally representative samples while minimizing expense, but effectively reduces the information contained in each degree of freedom. Called *design effects* (DEFFs; Kish, 1965, is often credited with introducing this concept) these effects of sampling must also be accounted for or the researcher risks misestimating effects and increasing the probability of making Type I errors. This is because modern sampling strategies can lead to violation of traditional assumptions of independence of observations. Specifically, without correcting for design effects, standard errors are often underestimated, leading to significance tests that are inappropriately sensitive (e.g., Johnson & Elliott, 1998; Lehtonen & Pahkinen, 2004).

In sum, two issues are introduced by complex sampling: a sample that in its original form potentially deviates substantially from representative of the population of interest, and a sample that violates assumptions of independence of observations, potentially leading to significant misestimation of significance levels in inferential statistical tests. The good news is that there are simple ways to account for these issues when doing quantitative analyses.

BEST PRACTICES IN ACCOUNTING FOR COMPLEX SAMPLING

In most samples of this nature, the data provider includes information in the data set (and in the user documentation) to facilitate appropriate use of the data. For example, weights for each individual, information about DEFFs for the overall sample and different subpopulations, as well as information on which primary sampling unit (PSU) and cluster each individual belongs to.

More information on these topics is available in most user manuals for those interested in the technical details of how each of these pieces of information are calculated and used.[5] Most modern statistical packages can easily incorporate these weights and design effects into analyses.

Applying appropriate weights creates a sample that is representative of the population of interest (e.g., eighth graders in the United States who remained in school through 12th grade, to continue the previous example from NELS 88). In most statistical software packages, doing this is as simple as identifying the variable that contains weights for each individual and then telling the software to apply those weights. For example, in SPSS a simple menu under *DATA* allows application of a weight, or a single line of syntax:

Weight by *<variablename>*.

The problem is that application of weights dramatically increases the sample size to approximately the size of the population (in NELS 88, for example, a sample of approximately 25,000 becomes the population of more than 3 million students), dramatically (and illegitimately) inflating the degrees of freedom used in inferential statistics. Previous best practices included scaling the weights, so that the weighted sample has the same weighted number of participants as the original, unweighted sample. I did this in some of my early research (e.g., Osborne, 1995, 1997), but scaling the weights does not take into account the design effects, which should further reduce the degrees of freedom available for the statistical tests.

Not all statistical software provides for accurate modeling of complex samples (e.g., SPSS requires users to purchase an additional module; in SAS, STATA, and SUDAAN, complex sampling appears to be incorporated, and software is also freely available, such as AM,[6] that correctly deals with this issue). For those without access to software that models complex samples accurately (again, as was the case long ago when I first started working with large data sets) one way to approximate best practices in complex sampling would be to further scale the weights to take into account design effects (e.g., if the DEFF = 1.80 for whatever sample or subsample a researcher is interested in studying, that researcher would divide all weights by 1.80, which has the effect of reducing degrees of freedom almost by half).

Obviously, the most desirable way of dealing with this issue is using software that has the capability to directly model the weight, primary sampling unit, and cluster directly, which best accounts for the effects of the complex sampling (e.g., Bozick et al., 2007; Ingels, 1994; Johnson & Elliott, 1998). In most cases, a simple set of commands informs the statistical software what weight you desire to use, what variable contains the PSU information, and what variable contains the cluster information, and the analyses are adjusted from that point on, automatically. Yet because not all will have access to this sort of software, in this chapter I compare and contrast both scaling (the way we had to do it in the "old days") and appropriately modeling the complex sample. You will see that if you do not have the capability to model complex samples in your software, the best old-school approach will not cause substantial problems.

DOES IT REALLY MAKE A DIFFERENCE IN THE RESULTS?

Some authors have argued that, particularly for complex analyses like multiple regression, it is acceptable to use unweighted data (e.g., Johnson & Elliott, 1998). To explore whether this really does have the potential to make a substantial difference in the results of an analysis, I present several analyses, below, under four different conditions that might reflect various strategies researchers would take to using this sort of data: (a) unweighted (taking the sample as is), (b) weighted only (population estimate), (c) weighted, using weights scaled to maintain original sample size and to account for DEFF (best approximation), and (d) using appropriate complex sampling analyses via AM.[7] For these examples, the ELS 2002 data set (introduced in Chapter 3) was used.

Condition

Unweighted. In this condition, the original sample (meeting condition G10COHRT = 1 and F1PNLWT > 0.00) was retained with no weighting or accommodation for complex sampling. This resulted in a sample of $N = 14,654$.

Weighted. In this condition, F1PNLWT was applied to the sample of 14,654 who met the inclusion criteria for the study. Application of F1PNLWT inflated the sample size to 3,388,462. This condition is a likely outcome when researchers with only passing familiarity with the nuances of weighting complex samples attempt to use a complex sample.

Scaled Weights. In this condition, F1PNLWT was divided by 231.232, bringing the sample size back to approximately the original sample size but retaining the representativeness of the population. Further, the weights were scaled by the design effect (1.88 for examples using only males, yielding a final sample of 3,923 males, or 2.33 for examples using all subjects, yielding a final sample of 6,289) to approximate use of best practices. This condition is a likely outcome when a researcher is sophisticated enough to understand the importance of correcting for these issues but does not have access to software that appropriately models the complex sampling.

Appropriately Modeled. In this case, AM software was used to appropriately model the weight, PSU, and cluster information provided in the data to account for all issues mentioned above. This is considered the "gold standard" for purposes of this analysis. Identical results should be obtained by any software that models probability samples, including SPSS with the complex samples module, SAS, STATA, and more.

Four different analyses were compared to explore the potential effects of failing to use best practices in modeling complex samples.

Large Effect in OLS Regression

In this example, 12th grade mathematics IRT achievement score (F1TX-M1IR) is predicted from base year reading IRT achievement score (BYTXRIRR) controlling for socioeconomic status (F1SES2). The results of this analysis across all four conditions are presented in Table 4.1.

As Table 4.1 shows, with an unusually strong effect (e.g., $\beta > 0.60$) there is not a substantial difference in the effect regardless of whether the complex sampling design is accounted for or not. However, note that the standard errors vary dramatically across condition. Note also that the scaled weights condition closely approximates the appropriately modeled condition. However, as following analyses will show, this is possibly the exception, rather than the rule.

Modest Effect in Binary Logistic Regression

To test the effects of condition on a more modest effect, African American males were selected for a logistic regression predicting dropout (F1DOSTAT; $0 =$ never, $1 =$ dropped out), from the importance of having children, controlling for standardized reading test scores in 10th grade.

The results of these analyses are presented in Table 4.2 on page 79. The results indicate that the conclusions across all four analyses are similar—that

Table 4.1　Large Effect: OLS Regression Predicting 12th Grade Math Achievement From 10th Grade Reading Achievement

Analysis	Group	b	SE	t (df)	p <	Beta
SPSS, no weighting	WhiteM	1.009	0.019	14.42 (3858)	.0001	.647
	AfAmM	0.959	0.040	23.91 (807)	.0001	.638
SPSS, weight only	WhiteM	1.027	0.001	872.25 (927909)	.0001	.658
	AfAmM	0.951	0.003	379.40 (201334)	.0001	.642
SPSS, weights scaled for N, DEFF	WhiteM	1.027	0.025	41.806 (2132)	.0001	.658
	AfAmM	0.951	0.052	18.138 (460)	.0001	.642
AM weight, PSU, Strata modeled	WhiteM	1.027	0.023	45.35 (362)	.0001	N/A
	AfAmM	0.951	0.049	19.41 (232)	.0001	

Note: males only; BYTXRIRR predicting F1TXM1IR controlling for F1SES2.

as the importance of having children increases, the odds of dropping out decrease among African American males. However, there are several important differences across the conditions. First, the standard error of *b* varies dramatically across the four analyses. Second, the results from the scaled weights analyses and the appropriately modeled analysis were again similar. Finally, this analysis is an example of a potential Type I error: using the original sample with no weights or nonscaled weights produces a clear rejection of the null hypothesis, while the appropriately weighted analysis might not if one uses a rigid *p* < .05 cutoff criterion for rejection of the null hypothesis (which is not something I personally recommend).

Null Effect in ANOVA

To test the effects of condition on an analysis where the null hypothesis should be retained (no effect), an ANOVA was performed examining sex differences (F1SEX) in the importance of strong friendships (F1S40D). Using our gold standard of modeling the complex sample effects via AM, as Table 4.3 indicates, there should be no differences across groups.

Table 4.2   Modest Effect: Logistic Regression Predicting Dropout From Importance Having Children

Analysis	b	SE	Wald	p <	Exp(b)
SPSS, no weighting	−0.09	0.146	5.59	.018	0.709
SPSS, weight only	−0.346	0.008	1805.85	.0001	0.708
SPSS, weights scaled for N, DEFF	−0.344	0.170	4.154	.042	0.708
AM weight, PSU, Strata modeled	−0.346	0.177	3.806	.052	N/A

Note: African American males only; F1DOSTAT never versus DO only; controlling for BYTXRSTD.

Table 4.3   Null Effect: Sex Differences in Importance of Strong Friendships (F1S40D)

Analysis	Group	Mean	SE mean	t (df)	p <
SPSS, no weighting	Male	2.827	0.0050	−1.67 (14,539)	.095
	Female	2.838	0.0048		
SPSS, weight only	Male	2.822	0.0003	−25.53 (3,360,675)	.0001
	Female	2.833	0.0003		
SPSS, weights scaled for N, DEFF	Male	2.822	0.0077	−1.100 (6,236)	.27
	Female	2.833	0.0075		
AM weight, PSU, Strata modeled	Male	2.822	0.0060	−1.366 (386)	.17
	Female	2.833	0.0060		

As Table 4.3 shows, this is a good example of the risks associated with failing to appropriately model or approximate complex sampling weights and design effects. A researcher using only the original weights would conclude there is evidence of sex differences in the importance of strong friendships amongst high school students when in fact there should not be. Finally, there is again similarity between the third (scaled weights) and fourth condition (AM analysis) indicating that the approximation in this case yields similar results to the AM analysis.

Null Effect in OLS Regression

In the final example, a multiple regression analysis predicted cumulative ninth to 12th grade GPA (F1RGPP2) from school poverty (percentage of students with free or reduced lunch; BY10FLP) controlling for dummy-coded race (based on F1RACE), and whether the school was public or private (BYSCTRL).

As Table 4.4 shows, in this case a stark contrast exists between appropriately modeled complex sampling and less ideal analyses. In this example, researchers using the unweighted sample or a weighted sample would make a Type I error, rejecting the null hypothesis and concluding there is a significant (albeit weak) relationship between school poverty and student GPA once other background variables were covaried. The last two conditions (scaled weights and AM modeling) produced similar results, indicating no significant effect. This is contrary to the results from the inappropriately modeled analyses.

SO WHAT DOES ALL THIS MEAN?

While this might seem an esoteric topic to many researchers, a wealth these types of data sets is easily accessible to researchers from all areas of science, and it is probably beneficial for these data sets to be fully explored. However, some have found evidence that researchers do not always model the complex sampling frame appropriately (Johnson & Elliott, 1998). When this happens,

Table 4.4   Null Effect: Predicting Student GPA From School Poverty, Controlling for Race, School Sector

Analysis	*b*	*SE*	*t (df)*	*p <*
SPSS, no weighting	−0.21	0.069	−2.98 (5,916)	.003
SPSS, weight only	−0.01	0.005	−2.09 (1,124,550)	.04
SPSS, weights scaled for *N*, DEFF	−0.01	0.11	−0.09 (2,078)	.93
AM weight, PSU, Strata modeled	−0.01	0.17	−0.058 (228)	.95

researchers may be at risk for drawing false conclusions. In three of the four examples included earlier, researchers might be at serious risk of drawing incorrect conclusions if they fail to take the sampling effects into account. In two of the four analyses, researchers would clearly make a Type I error, while in the logistic regression example it is less clear but still troubling.

Further, most of the analyses highlight how unweighted samples can misestimate not only parameter estimates, but also standard errors. This is because the unweighted sample is usually not representative of the population as a whole and contains many eccentricities, such as oversampling of populations of interest and perhaps nonrandom dropout patterns. Weighting provides a better parameter estimate, but, unless further measures are taken, serious errors can occur in hypothesis testing and drawing of conclusions because of inappropriately inflated degrees of freedom (in this case inflating *df* from approximately 15,000 to more than 3 million). Thus, while it requires extra effort to appropriately model the complex samples in these data sets, it is a necessary step to have confidence in the results arising from the analyses.

FOR FURTHER ENRICHMENT

1. Examine a study in your field that utilized a public data set like the ones described in this chapter. Did the authors use best practices in accommodating the sampling issues?

2. Find a data set in your field of interest that utilized complex sampling. Through reviewing the user manuals, identify the weighting variables and what design effects you might need to account for. Find out how to utilize this information in the statistical software you most commonly use.

3. Pick a relatively simple analysis (simple one-way ANOVA or simple correlation) and perform analyses of interest to you using both appropriate handling of the complex sampling and inappropriate handling of the sampling. Compare results to see how serious an error you are likely to make if you fail to appropriately model sampling in your analyses. If you do not have access to other data sets, earlier in the chapter I mentioned popular data sets in a variety of social science disciplines.

4. Pick a commonly used data set in your field that requires the use of complex sampling. Perform a search of scholarly articles published using that

data set and describe what percentage of the authors appropriately modeled the sampling issues. If you find interesting data, share it with me (jason-wosborne@gmail.com) and I will post it on the book's website.

NOTES

1. Thanks to John Wirt from the National Center for Educational Statistics and David Miller from the American Institute for Research for their mentorship on this issue. Further acknowledgements to a mentor from too long ago at the University of Buffalo, Robert Nichols, who helped me learn to love working with complex data sets.

2. Available through the NCES website (http://nces.ed.gov/) or the Interuniversity Consortium for Political and Social Research website (http://www.icpsr.umich.edu).

3. Available through the CDC website (http://www.cdc.gov/nchs/index.htm).

4. Available through the bureau's website (http://bjs.ojp.usdoj.gov/index.cfm?ty=dctp&tid=3).

5. In many data sets there are multiple options for weights. For example, in NELS 88, a survey of eighth grade students who were then followed for many years, there is a weight only for individuals interested in using the first (BY) data collection. A similar weight exists for each other data collection point (F1, F2, F3, and so on). Yet not all students present in BY are present also in F1 and F2, so if I want to perform an analysis following students from 8th grade to 10th and 12th grade, there is a weight (called a *panel* weight) for longitudinal analyses as well. This highlights the importance of being thoroughly familiar with the details of the user manual before using data from one of these studies.

6. Available from the AM Statistical website (http://am.air.org/).

7. In order to examine the effects of utilization of best practices in modeling complex samples, the original tenth grade (G10COHRT = 1) cohort from the Education Longitudinal Study of 2002 (along with the first follow-up) public release data was analyzed. Only students who were part of the original cohort (G10COHRT = 1) and who had weight over 0.00 on F1PNLWT (the weight for using both 10th and 12th grade data collection time points) were retained so that the identical sample is used throughout all analyses.

REFERENCES

Bozick, R., Lauff, E., & Wirt, J. (2007). *Education Longitudinal Study of 2002 (ELS: 2002): A first look at the initial postsecondary experiences of the sophomore class of 2002* (NCES 2008-308). Washington, DC: National Center for Education Statistics, Institute of Education Sciences, U.S. Department of Education.

Ingels, S. (1994). *National Education Longitudinal Study of 1988: Second follow-up: Student component data file user's manual*. Washington, DC: U.S. Deptartment of

Education, Office of Educational Research and Improvement, National Center for Education Statistics.

Johnson, D. R., & Elliott, L. A. (1998). Sampling design effects: Do they affect the analyses of data from the national survey of families and households? *Journal of Marriage and Family, 60*(4), 993–1001.

Kish, L. (1965). *Survey sampling.* New York: Wiley.

Lehtonen, R., & Pahkinen, E. (2004). *Practical methods for design and analysis of complex surveys.* Hoboken, NJ: Wiley.

Osborne, J. (1995). Academics, self-esteem, and race: A look at the underlying assumptions of the disidentification hypothesis. *Personality and Social Psychology Bulletin, 21*(5), 449–455.

Osborne, J. (1997). Race and academic disidentification. *Journal of Educational Psychology, 89*(4), 728–735.

❧ SECTION II ❧

BEST PRACTICES IN DATA CLEANING AND SCREENING

⁑ FIVE ⁑

SCREENING YOUR DATA
FOR POTENTIAL PROBLEMS

Debunking the Myth of Perfect Data

> *Part of a complete statistical analysis is an assessment of assumptions including any distributional assumptions.*
>
> (DeCarlo, 1997, p. 296)

In upcoming chapters I discuss the importance of screening your data for extreme scores (e.g., outliers) and performing data transformations to improve the normality of your variables, which can have important implications for the normality of your data. The goal of this chapter is to talk about some of the practical aspects of data screening using modern statistical software.

In quantitative research methods, the standard normal distribution (or the *bell-shaped curve*) is a symmetrical distribution with known mathematical properties.[1] Most relevant to our discussion, we know what percentage of a population falls at any given point of the normal distribution, which also gives us the probability that an individual with a given score (or above or below that score, as well) on the variable of interest would be drawn at random from a normally distributed population.

For example, we know that in a perfectly normal distribution, 68.26% of the population will fall within 1 standard deviation (*SD*) of the mean. That means that most individuals randomly sampled from a normally distributed population should fall relatively close to the mean. It also means we can calculate other interesting statistics, like percentage of individuals that should fall

How do they know my daughter is in the 5th percentile for weight?

When we took our infant daughter to the pediatrician, the first thing our nurse did was measure her height, weight, and head circumference. The pediatrician then told us what percentile she was for each measurement. How did she do that?

The process is similar for deciding whether a statistical test is "significant" at p < .05. The key to all of this, and much of parametric statistics, is the standard normal distribution (although not all percentiles are based on the normal distribution).

One of the fun properties of the standard normal distribution is that we know what percentage of the population falls above or below any given point. When these data are based on good statistics from the population, doctors such as our daughter's pediatrician can use them to tell nervous parents whether their child is below or above average for height and weight.

Using the same process, researchers can determine the probability of obtaining certain results (e.g., the probability two group means would be a certain distance apart if in the population there was no difference between the groups) and make a decision whether to reject a hypothesis.

But remember, if the data are not normally distributed, it is misleading to draw conclusions based on the standard normal distribution!

above or below a point. According to common statistics tables, we know that 34.13% of individuals fall between the mean and 1 standard deviation above the mean. We also know that 50% of individuals fall below the mean (again, remember we are assuming a normal distribution—this does not apply to variables not distributed normally!). Thus, an individual who is 1 standard deviation above the mean is at the 84.13rd percentile (50% + 34.13%). An individual 1 standard deviation below the mean is at the 15.87th percentile (50% − 34.13%).

Likewise, 95.44% of the population should fall within ± 2.0 standard deviations from the mean,[2] and that 99.74% of the population will fall within ± 3.0 standard deviations of the mean. You can see in Figure 5.1 an expectation that a particular percentage of the population will fall between any two points on a normally distributed variable.

Imagine at the pediatrician's visit, my 6-month-old child weighs 13.5 pounds and the mean for that age is 15.0 with a standard deviation of 3.0. That equals a z score of −0.50.

Figure 5.1   The Standard Normal Distribution

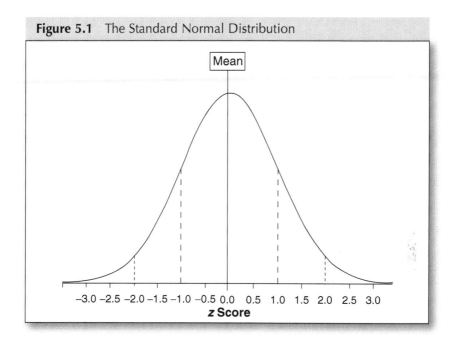

My child's weight is one half of 1 standard deviation below the mean. So she weighs slightly less than average. By looking up $z = -0.50$ in any z-score table (such as the one in the appendix of this chapter) you can see that this z score corresponds to 0.2776, meaning 27.76% of the population falls at or below this number. Another way of saying this is my child's weight is the 27.76th percentile. And no wonder; my daughter Olivia is *very active.*

Now imagine that you are taking the MCATs to get into medical school. You are applying to very selective schools, meaning that you must do very well compared to your peers in order to be accepted. According to my infor-mation, each scale on the test has a normal distribution with a mean of 8 and a standard deviation of 2.5. Thus, if you scored an 11, your z score would be:

$$z = \frac{(12-8)}{2.5} = 1.60 = 0.9452 \text{ or } 94.52\text{th percentile.}$$

In other words, you scored higher than 94.52% of the other students taking the MCATs that year, and the odds are good you will get accepted into the school of your choice. So how does this relate to statistical analyses? In brief, we also use our knowledge of this sort of process to understand how likely it is we would observe some pattern of results *if in fact the null hypothesis were true* (e.g., what is the probability you would see a correlation of −.32 in your sample if in reality the population correlation was .00?). In general, then, we compare that probability to the conventional $p < .05$ and if the probability is less than .05 (i.e., if the odds we would get our results from a sample when in fact the population results are null) then we say we reject the null hypothesis and discuss the alternative.

The important thing to remember is that all our parametric statistics (which include most of the commonly used statistical tests such as regression and ANOVA, as well as many more advanced techniques) assume variables are normally distributed because they use information such as this to determine the probability of achieving those results if in fact the null hypothesis (e.g., no correlation, no differences between groups) was true. So in many cases, having variables that violate this assumption of normality can substantially bias the results of your analyses (Yuan, Bentler, & Zhang, 2005). From a scientific point of view, this can make you more likely to draw the wrong conclusion (e.g., make a Type I error asserting that an effect exists when in fact there is none, or making a Type II error, which is failing to see an effect when in fact there is one), which is obviously undesirable. In other words, most procedures that assume normal distributions are relatively *nonrobust* (meaning not immune) to even modest violations of this assumption (Micceri, 1989).

From a more practical point of view, subsequent chapters explore how improving the normality of your variables not only reduces the odds of making one of these errors of inference, but also can improve the effect sizes of your analyses, making them more accurate estimates of what is actually in the population of interest.

Before we get into the effects of nonnormality in future chapters, here we focus on different techniques to screen your data so that you can diagnose whether you have an issue with nonnormality or extreme scores. This is an important, yet often overlooked first step in statistical analysis (DeCarlo, 1997), as the majority of variables you are likely to be analyzing are probably not normally distributed (Micceri, 1989)

THE LANGUAGE OF DESCRIBING DISTRIBUTIONS

In general we use two different terms to describe the distribution of variables: *skew* and *kurtosis*. Skew refers to how symmetrical the variable is. As you can see in Figure 5.2, the students in my undergraduate educational psychology class tend to do well on my exams. The data is not remotely symmetrical as the curve in Figure 5.1, but rather is highly skewed. In this case, we would say that the distribution is *negatively skewed*, as the "tail" of the distribution (the elongated part of the curve where there are relatively few individuals) points toward the negative portion of the number line if it were extended below zero. If the distribution were reversed, as the data in Figure 5.3, we would say that distribution is *positively skewed* because the tail of the distribution is pointing toward the positive end of the number line.

Kurtosis is the other aspect of describing the shape of a distribution. It refers to the height of the variable in relation to its width. Again, using our standard normal distribution in Figure 5.1 as our gold standard, a *leptokurtotic* distribution is one that is too "slender" or tall relative to its tails. So a leptokurtotic distribution would be taller and narrower (with heavier tails and a higher peak) than the curve in Figure 5.1, and would have a higher or positive value for kurtosis (in many statistical software packages, kurtosis of 0.00 is perfectly normal). The student grades in Figure 5.2 are a good example of a

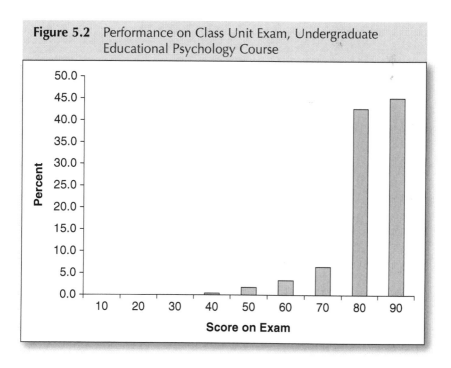

Figure 5.2 Performance on Class Unit Exam, Undergraduate Educational Psychology Course

Figure 5.3 Deaths From Horse Kicks, Prussian Army 1875–1894

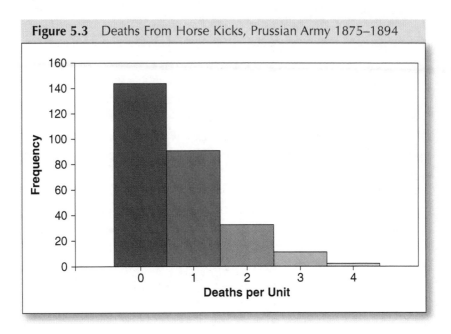

leptokurtotic (and highly skewed) distribution—the tails are too thin and long relative to the peak. A *platykurtotic* distribution is a distribution that is flatter and wider than a normally distributed variable, as though we took the distribution in Figure 5.1 and pushed down on the top, squashing it. Platykurtosis is also sometimes characterized as having "lighter tails than normal" (DeCarlo, 1997, p. 292; see also Pearson, 1905). A platykurtotic distribution would have a negative kurosis value.

Ceiling and Floor Effects

One topic related to normality is that of a ceiling or floor effect, introduced in Chapter 3. These are most commonly encountered when variation in responses are inhibited in some way, artificially attenuating the variation one would normally expect to see. For example, in educational research, giving students a test that is too hard or too easy can artificially attenuate variation. Giving second graders a multiple-choice high school calculus test would create a floor effect. Many will receive scores around 25%, representing random guessing. In this case, many students would have scored much worse than 25% if the measure of calculus ability was more carefully calibrated to be age appropriate. Thus, we can say many students find the floor of the measure. Conversely, giving high school students a second grade math test should produce a ceiling effect. Many will score 100% (if they truly are trying their best), but that does not truly assess their mathematical ability. We can say many of these students hit the ceiling of the measure, due to the mismatch between the ability of the student and the range of ability the test is assessing. Ceiling and floor effects are issues of calibration—matching the test to the population.

Another common example of this sort of issue can be found in mental or physical health inventories (e.g., O'Mahony, Rodgers, Thomson, Dobson, & James, 1998). For example, administering a wellness inventory intended for the general population to severely ill individuals (e.g., stroke patients or advanced cancer patients) could create floor effects. Likewise, administering a depression inventory intended for the general population to patients experiencing hospitalization for depression could create ceiling effects.

These effects create nonnormal distributions that are not always easily dealt with through methods discussed in coming chapters. Rather this is an issue best dealt with at the beginning of a study, ensuring the measures a researcher will use are appropriate (and validated) for the population of interest.

Again, remember that the reason why we care about the shape of a distribution is because if we assume a distribution is normal and it is not, all our assumptions about the probability of certain outcomes occurring are wrong, exposing us to increased likelihood of errors of inference.

TESTING WHETHER YOUR DATA ARE NORMALLY DISTRIBUTED

The Ocular Test

The most time-honored method of determining whether a variable is normally distributed is by looking at a histogram or other graphic representation of the distribution (modern statistical packages have excellent options for visual exploration of data). This is perhaps the most common and useful method researchers use. However, in my opinion, it is insufficient by itself, as decisions about normality based on visual inspection alone can be somewhat arbitrary.

I would suggest that you always look at a graphic representation of your data before doing *anything* else, as the human eye and brain are good at understanding nuances that simple numbers miss. Most researchers would recognize the data in Figure 5.1 as normal and the data in Figures 5.2 and 5.3 as non-normal, both skewed and leptokurtotic. However, in the 21st century, it is good to have objective evidence to corroborate conclusions from the ocular test.[3]

Examining Skew and Kurtosis Figures

Most statistical packages easily produce quantitative estimates of skew and kurtosis. There are various rules of thumb about what constitutes an acceptable skew or kurtosis. I often get concerned when I see skew or kurtosis moving toward 1.0 or −1.0, and have numerous examples of the beneficial effects of correcting skew of less than 1.0. Thus, it is difficult to give a definitive indication as to what is acceptable except to say that closer to normal is better than farther.

One further drawback to skew and kurtosis is that no consensus exists as to what constitutes a "significant" improvement in either. It is possible to imagine developing a measure using skew and the standard error of skew (or kurtosis and the standard error of kurtosis), but that may be more esoteric than necessary.

Obviously, as the data in Figure 5.1 was generated to be perfectly normal, it would have both a skew and kurtosis of 0.00. The data in Figure 5.2 has a skew of −1.75 and a kurtosis of 5.43 (indicating what is confirmed by visual inspection—that the tail of the distribution points to the left, and that the curve is narrower and taller, or "pointier" than desirable in a normal distribution). The data in Figure 5.3 is similarly nonnormal, with a skew of 1.24 (verifying our visual inspection that shows the tail of the distribution pointing to the right) and kurtosis of 1.20 (again, indicating a distribution that is narrower and taller, or "pointier" than a normal distribution.

An example of a platykurtotic distribution is obtained by examining student grades from Figure 5.2 but limiting the range to high-performing students (80% to 95%). This subsample yields a curve that is relatively symmetric (skew = −0.11) but is platykurtotic (kurtosis = −0.82, indicating it is flatter than a normal distribution), as shown in Figure 5.4.

Examining P-P Plots

P-P plots[4] examine the actual cumulative probabilities of your data from that expected from a theoretical normal distribution. If you have a perfectly

Figure 5.4 Grade Distribution of Scores Between 80 and 95

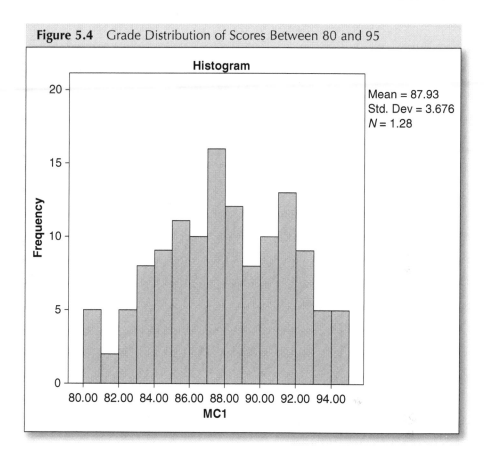

normal variable, the observed values (the dots) will fall exactly on the line (the expected values). In the P-P plot in Figure 5.5, you see the plot for socioeconomic status (SES) from a national data set (a very normal curve with a skew of 0.004 and kurtosis of −0.59). Thus, the normally distributed variable appears to follow the diagonal line very closely (essentially obscuring the line itself).

To the extent that you see substantial deviation from normal (as in Figure 5.6 on page 97, which comes from automobile crash test head injury data and has a skew of 1.67 and kurtosis of 4.52) you will see the observed data diverge from the line representing theoretical normality. This is merely another visual inspection tool for researchers.

Unfortunately, these plots share interpretive ambiguity with visual inspection and examination of skew and kurtosis statistics: there is once again no

Figure 5.5   A P-P Plot of a Mostly Normal Variable

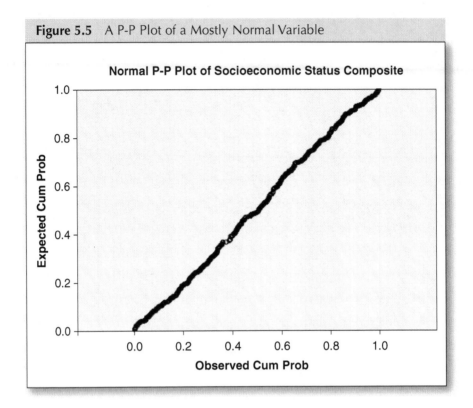

clear rule or guide to let you know how much of a deviation from normal is "too much." As I demonstrate in coming chapters, even seemingly modest deviations from normal can have implications for effect sizes.

Inferential Tests of Normality

Two of the most common inferential tests of normality—Kolmogorov-Smirnov (K-S) (with Lilliefors correction; see Lilliefors, 1967) and Shapiro-Wilk (S-W) (Shapiro & Wilk, 1965)—examine whether a variable conforms to a predetermined type of distribution (e.g., a normal distribution) or whether it differs *significantly*. Thus, these last two tests are examples of what might be one of the more objective ways to determine if your data are significantly different from normal. In all cases, the hypotheses tested are:

H_o: The variable distribution is not significantly different from normal.

H_a: The variable distribution is significantly different from normal.

Figure 5.6   A P-P Plot of a Negatively Skewed, Leptokurtic
Distribution

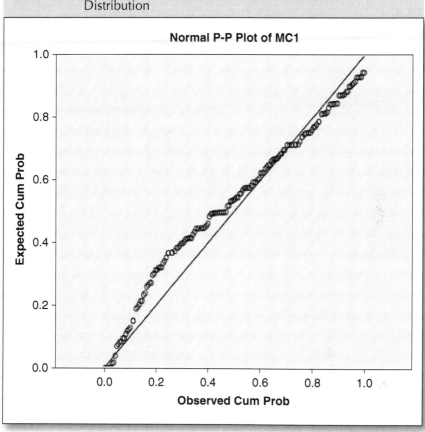

Recalling that the null hypothesis is that the variable is normally distributed, a significant (i.e., $p < .05$) result leads to the rejection of that hypothesis
and the conclusion the variable shows significant nonnormality and is then a
candidate for data cleaning in some way. S-W has often been discussed as
more accurate than K-S/Lilliefors (DeCarlo, 1997; Schoder, Himmelmann, &
Wilhelm, 2006; Shapiro, Wilk, & Chen, 1968). Yet in this type of analysis,
power from large samples may ironically make these tests undesirable.

How power can harm inferential tests of normality. This special type of
hypothesis testing is actually difficult to do in large-sample situations, as sensitivity to extremely minor deviations (i.e., unimportant deviations) from
normality becomes problematic quickly. The goal of using these tests is

betrayed if every test is significant, even for almost perfectly normal data. Thus, researchers need to interpret significant results with caution when samples are large (i.e., more than a couple hundred individuals).

Despite the K-S test (especially without the Lilliefors correction) being criticized in the literature for being insensitive to minor deviations, in larger-sample situations this might actually make it more desirable in the social sciences, where minor deviations from normality are practically unimportant (and usually unavoidable). As Table 5.1 shows, in a sample of more than 700 individuals, a relatively normal variable (SES) does not produce a significant K-S test statistic, but does under S-W. Both appear to be too sensitive to minor deviations from normality under very large sample conditions, so these tests must all be interpreted with caution (Steinskog, Tjøstheim, & Kvamstø, 2007) and in the context of what the goal of the researcher is (e.g., if the goal is wanting to be most sensitive to detecting deviations from normality then Shapiro-Wilk seems the best test).

Performing a K-S or S-W Test

Obviously, the details differ across software packages as to how to perform a K-S or S-W test. In SPSS, for example, you can perform a traditional K-S test by choosing ANALYSIS →NONPARAMETRIC TESTS → ONE SAMPLE (for the less sensitive K-S test) or you can go through ANALYSIS → DESCRIPTIVE STATISTICS → EXPLORE, selecting PLOT and checking NORMALITY PLOTS with tests, to perform a K-S test with Lilliefors correction (which appears to make it more sensitive to nonnormality).[5] Other statistical software has similar options.

As Table 5.1 shows, the K-S (with or without Lilliefors) test is nonsignificant for the two examples where it is probably *least* important for a researcher to deal with nonnormality (i.e., where the distributions were closest to normal) yet clearly identified the other two distributions as significantly different from normal and in need of attention. In contrast S-W may be too sensitive as it identified all four distributions as significantly different from normal (though in fairness, this test was designed to be more accurate in terms of identifying deviations from normality). In the chapters that follow, we will explore causes and solutions to substantial nonnormality.

Table 5.1 Results of Inferential Testing of Normality

	Ocular Test	Skew	Kurtos is	K-S (df)	p <	K-S With Lilliefors (df)	p <	S-W (df)	p <
Socioeconomic Status (Normal)	Normal	0.004	−0.59	0.75 (712)	.62	0.03 (712)	.20	0.99 (712)	.002
Student Grades	Negative skew + leptokurtotic	−1.75	5.43	1.65 (174)	.008	0.126 (174)	.0001	0.876 (174)	.0001
Student Grades (Only 80–95)	Symmetric but platykurtotic	−0.11	−0.82	0.81 (128)	.53	0.07 (128)	.19	0.98 (128)	.03
Horse Kicks	Positive skew + leptokurtotic	1.24	1.20	5.07 (280)	.0001	0.30 (280)	.0001	0.76 (280)	.0001

CONCLUSIONS

There is an art and a science to data screening and cleaning. The thoughtful researcher will use a variety of different pieces of information to determine the most reasonable course of action. Visual inspection of data will always be an important first step in understanding and screening that data, accompanied by quantitative information about the distributional qualities of the data (e.g., skew and kurtosis). Yet for many, that leaves the question of "how good is good enough" open to debate. Reviewers, thesis committee members, and even professors teaching quantitative methods courses are left open to justifiable debate and criticism if they use these pieces of information exclusively. It seems to me a much stronger and defensible position to be able to say that visual inspection, normality statistics, *and* inferential tests all support the argument that the data meet distributional assumptions.

Yet it is not always the case that all three pieces of information will point to the same conclusion. In this case, the professional, scholarly judgment of the statistician must come into play in making the best decisions about what steps might be necessary to prepare the data for analysis.

When Inferential Tests of Distributional Assumptions Might Not Be Valuable

Remember the K-S and S-W tests are attempting to detect deviations from normality, and that (like all inferential tests) the power to reject the null hypothesis (in this case the null hypothesis is the desired one to retain, to conclude that the data distribution is *not* significantly different from normal) is strongly influenced by sample size. For example, it might be that with a sample of 1,000 participants, it will be difficult to get a nonsignificant K-S or S-W test no matter how close to normally distributed the data are, because the power to detect minute deviations from normality is so great. Thus, in large samples, social scientists may find the inferential tests more of a guide than a final arbiter of distributional assumptions. A skilled statistician will utilize all information at hand, such as skew and kurtosis, as well as visual inspection of the data.

FOR FURTHER ENRICHMENT

1. Data sets mentioned in this chapter are available for download on the book's website. Download them and practice screening for nonnormality in the software you prefer. Identify how to perform a K-S test (with or without the Lilliefors correction) or the S-W test.

2. Explore a recent data set from your research, your advisor's research, or from a journal article you admire. Do the variables meet assumptions of normality according to the various methods discussed in this chapter?

3. Discuss basic data cleaning with another scholar in your field. Ask whether that person routinely screens data for normality. If not, ask why not. If so, ask what methods that person relies on to determine whether the assumption is met.

APPENDIX

Z-Score Table

Chart value corresponds to area below z score.

Table 5.2 Results of 100 Correlation Coefficients

z	0.09	0.08	0.07	0.06	0.05	0.04	0.03	0.02	0.01	0.00
−3.4	.0002	.0003	.0003	.0003	.0003	.0003	.0003	.0003	.0003	.0003
−3.3	.0003	.0004	.0004	.0004	.0004	.0004	.0004	.0005	.0005	.0005
−3.2	.0005	.0005	.0005	.0006	.0006	.0006	.0006	.0006	.0007	.0007
−3.1	.0007	.0007	.0008	.0008	.0008	.0008	.0009	.0009	.0009	.0010
−3.0	.0010	.0010	.0011	.0011	.0011	.0012	.0012	.0013	.0013	.0013
−2.9	.0014	.0014	.0015	.0015	.0016	.0016	.0017	.0018	.0018	.0019
−2.8	.0019	.0020	.0021	.0021	.0022	.0023	.0023	.0024	.0025	.0026
−2.7	.0026	.0027	.0028	.0029	.0030	.0031	.0032	.0033	.0034	.0035
−2.6	.0036	.0037	.0038	.0039	.0040	.0041	.0043	.0044	.0045	.0047

(Continued)

(Continued)

Z	0.09	0.08	0.07	0.06	0.05	0.04	0.03	0.02	0.01	0.00
−2.5	.0048	.0049	.0051	.0052	.0054	.0055	.0057	.0059	.0060	.0062
−2.4	.0064	.0066	.0068	.0069	.0071	.0073	.0075	.0078	.0080	.0082
−2.3	.0084	.0087	.0089	.0091	.0094	.0096	.0099	.0102	.0104	.0107
−2.2	.0110	.0113	.0116	.0119	.0122	.0125	.0129	.0132	.0136	.0139
−2.1	.0143	.0146	.0150	.0154	.0158	.0162	.0166	.0170	.0174	.0179
−2.0	.0183	.0188	.0192	.0197	.0202	.0207	.0212	.0217	.0222	.0228
−1.9	.0233	.0239	.0244	.0250	.0256	.0262	.0268	.0274	.0281	.0287
−1.8	.0294	.0301	.0307	.0314	.0322	.0329	.0336	.0344	.0351	.0359
−1.7	.0367	.0375	.0384	.0392	.0401	.0409	.0418	.0427	.0436	.0446
−1.6	.0455	.0465	.0475	.0485	.0495	.0505	.0516	.0526	.0537	.0548
−1.5	.0559	.0571	.0582	.0594	.0606	.0618	.0630	.0643	.0655	.0668
−1.4	.0681	.0694	.0708	.0721	.0735	.0749	.0764	.0778	.0793	.0808
−1.3	.0823	.0838	.0853	.0869	.0885	.0901	.0918	.0934	.0951	.0968
−1.2	.0985	.1003	.1020	.1038	.1056	.1075	.1093	.1112	.1131	.1151
−1.1	.1170	.1190	.1210	.1230	.1251	.1271	.1292	.1314	.1335	.1357
−1.0	.1379	.1401	.1423	.1446	.1469	.1492	.1515	.1539	.1562	.1587
−0.9	.1611	.1635	.1660	.1685	.1711	.1736	.1762	.1788	.1814	.1841
−0.8	.1867	.1894	.1922	.1949	.1977	.2005	.2033	.2061	.2090	.2119
−0.7	.2148	.2177	.2206	.2236	.2266	.2296	.2327	.2358	.2389	.2420
−0.6	.2451	.2483	.2546	.2514	.2578	.2611	.2643	.2676	.2709	.2743
−0.5	.2776	.2810	.2843	.2877	.2912	.2946	.2981	.3015	.3050	.3085
−0.4	.3121	.3156	.3192	.3228	.3264	.3300	.3336	.3372	.3409	.3446
−0.3	.3483	.3520	.3557	.3594	.3632	.3669	.3707	.3745	.3783	.3821
−0.2	.3859	.3897	.3936	.3974	.4013	.4052	.4090	.4129	.4168	.4207
−0.1	.4247	.4286	.4325	.4364	.4404	.4443	.4483	.4522	.4562	.4602
−0.0	.4641	.4681	.4721	.4761	.4801	.4840	.4880	.4920	.4960	.5000

Z	0.00	0.01	0.02	0.03	0.04	0.05	0.06	0.07	0.08	0.09
0.0	.5000	.5040	.5080	.5120	.5160	.5199	.5239	.5279	.5319	.5359
0.1	.5398	.5438	.5478	.5517	.5557	.5596	.5636	.5675	.5714	.5753
0.2	.5783	.5832	.5871	.5910	.5948	.5987	.6026	.6064	.6103	.6141
0.3	.6179	.6217	.6255	.6293	.6331	.6368	.6406	.6443	.6480	.6517
0.4	.6554	.6591	.6628	.6664	.6700	.6736	.6772	.6808	.6844	.6879
0.5	.6915	.6950	.6985	.7019	.7054	.7088	.7123	.7157	.7190	.7224
0.6	.7257	.7291	.7324	.7357	.7389	.7422	.7454	.7486	.7517	.7549
0.7	.7580	.7611	.7642	.7673	.7704	.7734	.7764	.7794	.7823	.7852

Z	0.00	0.01	0.02	0.03	0.04	0.05	0.06	0.07	0.08	0.09
0.8	.7881	.7910	.7939	.7967	.7995	.8023	.8051	.8078	.8106	.8133
0.9	.8159	.8186	.8212	.8238	.8264	.8289	.8115	.8340	.8365	.8389
1.0	.8413	.8438	.8461	.8485	.8508	.8531	.8554	.8577	.8599	.8621
1.1	.8643	.8665	.8686	.8708	.8729	.8749	.8770	.8790	.8810	8830
1.2	.8849	.8869	.8888	.8907	.8925	.8944	.8962	.8980	.8997	.9015
1.3	.9032	.9049	.9066	.9082	.9099	.9115	.9131	.9147	.9162	.9177
1.4	.9192	.9207	.9222	.9236	.9251	.9265	.9279	.9292	.9306	.9319
1.5	.9332	.9345	.9357	.9370	.9382	.9394	.9406	.9418	.9429	.9441
1.6	.9452	.9463	.9474	.9484	.9495	.9505	.9515	.9525	.9535	.9545
1.7	.9554	.9564	.9573	.9582	.9591	.9599	.9608	.9616	.9625	.9633
1.8	.9641	.9649	.9656	.9664	.9671	.9678	.9686	.9693	.9699	.9706
1.9	.9713	.9719	.9726	.9732	.9738	.9744	.9750	.9756	.9761	.9767
2.0	.9772	.9778	.9783	.9788	.9793	.9798	.9803	.9808	.9812	.9817
2.1	.9821	.9826	.9830	.9834	.9838	.9842	.9846	.9850	.9854	.9857
2.2	.9861	.9864	.9868	.9871	.9875	.9878	.9881	.9884	.9887	.9890
2.3	.9893	.9896	.9898	.9901	.9904	.9906	.9909	.9911	.9913	.9916
2.4	.9918	.9920	.9922	.9925	.9927	.9929	.9931	.9932	.9934	.9936
2.5	.9938	.9940	.9941	.9943	.9945	.9946	.9948	.9949	.9951	.9952
2.6	.9953	.9955	.9956	.9957	.9959	.9960	.9961	.9962	.9963	.9964
2.7	.9965	.9966	.9967	.9968	.9969	.9970	.9971	.9972	.9973	.9974
2.8	.9974	.9975	.9976	.9977	.9977	.9978	.9979	.9979	.9980	.9981
2.9	.9981	.9982	.9982	.9983	.9984	.9984	.9985	.9985	.9986	.9986
3.0	.9987	.9987	.9987	.9988	.9988	.9989	.9989	.9989	.9990	.9990
3.1	.9990	.9991	.9991	.9991	.9992	.9992	.9992	.9992	.9993	.9993
3.2	.9993	.9993	.9994	.9994	.9994	.9994	.9994	.9995	.9995	.9995
3.3	.9995	.9995	.9995	.9996	.9996	.9996	.9996	.9996	.9996	.9997
3.4	.9997	.9997	.9997	.9997	.9997	.9997	.9997	.9997	.9997	.9998

NOTES

1. $y = \frac{1}{\sqrt{2\pi}} e^{-x^2/2}$. (Spiegel, 1968).

2. That 95.0% fall within 1.96 standard deviation of the mean gives rise to the hallowed $p < .05$ criterion for null hypothesis significance testing. For some historical background on null hypothesis statistical testing, see Fisher (1925) and Neyman and Pearson (1936).

3. Thanks to my colleague Brett Jones, from Virginia Tech, who shared this term with me.

4. Not to be confused with Q-Q plots, which also serve to test for normality and compare the quantiles of the variable against the quantiles of the theoretical distribution.

5. The second, preferred method amongst statisticians applies the Lilliefors correction. Without this correction (as with the K-S test performed from the Non-Parametric menu option) the K-S test is considered to be biased.

REFERENCES

DeCarlo, L. (1997). On the meaning and use of kurtosis. *Psychological Methods, 2*(3), 292–307.

Fisher, R. A. (1925). *Statistical methods for research workers.* Edinburgh: Oliver & Boyd.

Lilliefors, H. (1967). On the Kolmogorov-Smirnov test for normality with mean and variance unknown. *Journal of the American Statistical Association, 62*(318), 399–402.

Micceri, T. (1989). The unicorn, the normal curve, and other improbable creatures. *Psychological Bulletin, 105*(1), 156–166.

Neyman, J., & Pearson, E. S. (1936). Contributions to the theory of testing statistical hypotheses. *Statistical Research Memoirs, 1*, 1–37.

O'Mahony, P. G., Rodgers, H., Thomson, R. G., Dobson, R., & James, O. F. W. (1998). Is the SF-36 suitable for assessing health status of older stroke patients? *Age and Ageing, 27*(1), 19–22.

Pearson, K. (1905). "Das Fehlergesetz und Seine Verallgemeinerungen Durch Fechner und Pearson" A rejoinder. *Biometrika, 4*(1/2), 169–212.

Schoder, V., Himmelmann, A., & Wilhelm, K. (2006). Preliminary testing for normality: Some statistical aspects of a common concept. *Clinical and experimental dermatology, 31*(6), 757–761.

Shapiro, S., & Wilk, M. (1965). An analysis of variance test for normality (complete samples). *Biometrika, 52*(3–4), 591.

Shapiro, S., Wilk, M., & Chen, H. (1968). A comparative study of various tests for normality. *Journal of the American Statistical Association, 63*(324), 1343–1372.

Spiegel, M. (1968). *Mathematics handbook of formulas and tables* (Vol. 18). New York: McGraw-Hill.

Steinskog, D. J., Tjøstheim, D. B., & Kvamstø, N. G. (2007). A cautionary note on the use of the Kolmogorov-Smirnov test for normality. *Monthly Weather Review, 135*(3), 1151–1157.

Yuan, K.-H., Bentler, P. M., & Zhang, W. (2005). The effect of skewness and kurtosis on mean and covariance structure analysis. *Sociological Methods & Research, 34*(2), 240–258.

⊰ SIX ⊱

DEALING WITH MISSING
OR INCOMPLETE DATA

Debunking the Myth of Emptiness

In almost any research you perform, there is the potential for missing or incomplete data. Missing data can occur for many reasons: participants can fail to respond to questions (legitimately or illegitimately—more on that later), equipment and data collecting or recording mechanisms can malfunction, subjects can withdraw from studies before they are completed, and data entry errors can occur. In later chapters I also discuss the elimination of extreme scores and outliers, which also can lead to missingness.

The issue with missingness is that nearly all classic and modern statistical techniques assume (or require) complete data, and most common statistical packages default to the least desirable options for dealing with missing data: deletion of the case from the analysis. Most people analyzing quantitative data allow the software to default to eliminating important data from their analyses, despite that individual or case potentially having a good deal of other data to contribute to the overall analysis.

It is my argument in this chapter that all researchers should examine their data for missingness, and researchers wanting the best (i.e., the most replicable and generalizable) results from their research need to be prepared to deal with missing data in the most appropriate and desirable way possible. In this chapter I briefly review common reasons for missing (or incomplete) data, compare and contrast several common methods for dealing with missingness, and demonstrate some of the benefits of using more modern methods (and some drawbacks of using the traditional, default methods) in the search for the best, most scientific outcomes for your research.

Is emptiness meaninglessness?

Modern researchers seem to view missing data as empty, useless, a void that should have been filled with information, a thing without pattern, meaning, or value.

Yet the ancient Greeks saw potential in emptiness. The Greek goddess Chaos (Khaos) represented unfilled space (initially the unfilled space between the earth and the heavens in the creation mythology), much as a blank canvas represents unfilled potential to an artist or a blank page to a writer. And ancient Olmec, Indian, and Arabic mathematicians saw usefulness in the mathematical quantification of nothing, what we now call zero (Colebrooke, 1817; Diehl, 2004).

The modern computer era is built upon use of 0s and 1s as indicators of important states, both meaningful and critical to the functioning of devices that are now ubiquitous. Just as our ancestors saw usefulness and information in absence, I propose to demonstrate that missingness can not only be informative, but in certain circumstances can also be filled with meaning and that those with missing data do not need to be banished from our analyses but rather can contribute to a more complete and accurate understanding of the population about which we wish to draw conclusions.

WHAT IS MISSING OR INCOMPLETE DATA?

The issue before us is whether we have complete data from all research participants on all variables (at all possible time points, if it is a repeated-measures design). If any data on any variable from any participant is not present, the researcher is dealing with missing or incomplete data. For the purposes of the rest of this chapter, we use the term *missing* to indicate that state of affairs. In many types of research, it is the case that there can be *legitimate missing data*. This can come in many forms, for many reasons. Most commonly, legitimate missing data is an absence of data when it is appropriate for there to be an absence. Imagine you are filling out a survey that asks you whether you are married,[1] and if so, how long you have been married. If you say you are not married, it is legitimate for you to skip the follow-up question on how long you have been married. If a survey asks you whether you voted in the last election, and if so, what party the candidate was from, it is legitimate to skip the second part if you did not vote in the last election.

In medical research, it is possible that whatever treatment a participant is receiving has eliminated the condition that person was getting treated for (since I am not a medical doctor, I will call that "being cured"). In a long-term study of people receiving a particular type of treatment, if you are no longer receiving treatment because you are cured, that might be a legitimate form of missing data. Or perhaps you are following employee satisfaction at a company. If an employee leaves the company (and thus is no longer an employee) it seems to me legitimate that person should no longer be responding to employee satisfaction questionnaires.

Large data sets, especially government data sets, are full of legitimately missing data, and researchers need to be thoughtful about handling this issue appropriately (as I hope you will be thoughtful about all issues around data cleaning). Note too that even in the case of legitimate missingness, missingness is meaningful. Missingness in this context informs and reinforces the status of a particular individual and can even provide an opportunity for checking the validity of an individual's responses. In cleaning the data from a survey on adolescent health risk behaviors many years ago, I came across some individuals who indicated on one question that they had never used illegal drugs, but later in the questionnaire, when asked how many times they had used marijuana, they answered that question indicating a number greater than 0. Thus, what should have been a question that was legitimately skipped was answered with an unexpected number. What could this mean? One possibility is that the respondent was not paying attention to the questions and answered carelessly or in error. Another possibility is that the initial answer (have you ever used illegal drugs) was answered incorrectly. It also is possible that some subset of the population did not include marijuana in the category of illegal drugs—an interesting finding in itself and one way in which researchers can use data cleaning to improve their subsequent research.

Legitimate missing data can be dealt with in different ways. One common way of dealing with this sort of data could be using analyses that do not require (or can deal effectively with) incomplete data. These include things like hierarchical linear modeling (HLM) (Raudenbush & Bryk, 2002) or survival analysis.[2] Another common way of dealing with this sort of legitimate missing data is adjusting the denominator (an important concept introduced in Chapter 3). Again taking the example of the marriage survey, we could eliminate non-married individuals from the particular analysis looking at length of marriage, but would leave nonmarried respondents in the analysis when looking at issues relating to being married versus not being married. Thus, instead of asking a slightly silly question of the data—"How long, on average, do all people, even unmarried people, stay married?"—we can ask two more refined questions: "What are the predictors of whether someone is currently married?" and "Of those who are currently married, how long on average have they been married?" In this case, it makes no sense to include nonmarried individuals in the data on how long someone has been married.

This example of dealing with legitimately missing data is relatively straightforward and mostly follows common sense. The best practice here is to make certain the denominator (the sample or subsample) is appropriate for the analysis. Be sure to report having selected certain parts of your sample for specific analyses when doing so. In the case of legitimate missing data, it is probably rare that a researcher would want to deal with it by imputing or substituting a value (as we discuss for illegitimately missing data below), as that again changes the research question being addressed to "If everyone was married, how long, on average, would they stay married?" That probably is not something that makes a tremendous amount of sense.

Illegitimately missing data is also common in all types of research. Sensors fail or become miscalibrated, leaving researchers without data until that sensor is replaced or recalibrated. Research participants choose to skip questions on surveys that the researchers expect everyone to answer. Participants drop out of studies before they are complete. Missing data also, somewhat ironically, can be caused by data cleaning. It is primarily this second type of missing data that I am most concerned with, as it has the potential to bias the results.

Few authors seem to explicitly deal with the issue of missing data, despite its obvious potential to substantially skew the results (Cole, 2008). For example, in a recent survey my students and I performed of highly regarded journals from the American Psychological Association, we found that more than one-third (38.89%) of authors discussed the issue of missing data in their articles (Osborne, Kocher, & Tillman, 2011). Do those 61% who fail to report anything relating to missing data have complete data (rare in the social sciences, but possible for some authors), do they have complete data because they removed all subjects with any missing data (undesirable, and potentially biasing the results, as we discuss next), did they deal effectively with the missing data and fail to report it (less likely, but possible), or did they allow the statistical software to treat the missing data via whatever the default method is, which most often leads to deletion of subjects with missing data? If our survey is representative of researchers across the sciences, we have cause for concern. Our survey found that of those researchers who did report something to do with missing data, most reported having used the classic methods of listwise deletion (complete case analysis) or mean substitution, neither of which are particularly effective practices (Schafer & Graham, 2002), as I demonstrate below. In only a few cases did researchers report doing anything constructive with the missing data, such as estimation or imputation. And in no case did we find that researchers analyzed the missingness to determine whether it was *missing completely at random* (MCAR), *missing at random* (MAR), or *missing not at random* (MNAR). This suggests there is a mythology in quantitative research that (a) individuals with incomplete data cannot contribute to the analyses, and that (b) removing them from the analyses is an innocuous action, which is only justified if you believe that missing data is missing completely at random (probably not the most common state).

CATEGORIES OF MISSINGNESS

When exploring missing data, it is important to come to a conclusion about the *mechanism of missingness*—that is, the hypothesized reason for why data are missing. This can range from arbitrary or random influences to purposeful patterns of nonresponse (e.g., most women in a study refuse to answer a question that is offensive or sensitive to women but that does not affect men in the same way).

Determination of the mechanism is important. If we can infer the data are missing at random (i.e., MCAR or MAR), then the nonresponse is deemed *ignorable*. In other words, random missingness can be problematic from a power perspective (in that it often reduces sample size or degrees of freedom for an analysis), but it would not potentially bias the results. However, data missing *not* at random (MNAR) could potentially be a strong biasing influence (Rubin, 1976).

Let us take an example of an employee satisfaction survey given to schoolteachers in a local district as an example of MCAR, MAR, and MNAR. Imagine that in September all teachers are surveyed (X), and then in January teachers are surveyed again (Y). Missing completely at random (MCAR) would mean that missingness in January is completely unrelated to any variable, including September satisfaction level, age, years of teaching, and the like. An example of this would be 50% of all respondents from September were randomly sampled to respond to the survey again in January, with all potential respondents completing surveys at both time points. In this case, having data for Y present or absent is completely explained by random selection. Put another way, missingness has no systematic relation to any variable present or unmeasured (such as age, sex, race, level of satisfaction, years teaching).

Now imagine that this surveying was part of the school district's initiative to keep teachers from leaving, and they wanted to focus on teachers with low satisfaction in September, perhaps with an intervention to help raise satisfaction of these low-satisfaction teachers. In this case, the missingness depends solely and completely on X, the initial score. Because the goal of the survey is to explore how these particular teachers fared, rather than all teachers in general, missingness is still considered ignorable and missing at random (MAR). If, on the other hand, other factors aside from initial satisfaction level were responsible (or partly responsible for missingness) such that perhaps only teachers whose satisfaction had improved responded (the teachers who continued to be substantially dissatisfied may be less likely to return the survey), then the data are considered missing not at random (MNAR) and are not ignorable (Rubin, 1976; Schafer & Graham, 2002) because they may substantially bias the results. In the case of MNAR, the average satisfaction of the follow-up group would be expected to be inflated if those who were most dissatisfied had stopped responding. If missingness were related to another external factor, such as if those teachers who were most dissatisfied were the most junior teachers (the teachers with least time in the profession), that also would qualify the missing data as MNAR.

In other words, it is only legitimate to assume that your observed data are representative of the intended population if data are convincingly missing at random or missing completely at random.[3] For simplicity, I will proceed through the rest of the chapter focusing on MCAR versus MNAR. MAR (ignorable missingness) is probably more common than MCAR but MNAR is probably most common, and thus, MCAR is merely presented as a comparison point. In truth, best practices in handling missing data appear to be equally effective regardless of whether the data are MCAR, MAR, or MNAR.

WHAT DO WE DO WITH MISSING DATA?

To illustrate some of the effects of missing data handling, I used data from the Education Longitudinal Study of 2002 (Ingels et al., 2004), grade 10 cohort to provide an example. For these analyses, no weights were applied. The complete sample of 15,163 students represents our example of the population (the advantage here is that we know the exact parameters of the population, something we often do not know). In this first example, I use the relatively strong correlation between math and reading achievement scores (BYTX-MIRR, BYTXRIRR), which produces what we define as the "population" correlation estimate (ρ) of .77, as indicated in Table 6.1 (row #1). (See also Figure 6.3 on page 134.)

Data Missing Completely at Random (MCAR)

To simulate MCAR situations, 20% of mathematics scores were randomly selected to be identified as missing. As a confirmation of the randomness of the missingness, two analyses were performed. First, as Table 6.1 shows, there was no mean difference in reading IRT scores between the missing and non-missing groups ($F_{(1, 15161)} = 0.56$, $p < .45$, $\eta^2 = .0001$). Second, there was no correlation between the missingness variable and any other substantive or ancillary variable (e.g., socioeconomic status, standardized reading IRT scores; all $r_{(15,163)}$ .002 to .006, $p < .57$ to .79). Another test of randomness was a logistic regression predicting missingness (0 = not missing, 1 = missing) from all other variables (math, reading, and socioeconomic status). When all three variables were in the equation, the overall equation was not significant ($p < .47$) and all 95% confidence intervals for the odds ratios for the three variables included 1.00, indicating no significant relationship between miss-ingness and any of the three variables.[4] Finally, another test of randomness is to perform an ANOVA to see if individuals with missing data on one variable are significantly different on other, similar variables (in this case, reading achievement). As you can see in Table 6.1, there is no significant difference in reading achievement between those with missing data on math achievement and those with valid math scores. Although not definitive, this sort of analysis in your data can give support to an inference of randomness or nonrandomness regarding the missing data.

Data Missing Not at Random—Low Scoring
Students More Likely to Be Missing (MNAR-Low)

To simulate one type of MNAR (labeled MNAR-low), cases at or below the 30th percentile on the math achievement test were given a 80% chance of being randomly labeled as missing on the math test, cases between the 30th and 50th percentile on the math test were given a 50% chance of being

Table 6.1 Summary of Effects of Missingness Corrections for Math Achievement Scores

	N	Mean Math IRT Score	SD Math IRT Score	Skew, Kurtosis Math IRT Score	Mean Reading IRT Scores— Not Missing[1]	Mean Reading IRT Scores— Missing[2]	F	Average Error of Estimates (SD)	Correlation With Reading IRT Score	Effect Size (r^2)
Original Data— "Population"	15,163	38.03	11.94	−0.02, −0.85					.77	.59
Missing Completely at Random (MCAR)	12,099	38.06	11.97	−0.03, −0.86	29.98	30.10	<1, ns		.77*	.59
Missing Not at Random (MNAR), Low	12,134	43.73	9.89	−0.50, 0.17	33.63	23.09	5,442.49, $p < .0001$, $\eta^2 = .26$		.70*	.49
Missing Not at Random (MNAR), Extreme	7,578	38.14	8.26	−0.01, 0.89	30.26	29.74	10.84, $p < .001$, $\eta^2 = .001$		.61*	.37
Missing Not at Random (MNAR), Inverse	4,994	37.60	5.99	0.20, 0.60	29.59	30.20	13.35, $p < .001$, $\eta^2 = .001$		−.20*	.04

112

	N	Mean Math IRT Score	SD Math IRT Score	Skew, Kurtosis Math IRT Score	Mean Reading IRT Scores— Not Missing[1]	Mean Reading IRT Scores— Missing[2]	F	Average Error of Estimates (SD)	Correlation With Reading IRT Score	Effect Size (r^2)
Mean Substitution										
MCAR	15,163	38.05	10.69	-0.02, -0.31				9.97 (6.34)	.69*	.47
MNAR-Low	15,163	43.73	8.02	-0.61, 1.83				16.71 (6.53)	.50*	.25
MNAR-Extreme	15,163	38.14	5.84	-0.02, 4.77				13.84 (5.00)	.38*	.14
MNAR-Inverse	15,163	37.60	3.44	0.36, 7.99				12.00 (6.15)	-.06*	.004
Strong Imputation										
MCAR	14,727[3]	38.19	11.72	-0.03, -0.84				3.89 (3.69)	.76*	.58
MNAR-Low	13,939[3]	40.45	10.43	-0.03, -0.63				5.26 (3.85)	.74*	.55
MNAR-Extreme	13,912[3]	38.59	9.13	-0.05, 0.53				5.17 (3.63)	.73*	.53
MNAR-Inverse	13,521[3]	38.31	6.64	-0.05, -0.82				6.77 (3.95)	.52*	.27

(Continued)

113

(Continued)

	N	Mean Math IRT Score	SD Math IRT Score	Skew, Kurtosis Math IRT Score	Mean Reading IRT Scores— Not Missing[1]	Mean Reading IRT Scores— Missing[2]	F	Average Error of Estimates (SD)	Correlation With Reading IRT Score	Effect Size (r^2)
Weak Imputation										
MCAR	14,532[4]	38.20	11.19	−0.07, −0.63				8.38 (5.93)	.73*	.53
MNAR-Low	13,720[4]	43.06	8.78	−0.35, 0.64				13.97 (6.52)	.60*	.36
MNAR-Extreme	13,489[4]	38.34	6.56	−.010 2.56				12.01 (5.06)	.52*	.27
MNAR-Inverse	12,977[4]	37.69	3.83	0.23, 5.34				12.16 (5.67)	.02	.00

Note. * $p < .0001$

1. Average reading scores for those students with valid math achievement scores.
2. Average reading scores for those students with missing math achievement scores.
3. There was missing data for F1TXM1IR leading to some scores being unable to be imputed.
4. There were occasional missing values on other variables leading to lower N.

114

randomly labeled as missing, and those over the 50th percentile on the math test were only given a 1% chance of being labeled as missing on the math test. This should simulate a highly biased situation where the best-performing students are more likely to respond to an item than the worst-performing students. As expected, MNAR-low produced an upwardly biased estimate of average performance—overestimating the mean performance due to more missing data from lower-performing students and slightly underestimating the standard deviation, also expected in this case due to less dispersion at the lower extreme of the distribution. As expected, achievement test scores were significantly correlated with missingness in this case ($r_{(15,163)}$ = -.51 and -.66 for reading and math achievement, respectively, both $p < .0001$) as was socioeconomic status ($r_{(15,163)}$ = -.28, $p < .0001$). Furthermore, logistic regression predicting missingness from achievement and socioeconomic status found all three variables were significant predictors of MNAR-low (all $p < .0001$), indicating that those with lower achievement (or SES) were more likely to be missing (as expected). Finally, as Table 6.1 shows, there were substantial mean differences in reading achievement between those with missing scores and those with valid math scores.

Data Missing Not at Random—Students at the Extremes More Likely to Be Missing (MNAR-Extreme)

A second type of MNAR (MNAR-extreme) was simulated by giving those students below the 30th percentile and above the 70th percentile on the math achievement test an 80% chance of being randomly identified as missing on the math test. Those in the center of the distribution were given only a 5% chance of being labeled as missing on the math test (Acock, 2005). This should have the effect of increased nonrandom missingness without substantially skewing the population average estimates.

As expected, MNAR-extreme produced the desired effects. Because the highest and lowest 30% of the students were more likely to be missing than the middle 40% (i.e., the missing data was symmetrically, but not randomly distributed), the distribution should closely match the mean of the original population, with dramatically reduced variance, and little or no difference in missing or nonmissing scores. As Table 6.1 shows, that is exactly what occurred. The average for MNAR-extreme closely approximates the population mean, underestimates the standard deviation, and produced significant, but unimportant differences between the two groups (an eta-squared of .001 is an extremely small effect size). Furthermore, we would not expect significant correlations between missingness and achievement or socioeconomic status, and correlations ranged from $r_{(15,163)} = -.03$ to $.02$. Finally, though the logistic regression indicated that missingness in this case was significantly related to reading achievement (Odds ratio $= 0.99$, $p < .0001$) and socioeconomic status (Odds ratio $= 1.10$, $p < .0001$), the odds ratios are close to 1.00, indicating a small effect size that is only significant by virtue of having more than 15,000 degrees of freedom. Thus, I can argue that while MNAR-extreme was decidedly non-random missingness, it did produce a largely symmetrical distribution.

Complete case analysis can lead to incomplete understanding.

Stuart, Azur, Frangakis, and Leaf (2009) give some interesting examples of how looking at only cases with complete data can lead to incomplete or inaccurate findings in the context of a national health survey. In one example, eliminating cases with missing data could lead us to conclude that individuals who start smoking earlier in life are more emotionally strong and less functionally impaired than individuals who started smoking later in life—a finding contrary to common sense and decades of research. They also found that under complete case analysis, those who drink more have *fewer internalizing problems* (e.g., depression, anxiety), another incongruous finding. Fortunately, after appropriate handling of missing data, these relationships were more consistent with the literature.

These real-life examples inspired me to create the fourth condition, MNAR-inverse because missing data apparently can lead to completely wrong conclusions in the real world.

Data Missing Not at Random That Inverts the Relationship Between Two Variables (MNAR-Inverse)

As a final challenge and test of missing data handling techniques, I created an extremely biased sampling technique that virtually eliminated those with both high reading and math scores, and those with both low reading and math scores, to have the effect of reversing the relationship between reading and math achievement (this is described more thoroughly in Appendix A of this chapter and also is available on the book's website). (See also Figure 6.4 on page 135.) By selectively sampling only those students on the downward diagonal, this produced a sample of almost $N = 5,000$ students that had a negative correlation ($r_{(4,994)} = -.20$).

Finally, MNAR-inverse also had the desired effect of producing a sample that at a glance does not look problematic. As Table 6.1 (5th row) shows, this MNAR-inverse sample is not substantially different from the other samples in mean math achievement (although the standard deviation underestimates the population variablility), and the shape of the distribution is not substantially different from the MNAR-extreme distribution. Furthermore, there is little difference between those missing and not missing on the reading achievement score (again, a very small effect size of eta-squared = .001). Other analyses showed no important correlations between missingness and achievement or socioeconomic status ($r_{(15,163)}$ ranged from .03 to .04), and a logistic regression predicting missingness from the same three variables showed only a small effect for socioeconomic status (Odds ratio = 1.08, $p < .0001$) indicating that those from more affluent families were more likely to be missing. If a researcher was unaware that the population correlation for these two variables should be .77, none of these minor effects hint at how biased this sample is due to nonrandom missingness—yet this example highlights the importance of dealing effectively with missing data.

THE EFFECTS OF LISTWISE DELETION

Traditional methods of dealing with missing data (and the default for many statistical packages) is to merely delete any cases with missing values on any variable in the analysis. A special case of this, called *pairwise deletion* or *available case analysis,* uses those cases with complete data on only those variables selected for a particular analysis. This means that the sample being analyzed can change depending on which variables are in the analysis, which could be problematic regarding replicability and increase the odds of errors of inference. Neither case is particularly desirable (Cole, 2008; Schafer & Graham, 2002). When data are MCAR, estimates are not biased, but under the more common MAR or MNAR conditions, misestimation and errors can result (Stuart, et al., 2009). Again, referring to Table 6.1, a simple example of the correlation between reading and math achievement test scores demonstrates this effect nicely.

As Table 6.1 shows, the original correlation coefficient for the population was $\rho = .77$ (variance accounted for = .59). When the data are MCAR, the population effect is estimated almost exactly. However, when data are MNAR, estimates begin to stray from the population parameter. In the MNAR-low sample, what might look like a minor misestimation ($r_{(12,134)} = .70$) is an underestimation of the effect size by almost 20% (coefficients of determination/percentage variance accounted for are .59 versus .49, a 16.9% underestimation). When the missing data causes a restriction of range situation (introduced in Chapter 3, showing restriction of range causing attenuation of correlation coefficients) represented by the MNAR-extreme sample, the misestimation is even more pronounced, producing a correlation coefficient of $r_{(7,578)} = .61$ (coefficient of determination of 0.37, which underestimates the population effect size by 37.29%). Finally, and most obviously, when the missingness is biased in a particular way, such as the MNAR-inverse example, it is possible that deletion of cases could lead researchers to draw the opposite conclusion regarding the nature of the relationship than exists in the population, as evidenced by the MNAR-inverse sample.

Thus, by deleting those with missing data, a researcher could be misestimating the population parameters, making replication less likely (for more examples of this effect, see Schafer & Graham, 2002, Table 2.).

Another undesirable effect of case deletion (even under MCAR) is loss of power. Most researchers use analyses with multiple variables. If each variable has some small percentage of randomly missing data, five variables with small percentages of missing data can add up to a substantial portion of a sample being deleted, which can have deleterious effects on power (as discussed in Chapter 2). Combined with what is likely an underestimation of the effect size, power can be significantly impacted when substantial portions of the sample are deleted when data are not MCAR. Thus, case deletion is only an innocuous practice when (a) the number of cases with missing data is a small percentage of the overall sample, and (b) the data are *demonstrably* MAR.

THE DETRIMENTAL EFFECTS OF MEAN SUBSTITUTION

I have seen two types of mean substitution. In one case, an observed variable (e.g., number of years of marriage) is unreported, the group or overall sample mean is substituted for each individual with missing data. The theory is that, in the absence of any other information, the mean is the best single estimate of any participant's score. The flaw in this theory is that if 20% of a sample is missing, even at random, substituting the identical score for a large portion of the sample artificially reduces the variance of the variable, and as the percentage of missing data increases, the effects of missing data become more profound. These effects have been known for many decades now (Cole, 2008; Haitovsky, 1968), yet many researchers still view mean substitution as a viable, or even progressive, method of dealing with missing data. As you will see below (and in Figure 6.1), mean substitution can create more inaccurate population estimates than simple case deletion when data are not MCAR.

To simulate this effect as a real researcher would face it, I substituted the mean of the math achievement variable calculated once the missing values were inserted into the variable.[5] As Table 6.1 shows, standard deviations are underestimated under MNAR situations.[6] For example, even under MCAR, the variability of math achievement is underestimated by 10.47% when mean substitution is used (and the effect would become more substantial as a larger percentage of the sample were missing), although the estimate of the mean is still accurate. In this case, the correlation effect size also is underestimated by 20.34% (coefficient of determination = 0.59 versus 0.47) just through virtue of 20% of the sample being MCAR and substituting the mean to compensate. Note also that mean substitution under MCAR appears to be less desirable than case deletion. In Figure 6.1, comparing MCAR with deletion and MCAR with mean substitution, you can see that the estimates of the population are more accurate when the missing cases are deleted.

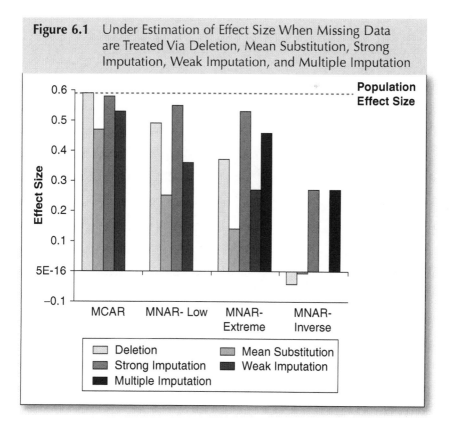

Figure 6.1 Under Estimation of Effect Size When Missing Data are Treated Via Deletion, Mean Substitution, Strong Imputation, Weak Imputation, and Multiple Imputation

To explore the errors mean substitution made, even under MCAR, the difference between the mean substituted and the original score was calculated and is presented in Figure 6.2. As you might expect from randomly missing data, the average error is almost 0 (-0.17), but there is a large range (-25.54 to 31. 15). Taking the absolute values of each error (presented in Figure 6.2), the average error of estimating scores via mean substitution is 9.97 with a standard deviation of 6.34.

The effects of mean substitution appear more dramatic under MNAR-low, despite being approximately the same overall number of missing cases. This is because the missing data in this case are likely to be low-performing students, and the mean is a poor estimate of their performance (average error in this case is 16.71, standard deviation is 6.53, much larger than under MCAR). Thus, under MNAR-low, mean substitution produces a biased mean, substantially underestimates the standard deviation by almost 33%, dramatically changes the shape of the distribution (skew, kurtosis), and leads to significant underestimation of the correlation between reading and math achievement. Under MNAR-low with mean substitution, the effect size for this simple correlation is underestimated by 57.63% (coefficient of determination = 0.59 versus 0.25). Note that MNAR with deletion produced better population estimates than mean substitution.

The example of MNAR-extreme also exposes the flaws of mean substitution. Note that because the missing data were symmetrical, the estimate of the

Figure 6.2 Misestimation of Math Scores Under Mean Substitution, Strong Imputation, MCAR

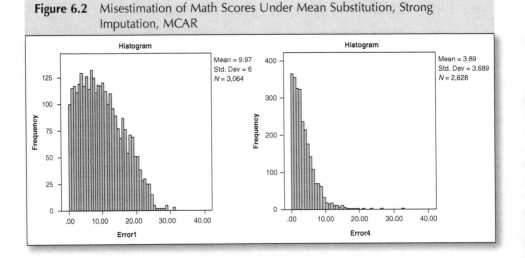

population mean was excellent both when cases were deleted and when mean substitution was used. However, the case of MNAR-extreme with mean substitution produced inaccurate estimates of population variability (SD = 5.84 versus population SD = 11.94, a 51.09% underestimation of the true variability in the population). Again, this is not a surprise as the average error from mean substitution is 13.84, standard deviation is 5.00. Furthermore, because of the high concentration of missing data in the tails of the distribution, the shape of the distribution becomes dramatically nonnormal. Finally, the effect size of the simple correlation between reading and math achievement scores is underestimated by 76.27% (0.59 versus 0.14), a notably poorer estimation than merely deleting cases under MNAR-extreme.

It should be no surprise that mean substitution does little to help the situation of MNAR-inverse. The correlation is simply a complete misestimation of the population parameter, has high error (but not as high as the two other MNAR samples, interestingly), and substantially underestimates population variability. Thus, this type of mean substitution does not appear to be an acceptable practice in which researchers should engage.

Mean substitution when creating composite scores based on multi-item questionniares. The other type of mean substitution involves administration of psychological scales (e.g., self-esteem, depression) where there are multiple, highly correlated questions assessing a single construct. In the case of the Rosenberg SVI, for example, where internal reliability estimates are often in excess of .90, the theory is that it is more desirable to substitute that individual's mean for the other items rather than to discard the individual from the data set. Thus, the idea that significant information is contained in the other highly correlated answers is an intriguing one, and used to generate other estimates discussed below. In this case, as item intercorrelations get higher, and the number of items increases, the bias does not appear to be substantial (Schafer & Graham, 2002), but this holds true only if the scale is unidimensional. In other words, if a scale has multiple independent aspects or subscales (e.g., depression is often not considered a unitary scale, and therefore averaging all the items would not be appropriate) it is only legitimate to average the items from the subscale the missing value belongs to.[7] This type of mean substitution is similar to imputation, discussed next, and when the imputation is based on strong relationships, it can be very effective. Thus, this type of mean substitution for missing scale items when internal consistency is strong and the scale is unidimensional appears to be a defensible practice. Of course, measurement scholars will argue that there are more modern methods of dealing with this sort of issue, and they are correct. If you are trained in more advanced measurement techniques, please use them.

THE EFFECTS OF STRONG AND WEAK IMPUTATION OF VALUES

Conceptually, the second type of mean substitution mentioned earlier is similar to imputation via multiple regression. It uses information available in the existing data to estimate a better value than the sample average, which as we saw in the previous section, is only effective at reducing the accuracy of the analysis. Essentially, imputation combines the complexity of predictive applications of multiple regression, which I think is excellently discussed in an article I wrote and which is freely available on the Internet (Osborne, 2000). In practice, assuming most variables have complete data for most participants, and they are strongly correlated to the variable with the missing data, a researcher can create a prediction equation using the variables with complete data, estimating values for the missing cases much more accurately than simple mean substitution.

To demonstrate this under the most ideal circumstances, I used two variables from the ELS 2002 data set that are correlated with the 10th grade math achievement variable that contains missing values: 12th grade math achievement (F1TXM1IR) and socioeconomic status (BYSES2). As imputation involves creating a regression equation based on the valid cases in a sample, for each simulation below I used only cases with nonmissing data to generate the regression equation, as a researcher faced with a real data set with missing data would have to do. For reference, I also calculated the regression equation for the population. These equations represent strong imputation, as the variance accounted for is very high (.40 to .80).

Prediction equation for population:

Math = 5.286 + 0.552(BYSES2) + 0.680(F1TXM1IR) $(r^2 = .80)$.

Prediction equation for MCAR sample:

Math = 5.283 + 0.533(BYSES2) + 0.681(F1TXM1IR) $(r^2 = .80)$.

Prediction equation for MNAR-low sample:

Math = 9.907 + 0.437(BYSES2) + 0.617(F1TXM1IR) (r^2 = .72).

Prediction equation for MNAR-extreme sample:

Math = 11.64 + 0.361(BYSES2) + 0.548(F1TXM1IR) (r^2 = .63).

Prediction equation for MNAR-inverse sample:

Math = 18.224 + -0.205(BYSES2) + 0.407(F1TXM1IR) (r^2 = .40).

It should not be surprising that the prediction equations became increasingly less similar to the population equation (and less effective) as I moved from MCAR to MNAR-low to MNAR-extreme to MNAR-inverse. However, given the extremely high predictive power of 12th grade math achievement scores in predicting 10th grade math achievement ($r_{(12,785)}$ = .89, which has a coefficient of determination of 0.79), prediction even in the worst case is strong. The relevant question is whether these equations will produce better estimations than mean substitution or complete case analysis.

As Table 6.1 and Figure 6.1 show, given this strong prediction, under MCAR the population mean and standard deviation, as well as the distributional properties, are closely replicated. Under MNAR-low, MNAR-extreme, and MNAR-inverse, the misestimation is significantly reduced, and the population parameters and distributional properties are more closely approximated than under mean substitution. Further, in all cases the errors of the estimates dropped markedly (as one might expect using such powerful prediction rather than mean substitution). Finally, under imputation, the estimates of the correlation between reading and math achievement test scores are much closer to approximating the population correlation than either deletion or mean substitution. This is particularly true for MNAR-inverse, where we see the true power of more progressive missing value handling techniques. Researchers using strong imputation would estimate a relationship between these two variables in the correct direction and, while underestimated, it is much closer to the population parameter than under any other technique.

Unfortunately, it is not always the case that one has another variable with a correlation of this magnitude with which to predict scores for missing values. Thus, to simulate a weaker prediction scenario, I used other variables from the same data set: BYSES2 (socioeconomic status), BYRISKFC (number of academic risk factors a student exhibits), and F1SEX (1 = male, 2 = female). Collectively, these three variables represent modest predictive power, with an r = .49, r^2 = .24, $p < .0001$ for the model. The predictive equations are as follows:

Prediction equation for population:

$$\text{Math} = 42.564 + 5.487(\text{BYSES2}) - 1.229(\text{F1SEX}) - 2.304(\text{BYRISKFC}) \ (r^2 = .24).$$

Prediction equation for MCAR sample:

$$\text{Math} = 42.701 + 5.468(\text{BYSES2}) - 1.241(\text{F1SEX}) - 2.368(\text{BYRISKFC}) \ (r^2 = .24).$$

Prediction equation for MNAR_low sample:

$$\text{Math} = 46.858 + 4.035(\text{BYSES2}) - 1.440(\text{F1SEX}) - 1.748(\text{BYRISKFC}) \ (r^2 = .17).$$

Prediction equation for MNAR_extreme sample:

$$\text{Math} = 40.149 + 3.051 \ (\text{BYSES2}) - 0.491(\text{F1SEX}) - 1.155(\text{BYRISKFC}) \ (r^2 = .13).$$

Prediction equation for MNAR_inverse sample:

$$\text{Math} = 40.416 + 0.548 \ (\text{BYSES2}) - 1.460(\text{F1SEX}) - 0.547(\text{BYRISKFC}) \ (r^2 = .03).$$

As you can see from this more realistic example (Table 6.1, and Figure 6.1), as the imputation gets weaker, the results get closer to mean substitution. In this case, the prediction was generally better than simple mean substitution, but not as good as strong imputation. As Table 6.1 shows, under MNAR-low, MNAR-extreme, and MNAR-inverse conditions, the variance of the population was misestimated, and in the case of MNAR-low, the population mean also was misestimated. The errors of estimation, while not as large as mean substitution, were still undesirably large. Finally, estimation of the population correlation between math and reading achievement tests were improved over mean substitution, but still misestimated compared to strong imputation.

So where does that leave us? Under the best circumstances, imputation appears to give the best results, even correcting the undesirable situation present in MNAR-inverse, particularly when prediction is strong and done well. When done poorly, imputation can cause distortion of estimates and lead to errors of inference (Little & Rubin, 1987), just as complete case analysis can (Stuart et al., 2009). In large samples with strongly correlated variables and low rates of missing data, this appears to be a good option from amongst the classic techniques thus far, although far more effective when data are missing at random than when missingness is biased in some way. However, recent research has shown that taking the extra effort of using advanced, modern estimation procedures can have benefits for those researchers with relatively high rates of missingness. It is beyond the scope of this chapter to get into all the details of all these different advanced techniques, but I will briefly address one of the more common ones for those curious in exploring further.

MULTIPLE IMPUTATION: A MODERN METHOD OF MISSING DATA ESTIMATION

Multiple imputation (MI) has emerged as one of the more common modern options in missing data handling with the ubiquity of desktop computing power. Essentially, multiple imputation uses a variety of advanced techniques—e.g., EM/maximum likelihood estimation, propensity score estimation, or Markov Chain Monte Carlo (MCMC) simulation—to estimate missing values, creating multiple versions of the same data set (sort of a statistician's view of the classic science fiction scenario of alternate realities or parallel universes) that explore the scope and effect of the missing data. These parallel data sets can then be analyzed via standard methods and results combined to produce estimates and confidence intervals that are often more robust than simple (especially relatively weak) imputation or previously mentioned methods of dealing with missing values (Schafer, 1997, 1999).

   When the proportion of missing data is small and prediction is good, single imputation described above is probably sufficient, although as with any prediction through multiple regression, it "overfits" the data, leading to less generalizable results than the original data would have (Osborne, 2000, 2008; Schafer, 1999).[8] The advantage of MI is generalizability and replicability—it explicitly models the missingness and gives the researcher confidence intervals for estimates rather than trusting to a single imputation. Some statistical software packages are beginning to support MI (e.g., SAS, R, S-Plus, SPSS—with additionally purchased modules and standalone software such as that available from Joseph Schafer at http://www.stat.psu.edu/~jls/software.html). Finally, and importantly, some MI procedures do *not* require that data be missing at random (e.g., in SAS there are several options for estimating values depending on the assumptions around the missing data). In other words, under a worst-case scenario of a substantial portion of missing data that is due to some significant bias, this procedure should be a good alternative (Schafer, 1999).

I used SAS's PROC MI procedure as it is relatively simple to use (if you are at all familiar with SAS)[9] and has the nice option of automatically combining the multiple parallel data sets into one analysis. For this analysis, I prepared a data set that contained the math and reading achievement test scores, as well as the three variables used for weak imputation (sex of student, socioeconomic status, and risk factors), and used the SAS defaults of EM estimation with five parallel data sets.

The traditional view within multiple imputation literature has been that five parallel data sets is generally a good number, even with high proportions of missing data. More recent studies suggest that 20 should be a minimum number of iterations (Graham, Olchowski, & Gilreath, 2007). In truth, with software that can perform MI automatically, there is no reason *not* to do more iterations. But in the case of this analysis, five parallel data sets achieved a relative efficiency of 96%, a good indicator. For illustrative purposes, Table 6.2 shows the five different imputations.

As you can see in Table 6.2 (and Figure 6.1), even using the weak relationships between the variables from the weak imputation example, the results are much better than the simple weak imputation (closer to strong imputation) and remarkably consistent. And the variance of the population, the shape of the variable distribution, and the estimation of the correlation between the two variables of interest are estimated much more accurately than any other method save having an extremely highly correlated variable to help with imputation. These estimates would then be combined to create a single estimate of the effect and confidence interval around that effect. In this case, the effect was so consistent that step was not necessary for this purpose.

Can multiple imputation fix the highly biased missingness in MNAR-inverse? As a final test of the power of MI, Table 6.3 shows the 20 EM imputations I performed to get a relative efficiency of 98% on the MNAR-inverse data.[10] By analyzing the 20 imputations through PROC MI ANALYZE, SAS provides the

Table 6.2 Example of Multiple Imputation Using Sas Proc MI and Weak Predictors Only, MNAR-Extreme Missingness Pattern

	N	Mean Math IRT Score	SD Math IRT Score	Skew, Kurtosis Math IRT Score	Correlation With Reading IRT Score	Effect Size (r^2)
Original Data— "Population"	15,163	38.03	11.94	−0.02, −0.85	.77	.59
Complete Case Analysis	7,578	38.14	8.26	−0.01, 0.89	.61*	.37
Mean Substitution	15,163	38.14	5.84	−0.02, 4.77	.38*	.14
Strong Imputation	13,912	38.59	9.13	−0.05, −0.53	.73*	.53
Weak Imputation	13,489	38.34	6.56	−0.10, 2.56	.52*	.27
EM Estimation						
Imputation 1	15,163	38.07	8.82	−0.03 0.16	.67*	.45
Imputation 2	15,163	37.90	8.79	−0.04 0.13	.68*	.46
Imputation 3	15,163	37.97	8.81	−0.03 0.15	.68*	.46
Imputation 4	15,163	38.07	8.80	−0.02 0.15	.67*	.45
Imputation 5	15,163	37.95	8.85	−0.02 0.13	.68*	.46
Markov Chain Monte Carlo Estimation						
Imputation 1	15,163	37.94	8.80	−0.03, 0.19	.68*	.46
Imputation 2	15,163	38.01	8.80	−0.02, 0.15	.67*	.45

(Continued)

(Continued)

Imputation 3	15,163	38.01	8.93	−0.03, 0.07	.69*	.47
Imputation 4	15,163	37.98	8.80	−0.04, 0.13	.68*	.46
Imputation 5	15,163	37.92	8.88	−0.02, 0.16	.68*	.46

Note. * $p < .0001$

average of the estimate, the standard error of the estimate, 95% confidence interval for the estimate, and more. In this case, the 20 iterations produced an average standardized regression coefficient (identical to correlation in this example) of 0.51, with a standard error of 0.00982, a 95% confidence interval of 0.49 to 0.52.

Ultimately, multiple imputation (and other modern missing value estimation techniques) are increasingly accessible to average statisticians and therefore represents an exciting frontier for improving data cleaning practice. As the results in Tables 6.2 and 6.3 show, even with only modestly correlated variables and extensive missing data rates, the MI techniques demonstrated here gave superior results to single, weak imputation for the MNAR-extreme and MNAR-inverse missingness patterns. These represent extremely challenging missingness issues often not faced by average researchers, but it should be comforting to know that appropriately handling missing data, even in extremely unfortunate cases, can still produce desirable (i.e., accurate, reproducible) outcomes. MI techniques seem, therefore, to be vastly superior to any other, traditional technique. Unfortunately, no technique can completely recapture the population parameters when there are such high rates of missingness, and in such a dramatically biased fashion. But these techniques would at least keep you, as a researcher, on safe ground concerning the goodness of inferences you would draw from the results.

MISSINGNESS CAN BE AN INTERESTING VARIABLE IN AND OF ITSELF

Missing data is often viewed as lost, an unfilled gap, but as I have demonstrated in this chapter, it is not always completely lost, given the availability

Table 6.3 MI Estimation for MNAR-Inverse Using Weak Predictor, MCMC Estimation

	N	Correlation With Reading IRT Score	Effect Size (r^2)
Original Data— "Population"	15,163	.77	.59
Complete Case Analysis	4,994	−.20*	.04
Mean Substitution	15,163	−.06*	.004
Strong Imputation	13,521	.61*	.37
Weak Imputation	12,977	.02	.00
Markov Chain Monte Carlo Estimation			
Imputation 1	15,163	.51*	.28
Imputation 2	15,163	.51*	.28
Imputation 3	15,163	.49*	.25
...			
Imputation 18	15,163	.50*	.25
Imputation 19	15,163	.50*	.25
Imputation 20	15,163	.51*	.27

Note. * $p < .0001$

of other strongly correlated variables. Going one step farther, missingness itself can be considered an outcome itself, and in some cases can be an interesting variable to explore. There is information in missingness. The act of refusing to respond or responding in and of itself might be of interest to researchers, just as quitting a job or remaining at a job can be an interesting variable. I always encourage researchers to create a *dummy variable*, representing whether a person has missing data or not on a particular variable, and do some analyses to see if anything interesting arises. Aside from attempting to determine if the data are MCAR, MAR, or MNAR, these data could yield important information.

Imagine two educational interventions designed to improve student achievement, and further imagine that in one condition there is much higher dropout than in the other condition, and further that the students dropping out are those with the poorest performance. Not only is that important information for interpreting the results (as the differential dropout would artificially bias the results), but it might give insight into the intervention itself. Is it possible that the intervention with a strong dropout rate among those most at risk indicates that the intervention is not supporting those students well enough? Is it possible that intervention is alienating the students in some way, or it might be inappropriate for struggling students?

All of this could be important information for researchers and policymakers, but many researchers discard this potentially important information. Remember, you (or someone) worked hard to obtain your data. Do not discard anything that might be useful!

SUMMING UP: WHAT ARE BEST PRACTICES?

This chapter ended up being a longer journey than I had intended. The more I delved into this issue, the more I found what (I thought) needed to be said, and the more examples needed to be explored. There are some very good books by some very smart people dealing solely with missing data (e.g., Little & Rubin, 1987; Schafer, 1997), and I have no wish to replicate that work here. The goal of this chapter was to convince you, the researcher, that this is a topic worthy of attention, that there are good, simple ways to deal with this issue, and that effectively dealing with the issue makes your results better.

Because we often gather data on multiple related variables, we often know (or can estimate) a good deal about the missing values. Aside from examining missingness as an outcome itself (which I strongly recommend), modern computing affords us the opportunity to fill in many of the gaps with high-quality data. This is not merely "making up data" as some early, misinformed researchers claimed. Rather, as my examples show, the act of estimating values and retaining cases in your analyses most often leads to more replicable findings as they are generally closer to the actual population values than analyses that discards those with missing data (or worse, substitutes means for the missing values). Thus, using best practices in handling missing data makes the results a better estimate of the population you are interested in. And it is surprisingly easy to do, once you know how.

Thus, it is my belief that best practices in handling missing data include the following.

- First, do no harm. Use best practices and careful methodology to minimize missingness. There is no substitute for complete data[11] and some careful forethought can often save a good deal of frustration in the data analysis phase of research.
- Be transparent. Report any incidences of missing data (rates, by variable, and reasons for missingness, if possible). This can be important information to reviewers and consumers of your research and is the first step in thinking about how to effectively deal with missingness in your analyses.
- Explicitly discuss whether data are missing at random (i.e., if there are differences between individuals with incomplete and complete data). Using analyses similar to those modeled in this chapter, you can give yourself and the reader a good sense of why data might be missing and whether it is at random. That allows you, and your audience, to think carefully about whether missingness may have introduced bias into the results. I would advocate that all authors report this information in the methods section of formal research reports.
- Discuss how you as a researcher have dealt with the issue of incomplete data and the results of your intervention. A clear statement concerning this issue is simple to add to a manuscript, and it can be valuable for future consumers as they interpret your work. Be specific—if you used imputation, how was it done, and what were the results? If you deleted the data (complete case analysis) justify why.

Finally, as I mentioned in Chapter 1, I would advocate that all authors report this information in the methods section of formal research reports and that all journals and editors and conferences mandate reporting of this type. If no data is missing, state that clearly so consumers and reviewers have that important information as well.

FOR FURTHER ENRICHMENT

1. Download from the book's website some of the missing data sets I discuss in this chapter, and see if you can replicate the results I achieved through

various means. In particular, I would challenge you to attempt multiple imputation.

2. Choose a data set from a previous study you conducted (or your advisor did) that had some missing data in it. Review how the missing data was handled originally. (I also have another data set online that you can play with for this purpose.)

   a. Conduct a missingness analysis to see if those who failed to respond were significantly different than those who responded.
   b. Use imputation or multiple imputation to deal with the missing data.
   c. Replicate the original analyses to see if the conclusions changed.
   d. If you found interesting results from effectively dealing with missing-ness, send me an e-mail letting me know. I will gather your results (anonymously) on the book's website, and may include you in future projects.

3. Find a data set wherein missing data were appropriately dealt with (i.e., imputation or multiple imputation). Do the reverse of #2, above, and explore how the results change by instead deleting subjects with missing data or using mean substitution.

APPENDIXES

Appendix A: SPSS Syntax for Creating Example Data Sets

If you are interested in the details of how I created these various missing data sets, I am including the SPSS syntax. Also, because the MNAR-inverse data set is a particularly odd one (and one I am particularly proud of), I include scatterplots of the data points prior to and after missingness was imposed.

```
**************************************************.
***missing NOT at random- lower scores more likely
to be missing
****************************************.
if (bytxmirr< 30.725) prob2=.80.
if (bytxmirr ge 30.725 and bytxmirr < 38.13)
prob2=0.50.
```

```
if (bytxmirr ge 38.13) prob2=0.01.
execute.
COMPUTE missing2=RV.BINOM(1,prob2).
EXECUTE.
compute math2=bytxmirr.
do if (missing2=1).
compute math2=-9.
end if.
recode math2   (-9=sysmis).
execute.
**************************************************.
***missing NOT at random- lower scores and higher
scores more likely to be missing
**************************************.
if (bytxmirr< 30.725) prob3=.80.
if (bytxmirr ge 30.725 and bytxmirr < 45.74)
prob3=0.05.
if (bytxmirr ge 45.74) prob3=0.80.
execute.
COMPUTE missing3=RV.BINOM(1,prob3).
EXECUTE.
compute math3=bytxmirr.
do if (missing3=1).
compute math3=-9.
end if.
recode math3   (-9=sysmis).
execute.
**************************************************.
***missing NOT at random- inverted relationship
**************************************.
compute prob4=0.001.
compute missing4=0.
if (bytxmirr<38.13 and bytxrirr<20.19) prob4=.99.
if (bytxmirr<34.55 and bytxrirr<23.75) prob4=.99.
if (bytxmirr<30.73 and bytxrirr<27.29) prob4=.99.
if (bytxmirr<26.47 and bytxrirr<33.69) prob4=.99.
if (bytxmirr<21.48 and bytxrirr<36.65) prob4=.99.
```

```
if (bytxmirr>34.55 and bytxrirr>39.59) prob4=.99.
if (bytxmirr>38.13 and bytxrirr>36.65) prob4=.99.
if (bytxmirr>41.92 and bytxrirr>33.69) prob4=.99.
if (bytxmirr>45.75 and bytxrirr>30.61) prob4=.99.
if (bytxmirr>49.41 and bytxrirr>27.29) prob4=.99.
COMPUTE missing4=RV.BINOM(1,prob4).
EXECUTE.
compute math4=bytxmirr.
do if (missing4=1).
compute math4=-9.
end if.
recode math4 (-9=sysmis).
execute.
```

Figure 6.3 Original Relationship Between Math and Reading Score

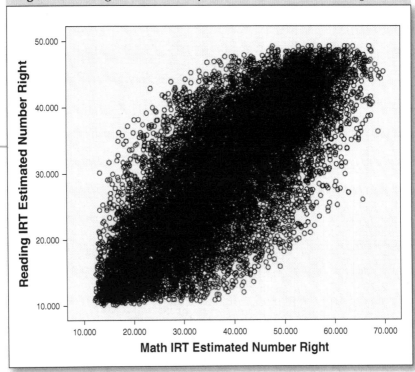

Figure 6.4 Inverse Relationship Between Math and Reading Score Creating MNAR-Inverse

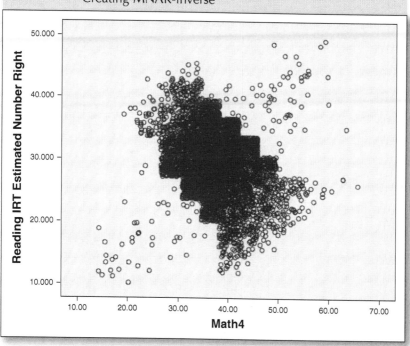

Appendix B: SAS Syntax for Performing Multiple Imputation

This SAS Syntax was used to generate multiple imputation data sets, analyze them, and report summary statistics.

```
proc MI  data=MNAR_EXT_NEW out=work.MNAREXT_MIout1;
mcmc chain=single impute=full initial=em nbiter=200
niter=100;
Run;
proc reg  data=work.mnarext_miout1  outest=MNAR_
ext_est covout;
    model BYTXRIRR=math3;
    by _imputation_;
    run;
```

```
proc mianalyze data=work.mnar_ext_est;
modeleffects intercept math3;
run;
```

NOTES

1. And, of course, if this was good research, I would assume follow-up questions would ask if the respondent is in a committed, long-term relationship as well to capture the effect of being in a stable relationship with another person regardless of whether that relationship was technically an officially recognized marriage. I leave that to all the relationship researchers out there to figure out—I am just a humble quaint guy trying to help clean data.

2. Which can deal with issues like participants leaving the study (right-censored or truncated data) or entering the study at a particular point (left-censored or truncated data).

3. Once again, let us be clear that values that are "out of scope" or legitimately missing, such as nonsmokers who skip the question concerning how many cigarettes are smoked a day, are not considered missing and are not an issue (Schafer & Graham, 2002). In this example, let us imagine that non–classroom teachers (e.g., guidance counselors, teacher assistants, or other personnel) who took the initial survey were not included in the follow-up because they are not the population of interest—i.e., classroom teachers. This would be legitimate missing data.

4. Which, honestly, is darned impressive, considering how much power there was in this analysis to detect *any* effect, no matter how small.

5. This is important because, as a researcher, you would not know the true population mean, and thus would be substituting an already biased mean for the missing values.

6. Note as well that case deletion also produces artificially reduced estimates of the population standard deviation under MNAR.

7. This also is implemented relatively easily in many statistical packages. For example, the SPSS syntax command below creates an average called "average" by averaging the items if at least five of the six values are present. As mentioned in the text, this is only desirable if these items have good internal consistency.

```
Compute average=mean.5(item01, item02,
item03, item04, item05, item06).
```

8. This is a bit of an esoteric topic to many researchers, so I will be brief and refer you to the cited references if you are interested in further information. Almost by definition, multiple regression creates an ideal fit between variables based on a particular data set. It squeezes every bit of relationship out of the data that it can. This is called *overfitting* because if you take the same equation and apply it to a different

sample (e.g., if we were to predict math achievement from reading achievement and socioeconomic status in a new sample) the prediction equations are often not as accurate. Thus, the relationships in a new sample are likely to be lower, leading to "shrinkage" in the overall relationship. Thus, in the prediction literature double cross-validation is a good practice, where samples are split in two and prediction equations generated from each are validated on the other half-sample to estimate how generalizable the prediction equation is. Multiple imputation takes this to another level, essentially, by creating several different parallel analyses to see how much variability there is across samples as a function of the missing data estimation. A very sensible concept!

9. An excellent introduction and guide to this procedure and process is Yuan (2000). Though some beginning users find SAS challenging, multiple imputation through SAS is relatively painless and efficient, accomplished through only a few lines of syntax. Once programmed, the actual multiple imputation procedure that produced 20 parallel data sets, analyzed them, and reported the summary statistics took less than 60 seconds on my laptop. For reference, I have appended the SAS syntax used to perform the first multiple imputation at the end of this chapter.

10. As the proportion of data missing increases, it is sometimes desirable to increase the number of imputed data sets to maintain a high relative efficiency. Given the ease of using SAS to create and analyze these data, and the speed of modern computers, there is little reason *not* to do so.

11. Except in certain specialized circumstances where researchers purposely administer selected questions to participants or use other advanced sampling techniques that have been advocated for in the researching of very sensitive topics.

REFERENCES

Acock, A. (2005). Working with missing values. *Journal of Marriage and Family, 67*(4), 1012–1028.

Cole, J. C. (2008). How to deal with missing data. In J. W. Osborne (Ed.), *Best practices in quantitative methods* (pp. 214–238). Thousand Oaks, CA: Sage.

Colebrooke, H. (1817). *Algebra with arithmetic of Brahmagupta and Bhaskara.* London: John Murray.

Diehl, R. (2004). *The Olmecs: America's first civilization.* London: Thames & Hudson.

Graham, J., Olchowski, A., & Gilreath, T. (2007). How many imputations are really needed? Some practical clarifications of multiple imputation theory. *Prevention Science, 8*(3), 206–213.

Haitovsky, Y. (1968). Missing data in regression analysis. *Journal of the Royal Statistical Society. Series B (Methodological), 30*(1), 67–82.

Ingels, S., Pratt, D., Rogers, J., Siegel, P., Stutts, E., & Owings, J. (2004). *Education Longitudinal Study of 2002: Base year data file user's manual* (NCES 2004-405). Washington, DC: U.S. Department of Educations, National Center for Education Statistics.

Little, R., & Rubin, D. (1987). *Statistical analysis with missing data.* New York: Wiley.

Osborne, J. W. (2000). Prediction in multiple regression. *Practical Assessment, Research & Evaluation, 7*(2).

Osborne, J. W. (2008). Creating valid prediction equations in multiple regression: Shrinkage, double cross-validation, and confidence intervals around prediction. In J. W. Osborne (Ed.), *Best practices in quantitative methods.* (pp. 299–305). Thousand Oaks, CA: Sage.

Osborne, J. W., Kocher, B., & Tillman, D. (2011). *Sweating the small stuff: Do authors in APA journals clean data or test assumptions (and should anyone care if they do)?* Unpublished Manuscript, North Carolina State University.

Raudenbush, S. W., & Bryk, A. S. (2002). *Hierarchical linear models: Applications and data analysis methods* (Vol. 1). Thousand Oaks, CA: Sage.

Rubin, D. (1976). Inference and missing data. *Biometrika, 63*(3), 581–592.

Schafer, J. (1997). *Analysis of incomplete multivariate data.* London: Chapman & Hall/ CRC.

Schafer, J. (1999). Multiple imputation: A primer. *Statistical Methods in Medical Research, 8*(1), 3–15.

Schafer, J., & Graham, J. (2002). Missing data: Our view of the state of the art. *Psychological Methods, 7*(2), 147–177.

Stuart, E. A., Azur, M., Frangakis, C., & Leaf, P. (2009). Multiple imputation with large data sets: A case study of the children's mental health initiative. *American Journal of Epidemiology, 169*(9), 1133–1139.

Yuan, Y. (2000). *Multiple imputation for missing data: Concepts and new development.* Paper presented at the Proceedings of the Twenty-Fifth Annual SAS Users Group International Conference, Cary, N.C. Retrieved from http://support.sas.com/rnd/ app/papers/multipleimputation.pdf

SEVEN

EXTREME AND INFLUENTIAL DATA POINTS

Debunking the Myth of Equality

Next time you read an article from a top journal in your field, look for any mention of looking for influential data points (or extreme scores or outliers). Odds are you will find none (as my students and I have found in several surveys across several disciplines). Authors spend a great deal of time describing the importance of the study, the research methods, the sample, the statistical analyses used, results, and conclusions based on those results, but rarely mention having screened their data for outliers or extreme scores (sometimes referred to as influential data points). Many conscientious researchers do check their data for these things, perhaps neglecting to report having done so, but more often than not, this step is skipped in the excitement of moving directly to hypothesis testing. After all, researchers often spend months or years waiting for results from their studies, so it is not surprising they are excited to see the results of their labors. Yet jumping directly from data collection to data analysis without examining data for extreme scores or inappropriately influential scores can, ironically, decrease the likelihood that the researcher will find the results they so eagerly anticipate.

Researchers from the dawn of the age of statistics have been trained in the effects of extreme scores, but more recently, this seems to have waned. In fact, a recent article of mine examining publications in respected educational psychology journals (Osborne, 2008) found that only 8% of these articles reported testing any sort of assumption, and almost none specifically discussed having examined data for extreme scores. There is no reason to believe that the situation is different in other disciplines. Given what we know of the importance of assumptions to accuracy of estimates and error rates (Micceri, 1989; Yuan, Bentler, & Zhang, 2005), this is troubling, and it leads to the conclusion that research in the social sciences is probably at increased risk for errors of inference, problems with generalizability, and suboptimal outcomes. One can only conclude that most researchers assume that extreme scores do not exist, or that if they exist, they have little appreciable influence on their analyses. Hence, the goal of this chapter is to debunk the myth of equality, the myth that all data points are equal. As this chapter shows, extreme scores have disproportionate, usually detrimental, effects on analyses.

Some techniques, such as "robust" procedures and nonparametric tests (which do not require an assumption of normally distributed data) are often considered to be immune from these sorts of issues. However, parametric tests are rarely robust to violations of distributional assumptions (Micceri, 1989) and nonparametric tests benefit from clean data, so there is no drawback to cleaning your data and looking for outliers and fringeliers, whether you are using parametric or nonparametric tests (e.g., Zimmerman, 1994, 1995, 1998).

The goal of this step is to decrease the probability you will make a significant error of inference, as well as to improve generalizability, replicability, and accuracy of your results by making sure your data includes only those data points that belong there.

WHAT ARE EXTREME SCORES?

Figure 7.1, on page 142, visually shows the concept of the extreme score, including the outlier and the fringelier. Although definitions vary, an outlier is generally considered to be a data point that is far outside the norm for a variable or population (e.g., Jarrell, 1994; Rasmussen, 1988; Stevens, 1984). It is an observation that "deviates so much from other observations as to arouse suspicions that it was generated by a different mechanism" (Hawkins, 1980, p. 1). Hawkins's description of outliers reinforces the notion that if a value is very different because it reflects different processes (or populations), then it does not belong in the analysis at hand. Outliers also have been defined as values that are "dubious in the eyes of the researcher" (Dixon, 1950, p. 488) and contaminants (Wainer, 1976), all of which lead to the same conclusion: extreme scores probably do not belong in your analyses. That is not to say that these extreme scores are not of value. As discussed next, they most likely should be examined more closely and in depth.

The scholarly literature on extreme scores reveals two broad categories: scores typically referred to as *outliers,* which are clearly problematic in that they are far from the rest of the distribution, and *fringeliers,* which are scores hovering around the fringes of a normal distribution that are unlikely to be part of the population of interest but less clearly so (Wainer, 1976, p. 286). We can operationalize fringeliers as those scores around ± 3.0 standard deviations (*SD*) from the mean, which represents a good (but by no means the only possible) rule of thumb for identifying scores that merit further examination.

Why are we concerned with scores around ± 3.0 standard deviations from the mean? Recall from Chapter 5 that the standard normal distribution is symmetrical distribution with known mathematical properties. Most relevant to our discussion, we know what percentage of a population falls at any given point of the normal distribution, which also gives us the probability that an individual with a given score on the variable of interest would be drawn at random from a normally distributed population. So, for example, we know that in a perfectly normal distribution, 68.2% of the population will fall within 1 standard deviation of the mean, about 95% of the population should fall within 2 standard deviations from the mean, and 99.74% of the population will fall within 3 standard deviations. In other words, the probability of randomly sampling an individual more than 3 standard deviations from the mean in a normally distributed population is 0.26%, which gives me good justification for considering scores outside this range as suspect.

Because of this, I tend to be suspicious that data points outside ± 3.0 standard deviations from the mean are *not part of the population of interest,* and furthermore, despite being plausible (though unlikely) members of the population of interest, these scores can have a disproportionately strong influence on parameter estimates and thus need to be treated with caution. In general, since both outliers and fringeliers represent different magnitudes of the same problem (single data points with disproportionately high influence on statistics) I refer to them here collectively as *extreme values.*

HOW EXTREME VALUES AFFECT STATISTICAL ANALYSES

Extreme values can cause serious problems for statistical analyses. First, they generally increase error variance and reduce the power of statistical tests by altering the skew or kurtosis of a variable (which can become very problematic

Figure 7.1   Extreme Scores: Outliers and Fringeliers

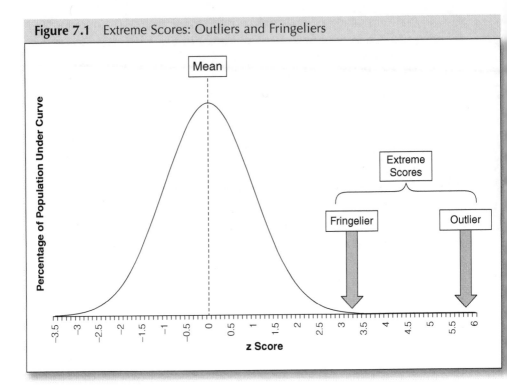

in multivariate analyses). As many statistical tests compare variance accounted for to error (unexplained) variance, the more error variance in the analyses, the less likely you are to find a statistically significant result when you should (increasing the probability of making a Type II error).

Second, they can seriously bias or influence estimates that may be of substantive interest, such as means, standard deviation, and the like (for more information on these points, see Rasmussen, 1988; Schwager & Margolin, 1982; Zimmerman, 1994). Since extreme scores can substantially bias your results, you may be more likely to draw erroneous conclusions, and any conclusions you do draw will be less replicable and generalizable, two important goals of scientific quantitative research.

I explore each of these effects and outcomes in this chapter.

WHAT CAUSES EXTREME SCORES?

Extreme scores can arise from several different mechanisms or causes. Anscombe (1960) sorts extreme scores into two major categories: those arising from errors in the data and those arising from the inherent variability of the data. I elaborate on this idea to summarize six possible reasons for data points that may be suspect.

Let me first be careful to note that not all extreme scores are illegitimate contaminants, and not all illegitimate scores show up as extreme scores (Barnett & Lewis, 1994). Although the average American male stands about 5′ 10″ tall, there are 7-foot-tall males and 4-foot-tall males. These are legitimate scores, even though they are relatively extreme and do not describe the majority of the American male population. Likewise, it is possible that a score of 5′5″ (what seems to be a very legitimate score) could be an error, if the male was in reality 6′5″ but the data was recorded incorrectly.

It is therefore important to consider the range of causes that may be responsible for extreme scores in a given data set. What should be done about an outlying data point is very much a function of the inferred cause.

The Case of the Mysterious 99s

Early in my career I was working with data from the U. S. National Center for Educational Statistics (NCES), analyzing student psychological variables such as self-esteem. With many thousands of subjects and previous research showing strong correlations between the variables we were researching, I was baffled to discover correlations that were substantially lower than what we expected.

Exasperated, I informed a professor I was working with of the problem, who merely smiled and suggested checking the data for outliers.

Figure 7.2 The Case of the Mysterious 99s

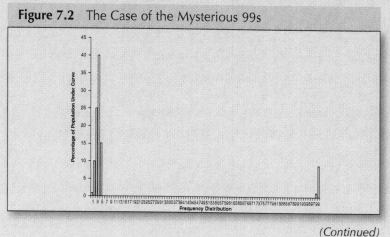

(Continued)

(Continued)

Immediately the problem became apparent. Items, such as the one in Figure 7.2, had responses from 1-5, a typical Likert-type scale item, and then a small but significant number of 98s and 99s. I learned that many researchers and government data sets use numeric codes for missing data, rather than just leaving the data field blank. There are good reasons for this.

First, in earlier days, computers had difficulty handling blanks in data, so entering numeric codes for missing data was important. Second, there are sometimes different reasons for missing data, and the NCES had different codes so they could analyze the missingness in the data (as we discussed in Chapter 6). Identifying 99 and 98 as missing data immediately solved the problem, but I never forgot the lesson: always check for extreme scores!

1. *Extreme Scores From Data Errors.* Extreme scores, particularly outliers, are often caused by human error, such as errors in data collection, recording, or entry. Data gathered during research can be recorded incorrectly and mistakes can happen during data entry. One survey I was involved with gathered data on nurses' hourly wages, which at that time averaged about $12.00 per hour with a standard deviation of about $2.00 per hour. In our data set one nurse had reported an hourly wage of $42,000.00, clearly not a legitimate hourly wage in nursing. This figure represented a data collection error (specifically, a failure of the respondent to read the question carefully—she reported *yearly* wage rather than *hourly* wage). The good news about these types of errors is that they can often be corrected by returning to the original documents or even possibly contacting the research participant, thus potentially eliminating the problem. In cases such as this, another option is available—estimation of the correct answer. We used anonymous surveys, so we could not contact the nurse in question, but because the nature of the error was obvious, we could convert this nurse's salary to an estimated hourly wage because we knew how many hours per week and how many weeks per year she worked.

Data entry is a significant source of extreme scores, particularly when humans are hand-entering data from printed surveys (the rise of web-based surveys are helpful in this regard). Recently, I was analyzing some hand-entered data from a Likert scale where values should range from 1 to 7, yet I found some *0* and *57* values in the data. This obviously arose from human entry error, and returning to the original surveys allowed for entry of correct values.

If extreme scores of this nature cannot be corrected they should be eliminated as they do not represent valid population data points, and while it is tempting to assume the 0 was supposed to be a 1 or 2 (which is right above the 0 on a numeric keypad) and the 57 was supposed to probably be a 5 (and the data entry person hit both keys accidentally) researchers *cannot make those assumptions* without reasonable rationale to do so. If you do such a thing, be sure to be transparent and report having done so when you present your results.

A final, special case of this source of extreme score is when researchers (such as government agencies) use numeric codes for missing data, but researchers fail to identify those codes to the statistical software as missing. This is a simple process that all modern statistical software does easily, but can be disastrous to analyses if these codes are in the data but researchers fail to realize this (see sidebar, The Case of the Mysterious 99s).

2. *Extreme Scores From Intentional or Motivated Misreporting.* Sometimes participants purposefully report incorrect data to experimenters or surveyors. In Chapter 10, I explore various motivations for doing so, such as impression management or malingering. Yet these types of motives might not always result in extreme scores (social desirability pressures often push people toward average rather than toward unrealistic extremes).

This also can happen if a participant makes a conscious effort to sabotage the research, is fatigued, or may be acting from other motives. Motivated misreporting also can happen for obvious reasons when data are sensitive (e.g., teenagers misreporting drug or alcohol use, misreporting of sexual behavior, particularly if viewed as shameful or deviant). If all but a few teens underreport a behavior (for example, cheating on a test or driving under the influence of alcohol), the few honest responses might appear to be extreme scores when in fact they are legitimate and valid scores. Motivated overreporting can occur when the variable in question is socially desirable (e.g., income, educational attainment, grades, study time, church attendance, sexual experience) and can work in the same manner.

Environmental conditions can motivate misreporting, such as if an attractive female researcher is interviewing male undergraduates about attitudes on gender equality in marriage. Depending on the details of the research, one of two things can happen: inflation of all estimates, or production of extreme scores. If all subjects respond the same way, the distribution will shift upward, not generally causing extreme scores. However, if only a small subsample of the group responds this way to the experimenter, or if some of the male undergraduates are interviewed by male researchers, extreme scores can be created.

Identifying and reducing this issue is difficult unless researchers take care to triangulate or validate data in some manner.

3. *Extreme Scores From Sampling Error or Bias.* As I discuss in Chapter 3, sampling can help create biased samples that do not reflect the actual nature of the population. Imagine you are surveying university undergraduates about the extent of their alcohol usage, but due to your schedule, the only time you could perform interviews was 8:00 to 10:00 in the mornings Friday, Saturday, and Sunday. One might imagine that heavy alcohol users might not be willing or able to get up that early on the weekend, so your sample may be biased toward low usage. If most of your sample is biased toward nondrinkers, but a few average—drinking college students by chance slip into the sample, you may well see those as extreme scores when in fact they are part of the normal diversity in the population. Ideally, upon realizing this, you would correct your sampling plan to gather a representative sample of the population of interest.

Another cause of extreme scores is sampling error. It is possible that a few members of a sample were inadvertently drawn from a different population than the rest of the sample. For example, in the previously described survey of nurse salaries, nurses who had moved into hospital administration were included in the database we sampled from, as they had maintained their nursing license, despite our being primarily interested in nurses currently involved in routine patient care. In education, inadvertently sampling academically gifted or mentally retarded students is a possibility, and (depending on the goal of the study) might provide undesirable extreme scores. These cases should be removed if they do not reflect the target population.

4. *Extreme Scores From Standardization Failure.* Extreme scores can be caused by research methodology, particularly if something anomalous happened during a particular subject's experience. One might argue that a study of stress levels in schoolchildren around the country might have found some significant extreme scores if the sample had included schoolchildren in New York City schools during the fall of 2001 or in New Orleans following Hurricane Katrina in 2005. Researchers commonly experience such challenges—construction noise outside a research lab or an experimenter feeling particularly grouchy, or even events outside the context of the research lab, such as a student protest, a rape or murder on campus, observations in a classroom the day before a big holiday recess, and so on can produce extreme scores. Faulty or noncalibrated equipment is another common cause of extreme scores.

Let us consider two possible cases in relation to this source of extreme scores. In the first case, we might have a piece of equipment in our lab that was miscalibrated, yielding measurements that were extremely different from other days' measurements. If the miscalibration results in a fixed change to the score that is consistent or predictable across all measurements (for example, all measurements are off by 100) then adjustment of the scores is possible and appropriate. If there is no clear way to defensibly adjust the measurements, they must be discarded.

Other possible causes of extreme scores can cause unpredictable effects. Substantial changes in the social, psychological, or physical environment (e.g., a widely known crime, substantial noise outside the research lab, a natural disaster) can substantially alter the results of research in unpredictable ways, and these extreme scores should be discarded as they do not represent the normal processes you wish to study (e.g., if one were not interested in studying subjects' reactions to construction noise outside the lab, which I experienced one summer while trying to measure anxiety in a stereotype threat study).

5. *Extreme Scores From Faulty Distributional Assumptions.* Incorrect assumptions about the distribution of the data also can lead to the presence of suspected extreme scores (Iglewicz & Hoaglin, 1993). Blood sugar levels, disciplinary referrals, scores on classroom tests where students are well-prepared, and self-reports of low-frequency behaviors (e.g., number of times a student has been suspended or held back a grade) may give rise to bimodal, skewed, asymptotic, or flat distributions, depending on the sampling design and variable of interest, as Figure 7.3 shows.

The data in Figure 7.3, taken from an exam in one of the large undergraduate classes I teach, shows a highly skewed distribution with a mean of 87.50 and a standard deviation of 8.78. While one could argue the lowest scores on this test are extreme scores by virtue of distance from the mean, a better interpretation might be that the data should not be expected to be normally distributed. Thus, scores on the lower end of this distribution are in reality valid cases. In this case, a transformation could be used to normalize the data before analysis of extreme scores should occur (see Chapter 8 for details of how to perform transformations effectively) or analyses appropriate for nonnormal distributions could be used. Some authors argue that splitting variables such as this into groups (i.e., dichotomization) is an effective strategy for dealing with data such as this. I disagree, and demonstrate why in Chapter 11.

Figure 7.3   Performance on Class Unit Exam, Undergraduate
Educational Psychology Course

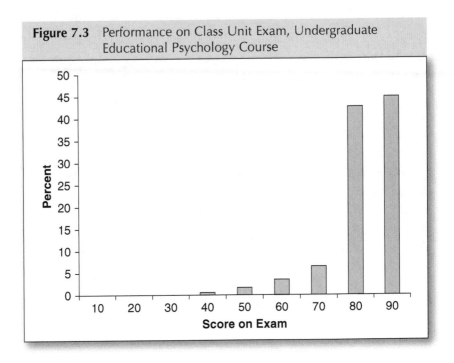

Similarly, the data may have a different structure than the researcher originally assumed, and long- or short-term trends may affect the data in unanticipated ways. For example, a study of college library usage rates during the month of August in the United States may find outlying values at the beginning and end of the month—exceptionally low rates at the beginning of the month when students are still on summer break and exceptionally high rates at the end of the month when students are just back in classes and beginning research projects. Depending on the goal of the research, these extreme values may or may not represent an aspect of the inherent variability of the data, and they may or may not have a legitimate place in the data set.

6. *Extreme Scores as Legitimate Cases Sampled From the Correct Population.* Finally, it is possible that an extreme score can come from the population being sampled legitimately through random chance. It is important to note that sample size plays a role in the probability of outlying values. Within a normally distributed population, it is more probable that a given data point will be drawn from the most densely concentrated area of the distribution, rather than one of the tails (Evans, 1999; Sachs, 1982). As a researcher casts a wider net and the data set becomes larger, the more the sample

resembles the population from which it was drawn, and thus the likelihood of legitimate extreme values, becomes greater.

Specifically, if you sample in a truly random fashion from a population that is distributed in an exact standard normal distribution, there is about a 0.25% chance you will get a data point at or beyond 3 standard deviations from the mean. This means that, on average, *about 0.25% of your subjects should be 3 standard deviations from the mean.* There is also a nontrivial probability of getting individuals far beyond the 3 standard deviation threshold. For example, in the United States, assume the average height for a woman is 5' 4" (64 inches), with a standard deviation of 2.5 inches.[1] While the odds are highest that a sample of women will be between 4' 11" and 5' 9", if one of our female volleyball players from North Carolina State University randomly happens to participate in your study, you could easily get a legitimate data point from a woman that is 6'0 ". Or if you had happened to ever meet my great-aunt Winifred Mauer, you could have included a woman about 4' 6" in your data set.

When legitimate extreme scores occur as a function of the inherent variability of the data, opinions differ widely on what to do. Due to the deleterious effects on power, accuracy, and error rates that extreme scores can have, I believe it is important to deal with the extreme score in some way, such as through transformation or a recoding/truncation strategy to both keep the individual in the data set and at the same time minimize the harm to statistical inference (for more on this point see Chapter 8). The alternative is removal.

EXTREME SCORES AS A POTENTIAL FOCUS OF INQUIRY

We all know that interesting research is often as much a matter of serendipity as planning and inspiration. Extreme scores can represent a nuisance, error, or legitimate data. They can be inspiration for inquiry as well. When researchers in Africa discovered that some women were living with HIV for many years longer than expected despite being untreated (Rowland-Jones et al., 1995), those rare cases constitute extreme scores compared to most untreated women infected with HIV, who die relatively rapidly. They could have been discarded as noise or error, but instead they served as inspiration for inquiry: what makes these women different or unique, and what can we learn from them? Legitimate exceptionality (rather than motivated misinformation or exaggeration motivated by social motives) can be the source of important and useful insight into processes and phenomena heretofore unexplored. Before discarding extreme scores, researchers should consider whether those data contain valuable information that may not necessarily relate to the intended study, but has importance in a more global sense.

I have a small sample and can't afford to lose data. Can I keep my extreme scores and still not violate my assumptions?

Yes, at least in some cases. But first, let's talk about why you want to keep your data, because keeping extreme scores can cause substantial problems. Are you dealing with a specialized population that precludes you from getting a large enough sample to have sufficient power? You should be aware that you might be better off without that data point anyway. Extreme scores that add substantial error variance to the analysis may be doing more harm than good.

If your extreme case is a *legitimate* member of the sample then it is acceptable to keep that case in the data set, provided you take steps to minimize the impact of that one case on the analysis.

Assuming you conclude that keeping the case is important, one means of accommodating extreme scores is the use of transformations or truncation. By using transformations, extreme scores can be kept in the data set with less impact on the analysis (Hamilton, 1992).

Transformations may not be appropriate for the model being tested, or may affect its interpretation in undesirable ways (see Chapter 8). One alternative to transformation is truncation, wherein extreme scores are recoded to the highest (or lowest) reasonable score. For example, a researcher might decide that in reality, it is impossible for a teenager to have more than 20 close friends. Thus, all teens reporting more than this value (even 100) would be recoded to 20. Through truncation the relative ordering of the data is maintained and the highest or lowest scores remain the highest or lowest scores, yet the distributional problems are reduced. However, this may not be ideal if those cases really represent bad data or sampling error.

To be clear on this point, even when the extreme score is either a legitimate part of the data or the cause is unclear, and even if you will study the case in more depth, that is a separate study. If you want the most replicable, honest estimate of the population parameters possible, Judd and McClelland (1989) suggest removal of the extreme data points, and I concur. However, not all researchers feel that way (Orr, Sackett, & DuBois, 1991). This is a case where researchers must use their training, intuition, reasoned argument, and thoughtful consideration in making decisions.

Interestingly, analysis of extreme scores is now becoming a growth industry in data forensics, where companies attempt to catch students cheating on high-stakes tests by looking at statistical anomalies like unusual patterns of answers, agreement across test-takers that indicates copying, and unusually large gain scores (Impara, Kingsbury, Maynes, & Fitzgerald, 2005).

Advanced Techniques for Dealing With Extreme Scores: Robust Methods

Instead of transformations or truncation, researchers sometimes use various "robust" procedures to protect their data from being distorted by the presence of extreme scores. These techniques can help accommodate extreme scores while minimizing their effects. Certain parameter estimates, especially the mean and least squares estimations, are particularly vulnerable to extreme scores, or have low breakdown values. For this reason, researchers turn to robust, or high breakdown, methods to provide alternative estimates for these important aspects of the data.

A common robust estimation method for univariate distributions involves the use of a trimmed mean, which is calculated by temporarily eliminating extreme observations at both ends of the sample (Anscombe, 1960). Alternatively, researchers may choose to compute a Windsorized mean, for which the highest and lowest observations are temporarily censored, and replaced with adjacent values from the remaining data (Barnett & Lewis, 1994).

Assuming that the distribution of prediction errors is close to normal, several common robust regression techniques can help reduce the influence of outlying data points. The least trimmed squares (LTS) and the least median of squares

A *Univariate Extreme* Score: is one that is relatively extreme when considering only that variable. An example would be a height of 36" in a sample of adults.

A *Bivariate Extreme* Score: is one that is extreme when considered in combination with other data. An example would be a height of 5'2" in a sample of adults. This score would not necessarily stand out from the overall distribution. However, in considering gender and height, if that height belonged to a male, that male would be considered an outlier within his group.

A *Multivariate Extreme* Score: is one that is extreme when considering more than two variables simultaneously. My nephew is 5'8", which is not extreme for a male, but considering he is only 10 years old, he is extreme when age is considered.

(LMS) estimators are conceptually similar to the trimmed mean, helping to minimize the scatter of the prediction errors by eliminating a specific percentage of the largest positive and negative extreme scores (Rousseeuw & Leroy, 1987), while Windsorized regression smooths the Y-data by replacing extreme residuals with the next closest value in the dataset (Lane, 2002). Rand Wilcox (e.g., Wilcox, 2008) is a noted scholar in the development and dissemination of these types of methods, and I would encourage readers interested in learning more about these techniques to read some of his work.

In addition to the above-mentioned robust analyses, researchers can choose from a variety of nonparametric analyses, which make few if any distributional assumptions. Unfortunately, nonparametric tests are sometimes less powerful than parametric analyses and can still suffer when extreme scores are present (e.g., Zimmerman, 1995).

IDENTIFICATION OF EXTREME SCORES

The controversy over what constitutes an extreme score has lasted many decades. I tend to do an initial screening of data by examining data points three or more standard deviations from the mean, in combination with visual inspection of the data in most cases.[2] Depending on the results of that screening, I may examine the data more closely and modify the extreme score detection strategy accordingly.

However, examining data for univariate extreme scores is merely a starting point, not an end point. It is not uncommon to find bivariate and multivariate extreme scores once you start performing data analyses. Bivariate and multivariate extreme scores are easily identified in modern statistical analyses through examination of things such as standardized residuals (where I also use the ±3.0 rule for identifying multivariate extreme scores) or diagnostics commonly provided in statistical packages, such as Mahalanobis distance and Cook's distance. The latter two indices attempt to capture how far individual data points are from the center of the data, and thus larger scores are considered more problematic than smaller scores. However, there is no good rule of thumb as to how large is too large, and researchers must use their professional judgment in deciding what data points to examine more closely.

For ANOVA-type analyses, most modern statistical software will produce a range of statistics, including standardized residuals. ANOVA analyses suffer from a special type of multivariate extreme score called a within-cell extreme score. In this case, within-cell extreme scores are data points that may not be extreme in the univariate analysis, but are extreme compared to the other data points within a particular cell or group (as in the example of my nephew's height in the earlier example above). Fortunately, most modern statistical packages will allow researchers to save standardized residuals in ANOVA, regression, and many other types of analyses, allowing for straightforward examination of data for extreme scores.

WHY REMOVE EXTREME SCORES?

Extreme scores have several specific effects on variables that otherwise are normally distributed. To illustrate this, I will use some examples from the National Education Longitudinal Study (NELS 88) data set from the National Center for Educational Statistics (http://nces.ed.gov/surveys/NELS88/). First, *socioeconomic status* (SES) represents a composite of family income and social status based on parent occupation (see Figure 7.4). In this data set, SES scores were reported as z scores (a distribution with a mean of 0.00 and a standard deviation of 1.0). This variable shows good (though not perfect) normality, with a mean of -0.038 and a standard deviation of 0.80. Skew is calculated to be -0.001 (where 0.00 is perfectly symmetrical).

Samples from this distribution should share these distributional traits as well. As with any sample, larger samples tend to better mirror the overall distribution than smaller samples. To show the effects of extreme scores on univariate distributions and analyses, my colleague Amy Overbay and I (Osborne & Overbay, 2004) drew repeated samples of $N = 416$, that included 4% extreme scores on one side of the distribution (very wealthy or very poor students) to demonstrate the effects of extreme scores even in large samples (I use a similar methodology to discuss the effects of extreme scores on correlation and regression and on t-tests and ANOVAs later in this chapter).

With only 4% of the sample (16 of 416) classified as extreme scores, you can see in Figure 7.5 the distribution for the variable changes substantially, along with the statistics for the variable. The mean is now -0.22, the standard deviation is 1.25, and the skew is -2.18. Substantial error has been added to the variable, and it is clear that those 16 students at the very bottom of the distribution do not belong to the normal population of interest. To confirm this sample was strongly representative of the larger population as a whole, removal of these extreme scores returned the distribution to a mean of -0.02, standard deviation = 0.78, skew = 0.01, not markedly different from the sample of more than 24,000.

Figure 7.4 Distribution of Socioeconomic Status

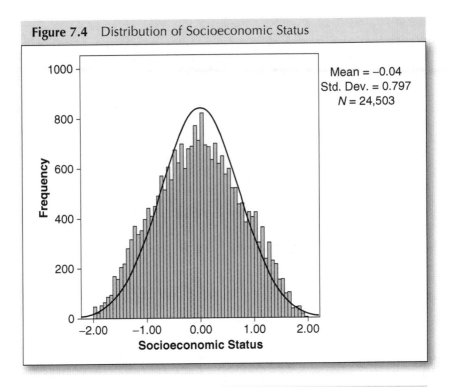

Mean = −0.04
Std. Dev. = 0.797
N = 24,503

Figure 7.5 Distribution of Socioeconomic Status With 4% Extreme Scores

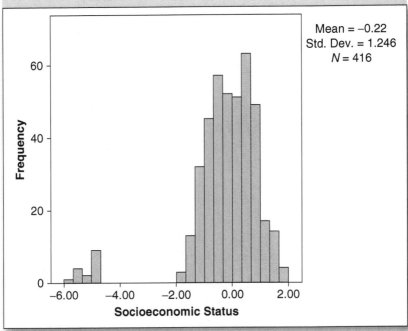

Mean = −0.22
Std. Dev. = 1.246
N = 416

Figure 7.6 Distribution of Socioeconomic Status With 4% Extreme Scores, Both Tails

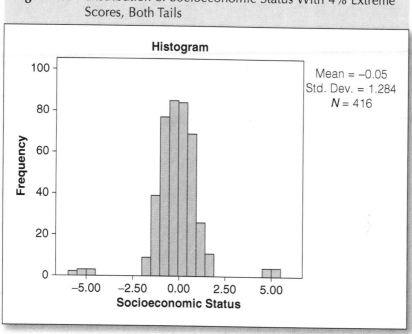

To emphasize the point that you need to examine your data visually, we repeated the process for drawing a sample of 416 from the same data, however this time half the extreme scores were in each tail of the distribution. As you can see in Figure 7.6, the distribution is still symmetrical and the mean is not significantly different from the original population mean (mean = -0.05, standard deviation = 1.28, skew = -0.03). In this case only the standard deviation is inflated because of added error variance caused by the extreme scores. This increase in error variance would have deleterious effects on any analyses you would want to perform if these extreme scores were not dealt with in some way.

Removing Univariate Extreme Scores

A simple way to handle this problem is to do a z transformation, converting all scores in a distribution to a z (standard normal distribution by subtracting the mean from each score and dividing by the standard deviation) distribution, which has a mean of 0.00 and standard deviation of 1.0, something most modern statistical packages can do automatically. You can then select cases with scores greater than -3.0 and less than 3.0 (or another cutoff point of your choosing) and continue analyses.

EFFECT OF EXTREME SCORES ON INFERENTIAL STATISTICS

Dr. Overbay and I also demonstrated the effects of extreme scores on the accuracy of parameter estimates and Type I and Type II error rates in analyses involving continuous variables such as correlation and regression, as well as discrete variable analyses such as t-tests and ANOVA.[3]

In order to simulate a real study in which a researcher samples from a particular population, we defined our population as the 23,396 subjects with complete data on all variables of interest in the NELS 88 data file (already introduced earlier in the book).[4] For the purposes of the analyses reported below, this population was sorted into two groups: "normal" individuals whose scores on relevant variables were between $z = -3.0$ and $z = 3.0$, and "extreme scores," who scored at least $z = \pm 3.0$ on one of the relevant variables.

To simulate the normal process of sampling from a population, but standardize the proportion of extreme scores in each sample, one hundred samples of $N = 50$, $N = 100$, and $N = 400$ each were randomly sampled (with replacement between each samples but not during the creation of a single sample) from the population of normal subjects. Then an additional 4% were randomly selected from the separate pool of extreme scores, bringing samples to $N = 52$, $N = 104$, and $N = 416$, respectively. This procedure produced samples that simulate samples that could easily have been drawn at random from the full population, but that ensure some small number of extreme scores in each sample for the purposes of our demonstration.

The following variables were calculated for each of the analyses below.

- *Accuracy* was assessed by checking whether the original statistics or cleaned statistics were closer to the population correlation. In these calculations the absolute difference was examined.
- *Error rates* were calculated by comparing the outcome from a sample to the outcome from the population. An error of inference was considered to have occurred if a particular sample yielded a different conclusion than was warranted by the population.

EFFECT OF EXTREME SCORES
ON CORRELATIONS AND REGRESSION

The first example looks at simple zero-order correlations. The goal was to demonstrate the effect of extreme scores on two different types of correlations:

correlations close to zero (to demonstrate the effects of extreme scores on Type I error rates) and correlations that were moderately strong (to demonstrate the effects of extreme scores on Type II error rates). Toward this end, two different correlations were identified for study in the NELS 88 data set: the correlation between locus of control and family size ("population" ρ = -.06), and the correlation between composite achievement test scores and socioeconomic status ("population" ρ = .46). Variable distributions were examined and found to be reasonably normal.

After all samples were drawn, correlations were calculated in each sample, both before removal of extreme scores and after. For our purposes, r = -.06 was not significant at $p < .05$ for any of the sample sizes, and r = .46 was significant at $p < .05$ for all sample sizes. Thus, if a sample correlation led to a decision that deviated from the "correct" state of affairs, it was considered an error or inference.

As Table 7.1 demonstrates, extreme scores had adverse effects upon correlations. In all cases, removal of extreme scores had significant effects on the magnitude of the correlations, and the cleaned correlations were more accurate (i.e., closer to the known "population" correlation) 70% to 100% of the time. Further, in most cases, errors of inference were significantly less common with cleaned than uncleaned data.

As Figure 7.7 shows, a few randomly chosen extreme scores in a sample of 100 can cause substantial misestimation of the population correlation. In the sample of almost 24,000 students, these two variables were correlated very strongly, r = .46. In this particular sample, the correlation with four extreme scores in the analysis was r = .16 and was not significant. If this was your study, and you failed to deal with extreme scores, you would have committed a Type II error asserting no evidence of an existing relationship when in fact there is a reasonably strong one in the population.

Removing Extreme Scores in Correlation and Regression

Merely performing univariate data cleaning is not always sufficient when performing statistical analyses, as bivariate and multivariate extreme scores are often in the normal range of one or both of the variables, so merely converting variables to z scores and selecting the range $-3.0 \leq z \geq 3.0$ may not work (as I mention above). In this type of analysis, a two-stage screening process is recommended. First, checking all univariate distributions for extreme scores before calculating a correlation or regression analysis should be done automatically. As you can see in Figure 7.8, after all extreme univariate

Table 7.1 The Effects of Extreme Scores on Correlations

Population ρ	N	Average Initial r	Average Cleaned r	t	% More Accurate	% Errors Before Cleaning	% Errors After Cleaning	t
r = -.06	52	.01	-.08	2.5*	95	78	8	13.40**
	104	-.54	-.06	75.44**	100	100	6	39.38**
	416	0	-.06	16.09**	70	0	21	5.13**
r = .46	52	.27	.52	8.1**	89	53	0	10.57**
	104	.15	.50	26.78**	90	73	0	16.36**
	416	.30	.50	54.77**	95	0	0	—

Note. 100 samples were drawn for each row. Extreme scores were actual members of the population who scored at least $z = \pm 3.0$ on the relevant variable.

With $N = 52$, a correlation of .274 is significant at $p < .05$. With $N = 104$, a correlation of .196 is significant at $p < .05$. With $N = 416$, a correlation of .098 is significant at $p < .05$, two-tailed.

* $p < .01$, ** $p < .001$.

Figure 7.7 Correlation of SES and Achievement, 4% Extreme Scores

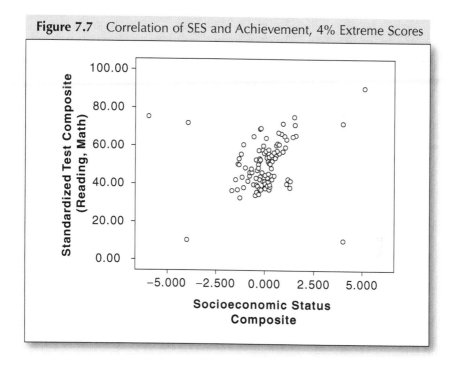

extreme scores were removed, some bivariate extreme scores remain. Most statistical programs allow you to save various statistics when you perform an analysis such as a regression. You will see several different types of residuals and many types of statistics. For simplicity, let us talk about two particular types: standardized residuals and distance indexes.

If you know what a residual is (the difference between the actual value of Y and the predicted value of Y from the analysis; also it can be conceptually defined as the vertical distance a data point is from the regression line), then a standardized residual is easy. It is essentially the z score of the residual and can be interpreted the same way as a univariate z score (e.g., higher numbers mean you are farther from the regression line, and standardized residuals outside the ± 3.0 range should be viewed suspiciously).[5]

Additionally, bivariate and multivariate extreme scores can exist in multiple directions (not just vertically from the regression line), but standardized residuals only identify scores that fall far from the regression line in a vertical direction. Thus, going back to our example in Figure 7.7, in Figure 7.9 the data points that are clearly extreme scores but are not vertically separated from the regression line (circled) would *not* be detected by examining standardized

Figure 7.8 Correlation of SES and Achievement, Bivariate Extreme
Scores Remain After Univariate Outliers Removed

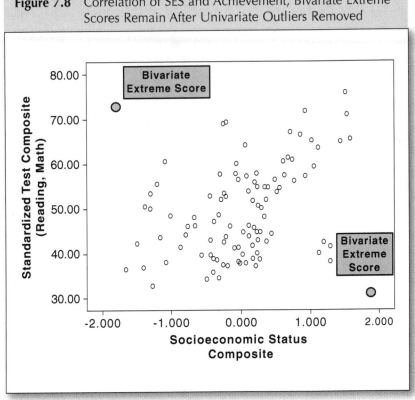

residuals as they are very near the regression line. Thus, while visual inspection is helpful, particularly with simple analyses containing only two variables, once we get past two variables we need other indices, especially as we get beyond two-dimensional space into multiple regression.

Indices of distance, such as Mahalanobis distance and Cook's distance, attempt to capture distance in more than one direction. While the details of their computations are beyond the scope of this chapter, imagine there is a center to the large group of data points in the middle of the scatterplot in Figure 7.9. As discussed above, the Mahalanobis distance and Cook's distance attempt to quantify distance from the center of the multivariate distribution and would likely pick up these extreme scores as being very far from the center of where most data points are, even though they are not vertically separated

Figure 7.9   Extreme Scores Not Detected by Standardized Residuals

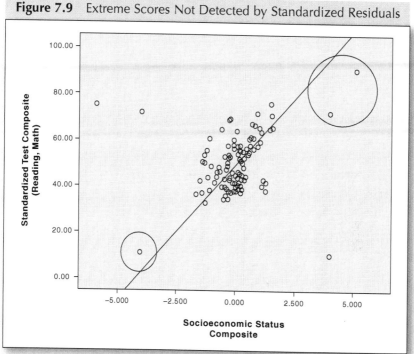

from the regression line. Using these indices to help with extreme score identification is relatively simple. Since statistical packages save these values as a
separate variable, you can easily select or remove cases based on these scores.

Note that the same process of decision making we covered in the previous
discussion of extreme scores should apply here as well—a case might be a
multivariate extreme score for many reasons, some of which are legitimate and
interesting and some not. You need to decide on an individual basis for each
analysis and data point how to handle them, with the same options (removal,
separate study, truncation or recoding, transformation, correction, and so on)
available.

EFFECT OF EXTREME SCORES ON T-TESTS AND ANOVAS

The second example deals with analyses that look at group mean differences,
such as t-tests and ANOVA. For the purpose of simplicity, I used t-tests for this
example, but these results easily generalize to more complex ANOVA-type

analyses. For these analyses, two different conditions were examined: when there were no significant differences between the groups in the population (sex differences in socioeconomic status produced a mean group difference of 0.0007 with a standard deviation of 0.80 and with 24,501 df produced a t of 0.29, which is not significant at $p < .05$) and when there were significant group differences in the population (sex differences in mathematics achievement test scores produced a mean difference of 4.06 and standard deviation of 9.75 and 24,501 df produced a t of 10.69, $p < .0001$). For both analyses, the effects of having extreme scores in only one cell as compared to both cells were examined. Distributions for both dependent variables were examined and found to be reasonably normal.

Similar to the previous set of analyses, in this example, t-tests were calculated in each sample, both before removal of extreme scores and after. For this purpose, t-tests looking at SES should not produce significant group differences, whereas t-tests looking at mathematics achievement test scores should. Two different issues were examined: mean group differences and the magnitude of the t. If an analysis from a sample led to a different conclusion than expected from the population analyses, it was considered an error of inference.

The results in Table 7.2 illustrate the unfortunate effects of extreme scores on ANOVA-type analyses, and they again highlight the importance of including this step in your routine data cleaning regimen. Removal of extreme scores produced a significant change in the mean differences between the two groups when there were no significant group differences expected, but tended not to when there were strong group differences (as these group differences were very strong to begin with). Removal of extreme scores produced significant change in the t statistics primarily when there were strong group differences. In both cases the tendency was for both group differences and t statistics to become more accurate in a majority of the samples. Interestingly, there was little evidence that extreme scores produced Type I errors when group means were equal, and thus removal had little discernable effect. But when strong group differences were revealed, extreme score removal tended to have a significant beneficial effect on error rates, although not as substantial an effect as seen in the correlation analyses.

The presence of extreme scores appears to produce similar effects regardless of whether they are concentrated only in one cell or are present in both.

Table 7.2 The Effects of Extreme Scores on ANOVA-Type Analyses

	N	Initial Mean Difference	Cleaned Mean Difference	t	% More Accurate Mean Difference	Average Initial t	Average Cleaned t	t	% Type I or II Errors Before Cleaning	% Type I or II Errors After Cleaning	t
Equal group means, extreme scores in one cell	52	0.34	0.18	3.70***	66	−0.20	0.12	1.02	2	1	< 1
	104	0.22	0.14	5.36***	67	0.05	0.08	1.27	3	3	< 1
	416	0.09	0.06	4.15***	61	0.14	0.05	0.98	2	3	< 1
Equal group means, extreme scores in both cells	52	0.27	0.19	3.21***	53	0.08	0.02	1.15	2	4	< 1
	104	0.20	0.14	3.98***	54	0.02	0.07	0.93	3	3	< 1
	416	0.15	0.11	2.28*	68	0.26	0.09	2.14*	3	2	< 1

(Continued)

163

(Continued)

	N	Initial Mean Difference	Cleaned Mean Difference	t	% More Accurate Mean Difference	Average Initial t	Average Cleaned t	t	% Type I or II Errors Before Cleaning	% Type I or II Errors After Cleaning	t
Unequal group means, extreme scores in one cell	52	4.72	4.25	1.64	52	0.99	1.44	−4.70***	82	72	2.41**
	104	4.11	4.03	0.42	57	1.61	2.06	−2.78**	68	45	4.70***
	416	4.11	4.21	−0.30	62	2.98	3.91	−12.97***	16	0	4.34***
Unequal group means, extreme scores in both cells	52	4.51	4.09	1.67	56	1.01	1.36	−4.57***	81	75	1.37
	104	4.15	4.08	0.36	51	1.43	2.01	−7.44***	71	47	5.06***
	416	4.17	4.07	1.16	61	3.06	4.12	−17.55***	10	0	3.13***

Note. 100 samples were drawn for each row. Extreme scores were actual members of the population who scored at least $z = \pm 3.0$ on the relevant variable.

$*p < .05, **p < .01, ***p < .001$

164

Detecting Extreme Scores in ANOVA-Type Analyses

Similar to regression type analyses, ANOVA-type analyses can contain bivariate or multivariate extreme scores not removed by simple univariate data cleaning. As mentioned previously, most statistical packages will save standardized residuals, which allows for identification of these types of extreme scores. In the case of ANOVA-type analyses, the residual is the difference between an individual score and the group mean, and by standardizing it, the same ± 3.0 standard deviation rule can apply.

TO REMOVE OR NOT TO REMOVE?

Some authors have made the argument that removal of extreme scores produces undesirable outcomes, such as making analyses less generalizable or representative of the population. I hope that this chapter persuades you that the opposite is in fact true: that your results probably will be more generalizable and less likely to represent an error of inference if you do conscientious data cleaning, including dealing with extreme scores where warranted (remember, there are many possible reasons for extreme scores, and the reason for them should inform the action you take). In univariate analyses, the cleaned data are closer to our example population than any sample with extreme scores—often by a substantial margin. In correlation and regression and in ANOVA-type analyses, my colleague and I demonstrated several different ways in which statistics and population parameter estimates are likely to be *more* representative of the population after having addressed extreme scores than before.

Though these were two fairly simple statistical procedures, it is straightforward to argue that the benefits of data cleaning extend to more complex analyses. More sophisticated analyses, such as structural equation modeling, multivariate analyses, and multilevel modeling, tend to have more restrictive and severe assumptions, not fewer, because they tend to be complex systems. Thus, it is good policy to make sure the data are as clean as possible when using more complex analyses. Ironically, even analyses designed to be robust to violations of distributional assumptions, such as nonparametric procedures, seem to benefit from solid, more normally distributed data.

FOR FURTHER ENRICHMENT

1. Data sets from the examples given in this chapter are available online on this book's website. Download some of the examples yourself and see how

removal of outliers generally makes results more generalizable and closer to the population values.

2. Examine a data set from a study you (or your advisor) have previously published for extreme scores that may have distorted the results. If you find any relatively extreme scores, explore them to determine if it would have been legitimate to remove them, and then examine how the results of the analyses might change as a result of removing those extreme scores. And if you find something interesting, be sure to share it with me. I enjoy hearing stories relating to real data.

3. Explore well-respected journals in your field. Note how many report having checked for extreme scores, and if they found any, how they dealt with them and what the results of dealing with them were (if reported). In many of the fields I explored, few authors explicitly discussed having looked for these types of issues.

NOTES

1. Data comes from the Health and Nutrition Examination Survey (HANES), performed by the U.S. Centers for Disease Control and Prevention (CDC).

2. Researchers (Miller, 1991; Van Selst & Jolicoeur, 1994) demonstrated that simply removing scores outside the ± 3.0 standard deviations can produce problems with certain distributions, such as highly skewed distributions characteristic of response latency variables, particularly when the sample is relatively small. If you are a researcher dealing with this relatively rare situation, Van Selst and Jolicoeur (1994) present a table of suggested cutoff scores for researchers to use with varying sample sizes that will minimize these issues with extremely nonnormal distributions. Another alternative would be to use a transformation to normalize the distribution prior to examining data for extreme scores.

3. Some readers will recognize that both regression and ANOVA are examples of general linear models. However, as many researchers treat these as different paradigms and there are slightly different procedural and conceptual issues in extreme scores, we treat them separately for the purpose of this chapter.

4. This is a different number from the univariate examples as there are different numbers of missing data in each variable, and for these analyses we removed all cases with missing data on *any* variable of interest. For more information on more appropriate ways of handling missing data, be sure to refer to Chapter 6.

5. However, standardized residuals are not perfect. In some cases a *studentized* residual is more helpful (studentized residuals are standardized residuals that account for the fact that extreme scores can inflate standard errors, thus potentially masking extreme scores, particularly in small data sets).

REFERENCES

Anscombe, F. J. (1960). Rejection of outliers. *Technometrics, 2*(2), 123–147.

Barnett, V., & Lewis, T. (1994). *Outliers in statistical data.* New York: Wiley.

Dixon, W. J. (1950). Analysis of extreme values. *Annals of Mathematical Statistics, 21*(4), 488–506.

Evans, V. P. (1999). Strategies for detecting outliers in regression analysis: An introductory primer. In B. Thompson (Ed.), *Advances in social science methodology* (Vol. 5, pp. 213–233). Stamford, CT: JAI Press.

Hamilton, L. (1992). *Regression with graphics: A second course in applied statistics*: Belmont, CA: Duxbury Press.

Hawkins, D. M. (1980). *Identification of outliers.* New York: Chapman & Hall.

Iglewicz, B., & Hoaglin, D. C. (1993). *How to detect and handle outliers.* Milwaukee, WI: ASQC Quality Press.

Impara, J., Kingsbury, G., Maynes, D., & Fitzgerald, C. (2005, April). *Detecting cheating in computer adaptive tests using data forensics.* Paper presented at the annual meeting of the National Council on Measurement in Education and National Association of Test Directors, Montreal, Canada.

Jarrell, M. G. (1994). A comparison of two procedures, the Mahalanobis Distance and the Andrews-Pregibon Statistic, for identifying multivariate outliers. *Research in the Schools, 1*, 49–58.

Judd, C. M., & McClelland, G. H. (1989). *Data analysis: A model comparison approach.* San Diego, CA: Harcourt Brace Jovanovich.

Lane, K. (2002, February). *What is robust regression and how do you do it?* Paper presented at the annual meeting of the Southwest Educational Research Association, Austin, TX.

Micceri, T. (1989). The unicorn, the normal curve, and other improbable creatures. *Psychological Bulletin, 105*(1), 156–166.

Miller, J. (1991). Reaction time analysis with outlier exclusion: Bias varies with sample size. *The Quarterly Journal of Experimental Psychology, 43*(4), 907–912.

Orr, J. M., Sackett, P. R., & DuBois, C. L. Z. (1991). Outlier detection and treatment in I/O Psychology: A survey of researcher beliefs and an empirical illustration. *Personnel Psychology, 44*, 473–486.

Osborne, J. W. (2008). Sweating the small stuff in educational psychology: How effect size and power reporting failed to change from 1969 to 1999, and what that means for the future of changing practices. *Educational Psychology, 28*(2), 1–10.

Osborne, J. W., & Overbay, A. (2004). The power of outliers (and why researchers should always check for them). *Practical Assessment, Research, and Evaluation, 9*(6), 1–12.

Rasmussen, J. L. (1988). Evaluating outlier identification tests: Mahalanobis D Squared and Comrey D. *Multivariate Behavioral Research, 23*(2), 189–202.

Rousseeuw, P., & Leroy, A. (1987). *Robust regression and outlier detection.* New York: Wiley.

Rowland-Jones, S., Sutton, J., Ariyoshi, K., Dong, T., Gotch, F., McAdam, S., Corrah, T. (1995). HIV-specific cytotoxic T-cells in HIV-exposed but uninfected Gambian women. *Nature Medicine, 1*(1), 59–64.

Sachs, L. (1982). *Applied statistics: A handbook of techniques* (2nd ed.). New York: Springer-Verlag.

Schwager, S. J., & Margolin, B. H. (1982). Detection of multivariate normal outliers. *The Annals of Statistics, 10*(3), 943–954.

Stevens, J. P. (1984). Outliers and influential data points in regression analysis. *Psychological Bulletin, 95*(2), 334–344.

Van Selst, M., & Jolicoeur, P. (1994). A solution to the effect of sample size on outlier elimination. *The Quarterly Journal of Experimental Psychology, 47*(3), 631–650.

Wainer, H. (1976). Robust statistics: A survey and some prescriptions. *Journal of Educational Statistics, 1*(4), 285–312.

Wilcox, R. (2008). Robust methods for detecting and describing associations. In J. W. Osborne (Ed.), *Best practices in quantitative methods* (pp. 263–279). Thousand Oaks, CA: Sage.

Yuan, K.-H., Bentler, P. M., & Zhang, W. (2005). The effect of skewness and kurtosis on mean and covariance structure analysis. *Sociological Methods & Research, 34*(2), 240–258.

Zimmerman, D. W. (1994). A note on the influence of outliers on parametric and non-parametric tests. *Journal of General Psychology, 121*(4), 391–401.

Zimmerman, D. W. (1995). Increasing the power of nonparametric tests by detecting and downweighting outliers. *Journal of Experimental Education, 64*(1), 71–78.

Zimmerman, D. W. (1998). Invalidation of parametric and nonparamteric statistical tests by concurrent violation of two assumptions. *Journal of Experimental Education, 67*(1), 55–68.

⁜ EIGHT ⁜

IMPROVING THE NORMALITY OF VARIABLES THROUGH BOX-COX TRANSFORMATION

Debunking the Myth of Distributional Irrelevance

In the social sciences, many of the statistical procedures you will encounter assume *normality* and *equality of variance* (e.g., homogeneity of variance or homoscedasticity, depending on the type of analysis). Yet how often do you read a research article in which the author describes testing the assumptions of the selected analysis? My experience is that authors rarely report attending to these important issues, which is a shame, because violation of certain assumptions can harm the validity and generalizability of the results, cause underestimation of effect sizes and significance levels, and inflate confidence intervals. Two common assumptions, normality and equality of variance, are easily tested during the initial data cleaning process. More importantly, issues arising from these tests are often easy to fix prior to analysis.

Data transformations are commonly used tools that can serve many functions in quantitative analysis of data, including improving normality and equalizing variance. There are as many potential types of data transformations as there are mathematical functions. Some of the more commonly discussed "traditional" transformations include: square root, converting to logarithmic (e.g., base 10, natural log) scales, inverting and reflecting, and applying trigonometric transformations such as sine wave transformations.

Unfortunately, if you have data that do not conform to the standard normal distribution, most statistical texts provide only cursory overview of best practices in transformation. I have, in previous papers (Osborne, 2002, 2008a), provided some detailed recommendations for best practices in utilizing traditional transformations (e.g., square root, log, inverse). One of the best practices I identified early on was anchoring the minimum value in a distribution at exactly 1.0 to improve the effectiveness of the transformations as some are severely degraded as the minimum deviates above 1.0 (and having values in a distribution less than 1.0 can either cause mathematical problems or cause data below 1.0 to be treated differently than those at or greater than 1.0).

The focus of this chapter is streamlining and improving data normalization that should be part of a routine data cleaning process. In the spirit of best practices, I introduce and explore the Box-Cox series of transformations (e.g., Box & Cox, 1964; Sakia, 1992), which has two significant advantages to the traditional transformations. First, Box-Cox expands on the traditional transformations to give the statistician the ability to fine-tune transformations for optimal normalization using an almost infinite number of potential transformations. Second, the syntax shared in this chapter (and the routines incorporated into programs like SAS) can easily transform data that are both positively and negatively skewed. More traditional transformations like square root or log transformations work primarily on positively skewed distributions. In the case of a negatively skewed variable, these traditional transformations require a cumbersome process that includes: (a) reflection (creating a mirror-image of the distribution), (b) anchoring at 1.0, (c) transformation, and (d) rereflection processes to return the variable to its original nature.

Box and Cox (1964) originally envisioned this transformation as a panacea for simultaneously correcting issues with normality, linearity, and homoscedasticity. While these transformations often improve all of these aspects of a distribution or analysis, Sakia (1992) and others have noted it does not always accomplish these challenging goals.

First, a cautionary note. While transformations are important tools, they should be used thoughtfully as they fundamentally alter the nature of the variable, making the interpretation of the results slightly more complex.[1] Thus, some authors suggest reversing the transformation once the analyses are done for reporting of means and standard deviations, graphing, and so on. Although it sounds simple, reversing a transformation so that you might substantively interpret estimates is a complex task fraught with the potential for introducing substantial bias (e.g., Beauchamp & Olson, 1973; Miller, 1984) that also might create potential for misunderstanding or misrepresentation of the actual nature of the analysis. This decision ultimately depends on the nature of the hypotheses and analyses, but is probably rarely needed in most research. I briefly discuss this issue later in the chapter.

WHY DO WE NEED DATA TRANSFORMATIONS?

Most common statistical procedures make two assumptions that are relevant to this topic: (a) an assumption that the variables (or their error terms, more technically) are normally distributed, and (b) an assumption of equality of variance (homoscedasticity or homogeneity of variance), meaning that the variance of the variable remains constant over the observed range of some other variable. In regression analyses, this second assumption is that the variance around the regression line is constant across the entire observed range of data. In ANOVA analyses, this assumption is that the variance in one group is not significantly different from that of other groups. Most statistical software packages provide ways to test both assumptions, and data transformations provide a way to remedy issues identified through testing these assumptions.

Significant violation of either assumption can increase your chances of committing Type I or II errors (depending on the nature of the analysis and violation of the assumption). Yet few researchers report testing these assumptions, and fewer still report correcting for violation of these assumptions (Osborne, 2008b). This is unfortunate, given that in most cases it is relatively simple to correct this problem through the application of data transformations. Even when one is using analyses considered robust to violations of these assumptions or nonparametric tests (that do not explicitly assume normally distributed error terms), attending to these issues can improve the results of the analyses (e.g., Zimmerman, 1995).

WHEN A VARIABLE VIOLATES THE ASSUMPTION OF NORMALITY

There are several ways to tell whether a variable deviates significantly from normal, as we saw in Chapter 5. While researchers tend to report favoring the "ocular test" (i.e., "eyeballing" the data or visual inspection of either the variable or the error terms) (Orr, Sackett, & DuBois, 1991), more sophisticated tools are available. These tools range from simple examination of skew (ideally between -0.80 and 0.80; closer to 0.00 is better) and kurtosis (closer to 3.0 is better in many software packages, closer to 0.00 in SPSS) to examination of P-P plots (plotted percentages should remain close to the diagonal line to indicate normality) and inferential tests of normality, such as the Kolmogorov-Smirnov (K-S) or Shapiro-Wilk (S-W) test. For the K-S or S-W tests, $p > .05$

indicates the distribution does *not* differ significantly from the standard normal distribution, thus meeting the assumption of normality. For more information on the K-S test and other similar tests, consult the manual for your software, as well as Goodman (1954), Lilliefors (1968), Rosenthal (1968), and Wilcox (1997).

TRADITIONAL DATA TRANSFORMATIONS FOR IMPROVING NORMALITY

Square Root Transformation

The Case of the Difficult Student and the Genesis of the Anchoring Rule

Early in my career, I was teaching graduate statistics courses at the University of Oklahoma, and as usual I had thoroughly indoctrinated my students in the art of data cleaning. Toward the end of the semester, while working with her own data, one student complained that the data transformations I had taught them were not working. No matter what transformation she tried (this was before I introduced my students to Box-Cox), she could not get her modestly skewed variable to become more normally distributed.

After verifying she was indeed performing the transformations correctly, we delved deeper into the data. The troublesome variable (student SAT scores) had an original range of 200 to 800. This problem led to the insight that applying transformations to variables with large minimum values can cause the transformations to be less effective, something I had never come across in all my statistics courses. Once we moved the distribution of the variable to have a minimum of 1.0 (by subtracting a constant from all scores), the transformations were more effective, giving her a more normally distributed variable to work with.

This "difficult student" with her unruly variable led me to write a paper in 2002 recommending anchoring all distributions at 1.0 prior to applying any transformation.

Many readers will be familiar with this procedure—when one applies a square root transformation, the square root of every value is taken (technically, a special case of a power transformation where all values are raised to the one-half power). However, as one cannot take the square root of a negative number. If the distribution of a variable includes negative values, a constant must be added to move the minimum value of the distribution above 0, preferably to 1.00. This recommendation (Osborne, 2002) reflects the fact that numbers between 0.00 and 1.0 behave differently than numbers 0.00, 1.00, and those larger than 1.00 (and the fact that adding a constant to all observations within a particular variable does not change the shape of the distribution of that variable). The square root of 1.00 and 0.00 remain 1.00 and 0.00, respectively, while numbers above 1.00 become smaller, and numbers between 0.00 and 1.00 become *larger* (the square root of 4 is 2, but the square root of 0.40 is 0.63). Thus, if you apply a square root transformation to a continuous variable that contains values between 0 and 1 as well as above 1, you are treating some numbers differently than others, which is not desirable. Square root transformations are traditionally thought of as good for normalizing Poisson distributions (most common with data that are counts of occurrences, such as number of times a student was suspended in a given year or the famous example, presented later in this chapter, of the number of soldiers in the Prussian Cavalry killed by horse kicks each year; Von Bortkiewicz, 1898) and equalizing variance.

Log Transformation(s)

Logarithmic transformations are actually a family of transformations, rather than a single transformation, and in many fields of science log-normal variables (i.e., normally distributed after log transformation) are relatively common. Log-normal variables seem to be more common when outcomes are influenced by many independent factors (e.g., biological outcomes; note that most variables in the social sciences are influenced by many factors as well). In brief, a logarithm is the power (exponent) a base number must be raised to in order to get the original

> **How Log Transformations Are Really a Family of Transformations**
>
> Log transformations express any number as a particular base raised to an exponent. Thus:
>
> $\log100(100)=1.000$, $\log100(10)=0.500$
> $\log50(100)=1.177$, $\log50(10)=0.589$
> $\log25(100)=1.431$, $\log25(10)=0.715$
> $\log10(100)=2.000$, $\log10(10)=1.000$
> $\log9(100)=2.096$, $\log9(10)=1.048$
> $\log8(100)=2.214$, $\log8(10)=1.107$
> $\log7(100)=2.367$, $\log7(10)=1.183$
> $\log6(100)=2.570$, $\log6(10)=1.285$
> $\log5(100)=2.861$, $\log5(10)=1.431$
> $\log4(100)=3.322$, $\log4(10)=1.661$
> $\log3(100)=4.192$, $\log3(10)=2.096$
> $\log e(100)=4.605$, $\log e(10)=2.302$
> $\log2(100)=6.644$, $\log2(10)=3.322$

number. Any given number can be expressed as y^x in an infinite number of ways. For example, if we were talking about base 10, 1 is 10^0, 100 is 10^2, 16 is $10^{1.2}$, and so on. Thus, $\log_{10}(100) = 2$ and $\log_{10}(16) = 1.2$. Another common option is the *natural logarithm,* where the constant e (2.7182818...) is the base. In this case the natural log of 100 is 4.605. As this example illustrates, a base in a logarithm can be almost any number, thus presenting infinite options for transformation. Traditionally, authors such as Cleveland (1984) have argued that a range of bases should be examined when attempting log transformations (see Osborne, 2002, for a brief overview on how different bases can produce different transformation results). The argument that a variety of transformations should be considered is compatible with the assertion that Box-Cox can constitute a best practice in data transformation.

Mathematically, the logarithm of a number less than or equal to 0 is undefined, and numbers in the range of 0 through 1.0 produce negative values, getting extremely large as values approach 0.00. Numbers above 1.0 produce positive values, though they do not become very large until they approach infinity. Thus, because numbers between 0 and 1.0 are treated differently than numbers above 1.0, a best practice should be to anchor a distribution submitted to this type of transformation at 1.00 (the recommendation in Osborne, 2002) or higher (see also Jobson, 1992).

Inverse Transformation

To take the inverse of a number (x) is to compute $1/x$ or x^{-1}. I personally dislike this transformation as it essentially makes very small numbers (e.g., 0.00001) very large, and very large numbers very small, thus reversing the order of your scores (this also is technically a class of transformations, as inverse square root and inverse of other powers are all discussed in the literature). Therefore one must be careful to either reflect or reverse the order distribution prior to applying an inverse transformation, or adjust interpretation of the results accordingly.

Arcsine Transformation

This transformation has traditionally been used for proportions (such as proportion of students passing a test at each school surveyed; recall that proportions only range from 0.00 to 1.00) and involves taking the arcsine of the

square root of a number, with the resulting transformed data reported in radi-
ans. Because of the mathematical properties of this transformation, the variable must be transformed to the range −1.00 to 1.00. While a perfectly valid
transformation, other modern techniques may limit the need for this transformation (e.g., rather than aggregating binary outcome data to a proportion,
analysts can use multilevel logistic regression on the original data).

Box-Cox Power Transformations

Most of the traditional transformations mentioned above are members of
a class of transformations called *power transformations*. Power transformations are merely transformations that raise all values of a variable to an exponent (power). For example, a square root transformation can be characterized
as $x^{1/2}$ and inverse transformations can be characterized as x^{-1}. And as mentioned above, log transformations embody a class of power transformations.
Although they are rarely discussed in texts, some authors have talked about
third and fourth roots (e.g., $x^{1/3}$, $x^{1/4}$) being useful in various circumstances. So
you might wonder why we should be limited to these options. Why not use $x^{0.9}$
or x^{-2} or x^4 or any other possible exponent if it improves the quality of the data?
In fact, for half a century and more statisticians have been talking about this
idea of using a continuum of transformations that provide a range of opportunities for closely calibrating a transformation to the needs of the data. Tukey
(1957) is often credited with presenting the initial idea that transformations
can be thought of as a class or family of similar mathematical functions. This
idea was modified by Box and Cox (1964) to take the form of the Box-Cox
series of transformations:[2]

$$y_i^\lambda = (y_i^\lambda - 1) / \lambda \text{ where } \lambda \neq 0;$$

$$y_i^\lambda = \log_e(y_i) \text{ where } \lambda = 0.$$

While not implemented in all statistical packages,[3] there are ways to estimate lambda, the Box-Cox transformation coefficient, through a variety of
means. Once an optimal lambda is identified, the transformation is mathematically straightforward to implement in any software package. Implementing
Box-Cox transformations within SPSS is discussed in detail at the end of this
chapter. Given that lambda is potentially a continuum from negative infinity
to positive infinity, we can theoretically calibrate this transformation to be

maximally effective in moving a variable toward normality. Additionally, as mentioned above, this family of transformations incorporates many traditional transformations:

$\lambda = 1.00$: no transformation needed; produces results identical to original data

$\lambda = 0.50$: square root transformation

$\lambda = 0.33$: cube root transformation

$\lambda = 0.25$: fourth root transformation

$\lambda = 2.00$: square transformation

$\lambda = 3.00$: cube transformation

$\lambda = 0.00$: natural log transformation

$\lambda = -0.50$: reciprocal square root transformation

$\lambda = -1.00$: reciprocal (inverse) transformation

$\lambda = -2.00$: reciprocal (inverse) square transformation

and so forth.

APPLICATION AND EFFICACY OF BOX-COX TRANSFORMATIONS

Bortkiewicz's Data on Prussian Cavalrymen Killed by Horse Kicks

This classic data set has long been used as an example of nonnormal (Poisson, or count) data. In this data set, Bortkiewicz (1898) gathered the number of cavalrymen in the Prussian army that had been killed each year from horse kicks between 1875 and 1894 by unit. As each unit had relatively few (ranging from 0 to 4 per year), this distribution is skewed (presented in Figure 8.1; skew = 1.24, kurtosis = 1.20), as is often the case in count data. Using square root, $\log_e$, or $\log_{10}$, will improve normality in this variable (resulting in skew of 0.84, 0.55, and 0.55, respectively). By using Box-Cox

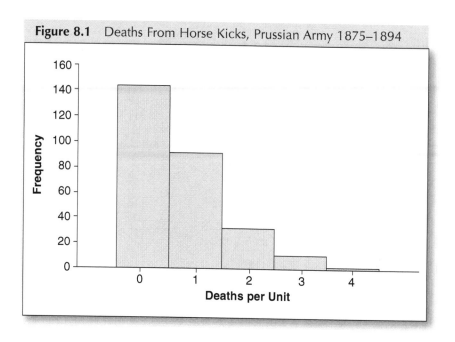

Figure 8.1 Deaths From Horse Kicks, Prussian Army 1875–1894

with a variety of lambda ranging from −2.00 to 1.00, we can determine that the optimal transformation after being anchored at 1.0 would be a Box-Cox transformation with $\lambda = -2.00$ (see Figure 8.2) yielding a variable that is almost symmetrical (skew = 0.11; note that even though transformations between $\lambda = -2.00$ and $\lambda = -3.00$ yield slightly better skew, it is not substantially better; note also that kurtosis remained suboptimal at −1.90).

University Size and Faculty Salary in the United States

Data from 1,161 institutions in the United States were collected on the size of the institution (number of faculty) and average faculty salary by the American Association of University Professors in 2005. As Figure 8.3 shows, the variable *number of faculty* is highly skewed (skew = 2.58, kurtosis = 8.09), and Figure 8.4 shows the results of Box-Cox transformations after being anchored at 1.0 over the range of lambda from −3.00 to 1.00. Because of the nature of these data (values ranging from 7 to more than 2,000 with a strong skew), this transformation attempt produced a wide range of outcomes across the 32 examples of Box-Cox transformations, from extremely bad outcomes (skew < −30.0 where $\lambda < -1.20$)

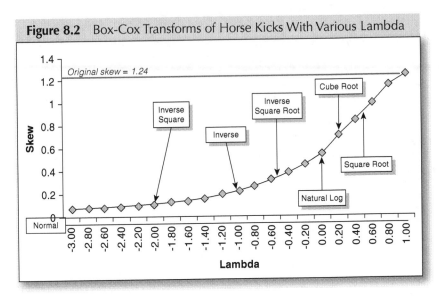

Figure 8.2   Box-Cox Transforms of Horse Kicks With Various Lambda

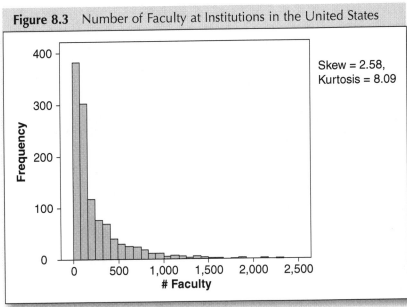

Figure 8.3   Number of Faculty at Institutions in the United States

to very positive outcomes of $\lambda = 0.00$ (equivalent to a natural log transformation) achieved the best result (skew = 0.11, kurtosis = −0.09 at $\lambda = 0.00$). (Figure 8.5 shows results of the same analysis when the distribution is anchored at other points beyond 1.0, such as the original mean (132.0) or 500. Once the anchor is

Figure 8.4 Box-Cox Transformation of University Size With Various Lambda Anchored at 1.00

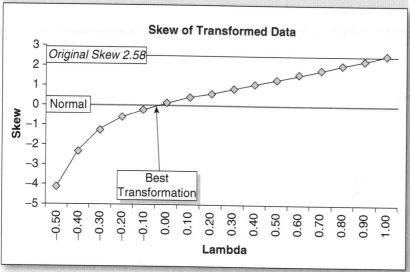

Figure 8.5 Box-Cox Transformation of University Size With Various Lambda Anchored at 132,500,10,000

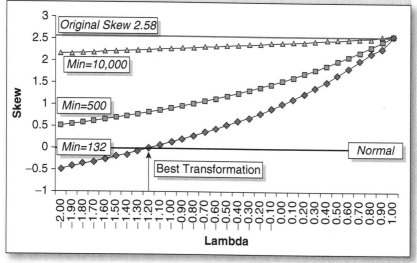

moved from 1.0, it becomes less likely that any level lambda will produce a normally distributed transformation. In the case of the variable when anchored at 132, one transform ($\lambda = -1.20$) achieves a skew of 0.00 but has a kurtosis of -1.11, arguably a poorer outcome than when the distribution was anchored at 1.0.

As noted (Osborne, 2002), as minimum values of distributions deviate from 1.00, power transformations tend to become less effective. To illustrate this, Figure 8.5 shows the same data anchored at a minimum of 500 and 10,000.[4] When anchored at 500, the results of the transformation are appreciably worse. It takes a much more severe transformation ($\lambda = -3.70$) to get the skew to approach 0.00, but kurtosis at this point is -1.28, again, not as good an outcome as when anchored at 1.0. And when the minimum value is 10,000, even the most severe transformations fail to bring the variable appreciably closer to normal (and in fact, some of the values of lambda produced distributions so severely nonnormal that SPSS could not calculate distributional characteristics).

As Figure 8.6 shows, once anchored at 1.0 and transformed appropriately, the distribution is much closer to normal.

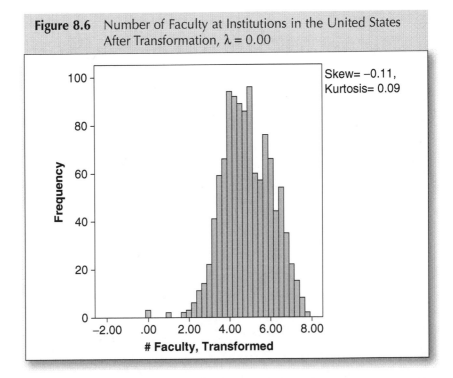

Figure 8.6 Number of Faculty at Institutions in the United States After Transformation, $\lambda = 0.00$

Faculty salary (associate professors) was more normally distributed to begin with, with a skew of 0.36 and kurtosis of 0.12. A Box-Cox transformation with lambda of 0.70 improved normality, but it is questionable whether it is necessary to transform a variable that is already approximating normality.

To demonstrate the benefits of normalizing data via Box-Cox, a simple correlation between number of faculty and associate professor salary (computed prior to any transformation) produced a correlation of $r_{(1,161)} = .49$, $p < .0001$ (model fit improved from $F_{(1, 1123)} = 362.90$ to $F_{(1, 1123)} = 850.60$ following transformation, a 134.39% increase). This represents a coefficient of determination (percentage variance accounted for) of 0.24, which is substantial yet probably underestimates the true population effect due to the substantial non-normality present. Once both variables were optimally transformed, the simple correlation was calculated to be $r_{(1,161)} = .66$, $p < .0001$. This represents a coefficient of determination (percentage variance accounted for) of 0.44, or an 81.50% increase in the coefficient of determination over the original.

Student Test Grades

Positively skewed variables are easily dealt with via the above procedures. Traditionally, a negatively skewed variable had to be *reflected* (reversed), anchored at 1.0, transformed via one of the traditional (square root, log, inverse) transformations, and reflected again. This is because these traditional methods of transformation tended to work only on positively skewed variables, and would increase skew on negatively skewed variables. While this reflect-and-transform procedure also works fine with Box-Cox, researchers can merely use a different range of lambda to create a transformation that deals with negatively skewed data. Here I use data from a test in an undergraduate class I taught several years ago. These 174 scores range from 48% to 100%, with a mean of 87.3% and a skew of −1.75 (kurtosis = 5.43) (see Figure 8.7). Anchoring the distribution at 1.0 by subtracting 47 from all scores, and applying Box-Cox transformations from $\lambda = 1.0$ to 4.0, we get the results presented in Figures 8.8 and 8.9, indicating a Box-Cox transformation with a $\lambda = 2.60$ produces a skew of −0.04 (kurtosis = −0.06).

REVERSING TRANSFORMATIONS

This area of discussion is relatively undeveloped in the social sciences, primarily because a need for it is rare. Most of our questions revolve around

Figure 8.7 Student Grades From an Undergraduate Psychology
Class

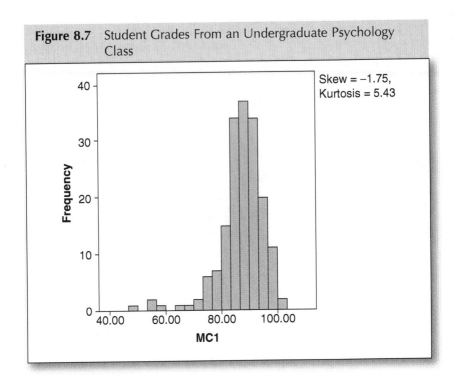

Figure 8.8 Box-Cox Transformation of Students Grades, Negatively
Skewed

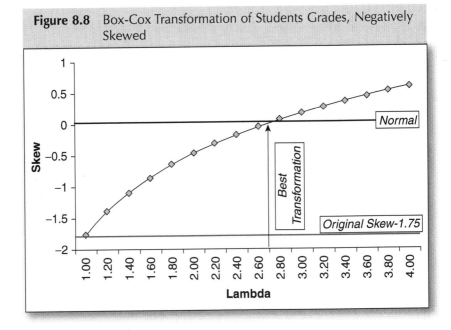

Figure 8.9   Student Grades Following Transformation λ = 2.60

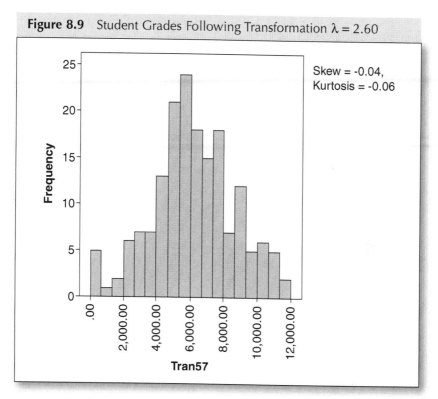

variables that are not concrete and specifically interpretable, but rather rela-
tional—what happens to one variable as another one increases, or are groups
significantly different on a particular measure. In these types of cases, there is
rarely a need to back-transform the values.

While it is relatively simple to manipulate the Box-Cox transformation to
calculate the reverse of the transform (in other words, to convert a transformed
value to the original value), other conceptual issues are important to discuss.

First, should you want to know what a particular transformed value corresponds to in the original variable metric (e.g., if you are graphing results or
providing information on critical points of interest), this formula reverses the
Box-Cox transformation:

$$y = [\hat{y}(\lambda) + 1)^{1/\lambda}] - C$$

Where $\hat{y}$ is the transformed value, λ is the Box-Cox coefficient used to
transform the variable, and C is the value subtracted or added to anchor the
minimum value of the distribution at 1.0. Note that if a constant was subtracted
to anchor the original distribution, that constant must be added here, and,

conversely, if a constant was added to anchor the original distribution, that constant must be subtracted here.

Look for an Excel spreadsheet that performs these calculations on the website for this book.

Conceptually, I find the arguments for or against back-transforming most important. The question of why you transformed a variable in the first place is important. In general, it improved the normality of the data, improving the analysis. To back-transform is to undo that benefit. Indeed, if you were to transform and then appropriately back-transform, you would end up with an identical distribution to that with which you started, ignoring rounding error.

Further, having transformed a variable for analysis, it is important to make that clear to the reader. The fifth root of a variable or natural log of a variable is a different variable than the original variable.

More thought needs to be given to this issue in the literature. Under what conditions is it desirable or important to back-transform and under what conditions is it unacceptable (or suboptimal)?

I would suggest the *only* time it is appropriate is if: (a) you have a variable that has specific, concrete interpretations (e.g., weight, age, income, grade point average, SAT score, IQ) and you are wanting to display the results graphically for reader interpretation, or (b) if you are attempting to establish critical cutoff scores for practitioners to use in settings where it would be impractical for them to convert observations to some other metric.

CONCLUSION

The goal of this chapter was to introduce Box-Cox transformations to researchers as a potential best practice in data cleaning. Many of us have been briefly exposed to data transformations, but few researchers appear to use them or report data cleaning of any kind (Osborne, 2008b). Box-Cox takes the idea of having a range of power transformations (rather than the classic square root, log, and inverse) available to improve the efficacy of normalizing and variance equalizing for both positively and negatively skewed variables.

As the examples presented in this chapter show, not only does Box-Cox easily handle substantially skewed data, but normalizing the data also can have a dramatic impact on effect sizes in analyses (in this case, improving the effect size of a simple correlation by more than 80%).

Further, many modern statistical programs (e.g., SAS) incorporate powerful Box-Cox routines, and in others (e.g., SPSS) it is relatively simple to use a script (see this chapter's appendix) to automatically examine a wide range of lambda to quickly determine the optimal transformation.

Data transformations can introduce complexity into substantive interpretation of the results (as they change the nature of the variable, and some can reverse the order of the data, and thus care should be taken when interpreting results). Sakia (1992) briefly reviews the arguments revolving around this issue, as well as techniques for using variables that have been power transformed in prediction or converting results back to the original metric of the variable. For example, Taylor (1986) describes a method of approximating the results of an analysis following transformation, and others (see Sakia, 1992) have shown that this seems to be a relatively good solution in most cases. Given the potential benefits of utilizing transformations (e.g., meeting assumptions of analyses, improving generalizability of the results, improving effect sizes) the drawbacks do not seem compelling in the age of modern computing.

FOR FURTHER ENRICHMENT

1. Explore how to implement Box-Cox transformations within the statistical software you use. Download one (or more) of the example data files from the book's website and see if you use Box-Cox transformations to normalize them as effectively as I did. Remember to use best practices, anchoring at 1.0.

2. Using a data set from your own research (or one from your advisor), examine variables that exhibit significant nonnormality. Perform an analysis prior to transforming them (e.g., correlation, regression, ANOVA), then transform them optimally using Box-Cox methods. Repeat the analysis, and note whether the normalization of the variables had any influence on effect sizes or interpretation of the results. If you find an interesting example, e-mail me a summary and I may feature it on the book's website.

APPENDIX

Calculating Box-Cox Lambda by Hand

If you desire to estimate lambda by hand, the general procedure is as follows.

- Divide the variable into at least 10 regions or parts.
- Calculate the mean and standard deviation for each region or part.

- Plot log(*SD*) versus log(mean) for the set of regions.
- Estimate the slope of the plot and use the slope (1-b) as the initial estimate of lambda.

To illustrate this procedure, I revisit the second example: number of faculty at a university. After determining the 10 cutpoints that divide this variable into even parts, selecting each part and calculating the mean and standard deviation, and then taking the $\log_{10}$ of each mean and standard deviation, Figure 8.10 shows the plot of these data. I estimated the slope for each segment of the line since there was a slight curve (segment slopes ranged from −1.61 for the first segment to 2.08 for the last) and averaged all, producing an average slope of 1.02. Interestingly, the estimated lambda from this exercise would be −0.02, very close to the empirically derived 0.00 used in the example above.

Figure 8.10   Figuring Lambda By Hand

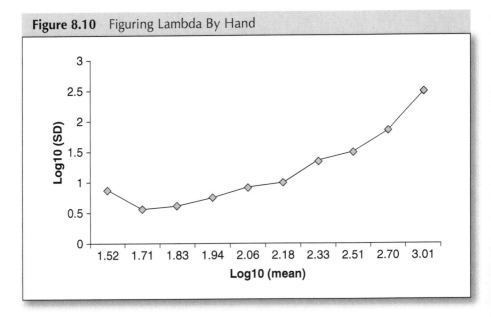

Estimating Lambda Empirically in
SPSS and Performing the Box-Cox Transformation

Using the following syntax, you can estimate the effects of Box-Cox using 32 different lambdas simultaneously, choosing the one that seems to work the best. Note that the first COMPUTE anchors the variable (NUM_TOT) at 1.0, as the minimum value in this example was 7. You need to edit this to move your variable to 1.0.

```
* * * * * * * * * * * * * * * * * * * * * * * * * * * * * * * * * * * * * * * * * * * * * * * * * * * * * * * *
* * *

* * * * * * * * * * *Syntax for exploring larger range of lambda
* * *

* * * * * * * * * * * On first line change NUM_TOT to variable you want to
transform,

* * * * * * * * * * * and -16 to anchor that variable at 1.0* * *.
* * *

* * * * * * * * * * * * * * * * * * * * * * * * * * * * * * * * * * * * * * * * * * * * * * * * * * * * * * * .
```

```
COMPUTE var1=num_tot-16.
execute.
VECTOR lam(61) /tran(61).
LOOP idx=1 TO 61.
- COMPUTE lam(idx)=-3.1 + idx * .1.
- DO IF lam(idx)=0.
-    COMPUTE tran(idx)=LN(var1).
- ELSE.
-   COMPUTE tran(idx)=(var1**lam(idx) - 1)/lam(idx).
- END IF.
END LOOP.
EXECUTE.
FREQUENCIES VARIABLES=var1 tran1 to tran61
   /format=notable
   /STATISTICS= SKEWNESS KURTOSIS
   /ORDER=ANALYSIS.
FREQUENCIES VARIABLES= lam1 to lam61
   /format=notable
   /STATISTICS= MINIMUM
   /ORDER=ANALYSIS.
```

Note that this syntax tests lambda from -3.0 to 3.0, which is the range most transformations should fall into, regardless of whether your variable is positively or negatively skewed. Although there is no reason to limit analyses to this range, I would be cautious about extending the transformations into more extreme ranges. If this range of lambda does not produce a satisfactory transformation, it is possible that something odd is going on (perhaps some extreme outliers, failure to anchor at 1.0, or the presence categorical variable) that indicates you should explore your data prior to attempting transformation.

To change the range of lambda, you can change the -3.1 starting value on following line:

```
- COMPUTE lam(idx)=-3.1 + idx * .1.
```

Changing the number at the end (0.1) changes the interval SPSS examines— in this case it examines lambda in 0.1 intervals, but changing the range and the interval can help fine-tune a transformation, should further refinement toward normality be desired.

Note: Thanks to Raynald Levesque for his webpage: http://www.spsstools.net/Syntax/Compute/Box-CoxTransformation.txt, which informed my SPSS syntax for estimating lambda.

NOTES

1. For example, instead of predicting student achievement test scores, you might be predicting the natural log of student achievement test scores, which alters the interpretation of the outcome and greatly complicates things if you want to substantively interpret unstandardized regression coefficients, means, or confidence intervals, or to create prediction equations.

2. Since Box and Cox (1964), other authors have introduced modifications of these transformations for special circumstances (e.g., data with negative values, which should be addressed via anchoring at 1.0) or peculiar data types less common in the social sciences. For example, John and Draper (1980) introduced their "modulus" transformation that was designed to normalize distributions that are relatively symmetrical but not normal (i.e., removing kurtosis where skew is not an issue). In practice, most researchers will get good results from using the original Box-Cox family of transformations, which is preferable to those new to this idea thanks to its computational simplicity.

3. SAS has a convenient and very well-done implementation of Box-Cox within *proc transreg* that iteratively tests a variety of lambda and identifies the several different good options for you. Many resources on the web, such as http://support.sas.com/rnd/app/da/new/802ce/stat/chap15/sect8.htm, provide guidance on how to use Box-Cox within SAS.

4. This is not unrealistic if this data represented something like salary, rather than number of faculty.

REFERENCES

Beauchamp, J. J., & Olson, J. S. (1973). Corrections for bias in regression estimates after logarithmic transformation. *Ecology, 54*(6), 1403–1407.

Bortkiewicz, L., von. (1898). *Das gesetz der kleinen zahlen.* Leipzig: G. Teubner.

Box, G. E. P., & Cox, D. R. (1964). An analysis of transformations. *Journal of the Royal Statistical Society, SeriesB, 26*(2), 211–234.

Cleveland, W. S. (1984). Graphical methods for data presentation: Full scale breaks, dot charts, and multibased logging. *The American Statistician, 38*(4), 270–280.

Goodman, L. A. (1954). Kolmogorov-Smirnov tests for psychological research. *Psychological Bulletin, 51*(2), 160–168.

Jobson, J. D. (1992). *Applied multivariate data analysis: Regression and experimental design.* New York: Springer-Verlag.

John, J. A., & Draper, N. R. (1980). An alternative family of transformations. *Applied Statistics, 29*(2), 190–197.

Lilliefors, H. W. (1968). On the Kolmogorov-Smirnov test for normality with mean and variance unknown. *Journal of the American Statistical Association, 62*(318), 399–402.

Miller, D. M. (1984). Reducing transformation bias in curve fitting. *The American Statistician, 38*(2), 124–126.

Orr, J. M., Sackett, P. R., & DuBois, C. L. Z. (1991). Outlier detection and treatment in I/O psychology: A survey of researcher beliefs and an empirical illustration. *Personnel Psychology, 44*, 473–486.

Osborne, J. W. (2002). Notes on the use of data transformations. *Practical Assessment, Research, and Evaluation., 8*(6). Retrieved from http://pareonline.net/getvn.asp?v=8&n=6.

Osborne, J. W. (2008a). Best practices in data transformation: The overlooked effect of minimum values. In J. W. Osborne (Ed.), *Best practices in quantitative methods* (pp. 197–204). Thousand Oaks, CA: Sage.

Osborne, J. W. (2008b). Sweating the small stuff in educational psychology: How effect size and power reporting failed to change from 1969 to 1999, and what that means for the future of changing practices. *Educational Psychology, 28*(2), 1–10.

Rosenthal, R. (1968). An application of the Kolmogorov-Smirnov test for normality with estimated mean and variance. *Psychological-Reports, 22*(2), 570.

Sakia, R. M. (1992). The Box-Cox transformation technique: A review. *The Statistician, 41*(2), 169–178.

Taylor, M. J. G. (1986). The retransformed mean after a fitted power transformation. *Journal of the American Statistical Association, 81*(393), 114–118.

Tukey, J. W. (1957). The comparative anatomy of transformations. *Annals of Mathematical Statistics, 28*(3), 602–632.

Wilcox, R. R. (1997). Some practical reasons for reconsidering the Kolmogorov-Smirnov test. *British Journal of Mathematical and Statistical Psychology, 50*(1), 71–78.

Zimmerman, D. W. (1995). Increasing the power of nonparametric tests by detecting and downweighting outliers. *Journal of Experimental Education, 64*(1), 71–78.

⚜ NINE ⚜

DOES RELIABILITY MATTER?

Debunking the Myth of Perfect Measurement

I n many branches of science, the variables we are interested in are also difficult to measure, making measurement error a particular concern.[1] Despite impressive advancements in measurement in recent years (particularly the broad dissemination of structural equation modeling, Rasch measurement methodologies, and item response theory, to name but a few), simple reliability of measurement remains an issue. In simple analyses such as simple correlation or regression, or univariate ANOVA, unreliable measurement causes relationships to be *underestimated* (or attenuated), increasing the risk of Type II errors. In the case of multiple regression or partial correlation, effect sizes of variables with poor reliability can be underestimated while causing other variables in the analysis to simultaneously be *overestimated*, as the full effect of the variable with poor measurement qualities might not be removed.

This is a significant concern if the goal of research is to accurately model the "real" relationships evident in the population, effects that would be replicable. Although most authors assume that reliability estimates (e.g., Cronbach alpha internal consistency estimates) of .70 and above are acceptable (e.g., Nunnally & Bernstein, 1994) and I (Osborne, 2008b) reported that the average alpha reported in top educational psychology journals was .83,[2] measurement of this quality still contains enough measurement error to make correction worthwhile (as illustrated below).

Many authors seem largely unconcerned with reliable measurement (by virtue of failing to report any facts relating to the quality of their measurement—see Osborne, 2008b). Others seem to believe that moderately good reliability is "good enough" to accurately model the population relationships and produce generalizable, accurate results. So, the goal in this chapter is to debunk the myth of perfect measurement—in other words, to encourage researchers to more rigorously assess the quality of their measurement, more fully understanding the effect of imperfect reliability on their results. In this chapter I argue that authors should be more thoughtful and careful about assuming their measurement is good enough if their goal is to obtain an accurate picture of the "true" relationship in the population.

WHAT IS A REASONABLE LEVEL OF RELIABILITY?

Reliability is a difficult topic to address in many sciences. There tend to be two ways of assessing reliability. Where scales or multiple indicators are involved, *internal consistency* is most often assessed through Cronbach's alpha.[3] Alpha is a function of two aspects of a scale or set of indicators: number of items and the average correlation between the items. This means that you can get a high alpha from either having a scale with strongly correlated items or a scale with many items (or both).

Conceptually, Cronbach's alpha is the average of all possible split-half correlations for a scale, which is also an estimate of the correlation of two random samples of items from a theoretical universe of items similar to those on a particular test or scale (Cronbach, 1951).[4] That is, if you took a particular scale and randomly split the items into two groups, making two parallel scales, and correlated those two halves of the scale, that would be an estimate of split-half reliability. If you did that an infinite number of times and averaged all the resulting correlations (both for actual items and the universe of similar theoretical items), that would be a close approximation of Cronbach's alpha. Thus, Cronbach's alpha was intended to provide an estimate of test/scale reliability without the drawbacks of actually having to compute split-half reliability, which has many conceptual and practical issues.[5] Note that alpha is *not* a measure of unidimensionality (an indicator that a scale is measuring a single construct rather than multiple related constructs) as is often thought (Cortina, 1993; Schmitt, 1996). Unidimensionality is an important assumption of alpha in that scales that are multidimensional will cause alpha to be underestimated if not assessed separately for each dimension, but high values for alpha are not necessarily indicators of unidimensionality (e.g., Cortina, 1993; Schmitt,

1996). I have seen examples of random items collected from different types of questionnaires leading to very acceptable levels of alpha if enough are used—regardless of whether they are measuring the same construct or very different constructs.

Furthermore, alpha should be considered a *lower boundary* of reliability in that actual reliability may be higher than alpha estimates (but is almost never lower than alpha in practice). Again, to the extent that item standard deviations are unequal, or that scales are multidimensional rather than unidimensional, actual reliability will be higher than estimated by alpha. Therefore, correcting statistics for low reliability based on alpha can, in some cases, lead to overcorrection, and thus should be approached with caution (Osborne, 2008a). As many authors have argued, the "acceptable" level of alpha depends on the use of the scale or measure, and there is probably no one universal cutoff point for acceptable levels of internal consistency. However, noting that $(1 - \alpha)^2$ is an estimate of the amount of error in a measure (coefficient of nondetermination), and in light of the pronounced effects reduced reliability can have on estimates of effect sizes (discussed below), researchers should be cautious in accepting measurement with a significant amount of error variance.

To this point I have only addressed one possible indicator of reliable measurement: internal consistency as measured by Cronbach's alpha. It is often the case that alpha is not the appropriate measure of reliability. For example, kappa (e.g., Cohen, 1968) is an indicator of agreement between raters, and test-retest correlations (e.g., weighing an individual twice with the same scale) are other common indicators of reliability that can be a measure of the reliability of a measurement. Each has methodological limitations and drawbacks that should be considered when employing them to correct for measurement error.

RELIABILITY AND SIMPLE CORRELATION OR REGRESSION

Since "the presence of measurement errors in behavioral research is the rule rather than the exception" and the "reliabilities of many measures used in the behavioral sciences are, at best, moderate" (Pedhazur, 1997, p. 172), it is important that researchers be aware of accepted methods of dealing with this issue. For simple correlation, the formula below (available in many references, such as Cohen, Cohen, West, & Aiken, 2002) provides an estimate of the "true" relationship between the independent variable (IV) and dependent variable (DV) in the population.

$$r_{12}^* = \frac{r_{12}}{\sqrt{r_{11}r_{22}}}$$

In this equation, r_{12} is the observed correlation, and r_{11} and r_{22} are the reliability estimates of the variables.[6] To illustrate use of this formula, I take an example from my own research (which I also return to later in this chapter).

Years ago I administered two scales measuring how psychologically invested students were in their education to 214 high school students. The two scales, the School Perceptions Questionnaire (SPQ), which I published (Osborne, 1997), and the Identification With School (IWS), published by a colleague, Kristin Voelkl-Finn (Voelkl, 1996, 1997). In practice, these scales tend to be strongly correlated, tend to have good internal consistency, and served as a good example of what can happen when reliability is sacrificed.

First, internal consistency estimates (Cronbach's alpha) were estimated for the SPQ via traditional means to be $\alpha = .88$ and for IWS was $\alpha = .81$, both of which are considered by traditional benchmarks to be good levels of internal consistency. After averaging the items to create composite scores and testing assumptions of simple correlation,[7] the correlation was calculated to be $r = .75$, which translates to a coefficient of determination (percentage variance accounted for) of .56. Again, this is considered a relatively strong correlation for the social sciences and is expected from two measures of similar constructs.

Using the equation above, we could correct this correlation to estimate the disattenuated, or "true" population correlation to be estimated at .89. Looking at effect size (percentage variance accounted for, often called the coefficient of determination) for these two correlations, we see a sizable improvement from .56 to .79. This represents a 40.29% increase in effect size or variance accounted for, or a 28.72% *underestimation* of the true correlation between these two variables if the assumption of perfectly reliable measurement was met.[8] Many are surprised that variables having such good reliability could still show such a dramatic misestimation of the true population effect. And some might be skeptical whether we can really estimate the true reliability of scales. Below I take the same data and use structural equation modeling (SEM) to estimate the true correlation between these two scales and the corrected estimate from our equation is remarkably close to the estimate generated by SEM.

Other examples of the effects of disattenuation (correcting estimates for attenuation due to poor reliability) are included in Table 9.1.

Table 9.1 Example Disattenuation of Simple Correlation Coefficients

Reliability Estimate	Observed Correlation Coefficient					
	r = .10 (.01)	r = .20 (.04)	r = .30 (.09)	r = .40 (.16)	r = .50 (.25)	r = .60 (.36)
.95	.11 (.01)	.21 (.04)	.32 (.10)	.42 (.18)	.53 (.28)	.63 (.40)
.90	.11 (.01)	.22 (.05)	.33 (.11)	.44 (.19)	.56 (.31)	.67 (.45)
.85	.12 (.01)	.24 (.06)	.35 (.12)	.47 (.22)	.59 (.35)	.71 (.50)
.80	.13 (.02)	.25 (.06)	.38 (.14)	.50 (.25)	.63 (.39)	.75 (.56)
.75	.13 (.02)	.27 (.07)	.40 (.16)	.53 (.28)	.67 (.45)	.80 (.64)
.70	.14 (.02)	.29 (.08)	.43 (.18)	.57 (.32)	.71 (.50)	.86 (.74)
.65	.15 (.02)	.31 (.10)	.46 (.21)	.62 (.38)	.77 (.59)	.92 (.85)
.60	.17 (.03)	.33 (.11)	.50 (.25)	.67 (.45)	.83 (.69)	---

Note. Reliability estimates for this example assume the same reliability for both variables. Percentage variance accounted for (shared variance minus coefficient of determination) is in parentheses.

For example, even when reliability is .80, correction for attenuation substantially changes the effect size (*increasing variance accounted for by about 50%* compared to simple attenuated correlations). When reliability drops to .70 or below, this correction yields a substantially different picture of the true nature of the relationship and potentially avoids Type II errors. As an example, an alpha of .70 equates conceptually to approximately half the variance in a measure being composed of error, half of the true score. Looking at Table 9.1, you can see that correcting for this level of reliability tends to double the effect size in the analysis. In other words, having an alpha of .70 can lead you to underestimate the effects in your analyses by 50%! How many articles in respected journals have reliability estimates at or below that important conceptual threshold?

RELIABILITY AND PARTIAL CORRELATIONS

With each independent variable added to a regression equation, the effects of less-than-perfect reliability on the strength of the relationship becomes more complex and the results of the analysis more questionable. With the addition of one independent variable with less-than-perfect reliability, each succeeding variable entered has the opportunity to claim part of the error variance left over by the unreliable variable(s). The apportionment of the explained variance among the independent variables thus will be incorrect and reflect a misestimation of the true population effect. In essence, low reliability in one variable can lead to substantial overestimation of the effect of another related variable. As more independent variables with low levels of reliability are added to the equation, the greater the likelihood that the variance accounted for is not apportioned correctly. This can lead to erroneous findings and increased potential for Type II errors for the variables with poor reliability, as well a Type I errors for the other variables in the equation. Obviously this gets increasingly complex as the number of variables in the equation grows and increasingly unacceptable in terms of replicability and confidence in results. In these cases, structural equation modeling could be considered a best practice.

A simple example, drawing heavily from Pedhazur (1997), is a case in which one is attempting to assess the relationship between two variables controlling for a third variable ($r_{12.3}$). When one is correcting for low reliability in all three variables, the formula below is used, where r_{11}, r_{22}, and r_{33} are reliabilities, and r_{12}, r_{23}, and r_{13} are relationships between variables. If one is only correcting for low reliability in the covariate, one could use the simplified version of the formula on the right.

$$r_{12.3}^* = \frac{r_{33}r_{12} - r_{13}r_{23}}{\sqrt{r_{11}r_{33} - r_{13}^2}\sqrt{r_{22}r_{33} - r_{23}^2}}$$

$$r_{12.3}^* = \frac{r_{33}r_{12} - r_{13}r_{23}}{\sqrt{r_{33} - r_{13}^2}\sqrt{r_{33} - r_{23}^2}}$$

Table 9.2 presents some examples of corrections for low reliability in the covariate (only) and in all three variables. Table 9.2 shows some of the many possible combinations of reliabilities, correlations, and the effects of correcting for only the covariate or all variables. Some points of interest: (a) as in Table 9.1, even small correlations see substantial effect size (r^2) changes when corrected for low reliability, in this case often toward reduced effect sizes (b) in some cases the corrected correlation is not only substantially different in magnitude, but also in direction of the relationship, and (c) as expected, the most dramatic changes occur when the covariate has a substantial relationship with the other variables.

Table 9.2 Values of $r_{12.3}$ After Correction Low Reliability

				Reliability of Covariate			Reliability of All Variables		
Examples				**.80**	**.70**	**.60**	**.80**	**.70**	**.60**
r_{12}	r_{13}	r_{23}	Observed $r_{12.3}$	$r_{12.3}$	$r_{12.3}$	$r_{12.3}$	$r_{12.3}$	$r_{12.3}$	$r_{12.3}$
.30	.30	.30	.23	.21	.20	.18	.27	.30	.33
.50	.50	.50	.33	.27	.22	.14	.38	.42	.45
.70	.70	.70	.41	.23	.00	-.64	.47	.00	—
.70	.30	.30	.67	.66	.65	.64	.85	.99	—
.30	.50	.50	.07	−.02	-.09	-.20	−.03	−.17	−.64
.50	.10	.70	.61	.66	.74	.90	—	—	—

Note. Some examples produce impossible values. These are denoted by --.

RELIABILITY AND MULTIPLE REGRESSION

Research has argued that regression coefficients are primarily affected by reliability in the independent variable (except for the intercept, which is affected by reliability of both variables), while true correlations are affected by reliability in both variables. Thus, researchers wanting to correct multiple regression coefficients for reliability can use the formula below, taken from Bohrnstedt (1983), which takes this issue into account.

$$\beta^*_{yx.z} = \left(\frac{\sigma_y}{\sigma_x}\right) \frac{r_{zz}r_{xy} - r_{yz}r_{xz}}{r_{xx}r_{zz} - r_{xz}^2}$$

Some examples of disattenuating multiple regression coefficients are presented in Table 9.3.

In these examples (which are admittedly and necessarily a very narrow subset of the total possibilities), corrections resulting in impossible values were rare, even with strong relationships between the variables and even when reliability is relatively weak.

Table 9.3 Example Disattenuation of Multiple Regression Coefficients

Reliability of All Variables	r_{xz}	Correlations r_{xy} and r_{yz}							
		$r = .10$	$r = .20$	$r = .30$	$r = .40$	$r = .50$	$r = .60$	$r = .70$	$r = .80$
.90	.10	.10	.20	.30	.40	.50	.60	.70	.80
	.40	.08	.15	.23	.31	.38	.46	.54	.62
	.70	.06	.13	.19	.25	.31	.38	.44	.50
.80	.10	.11	.22	.33	.44	.56	.67	.78	.89
	.40	.08	.17	.25	.33	.42	.50	.58	.67
	.70	.07	.13	.20	.27	.33	.40	.47	.53
.70	.10	.13	.25	.38	.50	.63	.75	.88	—
	.40	.09	.18	.27	.36	.45	.55	.64	.73
	.70	.07	.14	.21	.29	.36	.43	.50	.57
.60	.10	.14	.29	.43	.57	.71	.86	—	—
	.40	.10	.20	.30	.40	.50	.60	.70	.80
	.70	.08	.15	.23	.31	.38	.46	.54	.62

Notes. Calculations in this table utilized Bohrnstedt's formula, assumed all IVs had the same reliability estimate, assumed each IV had the same relationship to the DV, and assumed each IV had the same variance, in order to simplify the example. Numbers reported represent corrected r_{xz}.

RELIABILITY AND INTERACTIONS IN MULTIPLE REGRESSION

To this point the discussion has been confined to the relatively simple issue of the effects of low reliability, and correcting for low reliability, on simple correlations and higher-order main effects (partial correlations, multiple regression coefficients). However, many interesting hypotheses in the social sciences involve curvilinear or interaction effects. Of course, poor reliability in main effects is compounded dramatically when those effects are used in cross-products, such as squared or cubed terms or interaction terms. Aiken and West (1991) present a good discussion on the issue. An illustration of this effect is presented in Table 9.4.

As Table 9.4 shows that, even at relatively high reliabilities, the reliability of cross-products is relatively weak (except when there are strong correlations between the two variables). This, of course, has deleterious effects on power and inference. According to Aiken and West (1991), two avenues exist for dealing with this: correcting the correlation or covariance matrix for low reliability and then using the corrected matrix for the subsequent regression analyses, which of course is subject to the same issues discussed earlier, or using SEM to model the relationships in an error-free fashion.

Table 9.4   Effects of Measurement on the Reliability of Cross-Products (Interactions) in Multiple Regression

Reliability of X and Z	Correlation Between X and Z			
	$r = 0$	$r = .20$	$r = .40$	$r = .60$
.9	.81	.82	.86	.96
.8	.64	.66	.71	.83
.7	.49	.51	.58	.72
.6	.36	.39	.47	.62

Note. These calculations assume both variables are centered at 0 and that both X and Z have equal reliabilities. Numbers reported are cross-product reliabilities.

PROTECTING AGAINST OVERCORRECTING DURING DISATTENUATION

The goal of disattenuation is to be simultaneously accurate (in estimating the "true" relationships) and conservative in preventing overcorrecting. Overcorrection serves to further our understanding no more than leaving relationships attenuated.

Several scenarios might lead to inappropriate inflation of estimates, even to the point of impossible values. A substantial underestimation of the reliability of a variable would lead to substantial overcorrection, and potentially impossible values. This can happen when reliability estimates are biased downward by heterogeneous scales, for example. Researchers need to seek precision in reliability estimation in order to avoid this problem.

Given accurate reliability estimates, however, it is possible that sampling error, well-placed outliers, or even suppressor variables could inflate relationships artificially, and thus, when combined with correction for low reliability, produce inappropriately high or impossible corrected values. In light of this, I would suggest that researchers make sure they have checked for these issues prior to attempting a correction of this nature (researchers should check for these issues regularly anyway).

OTHER SOLUTIONS TO THE ISSUE OF MEASUREMENT ERROR

Fortunately, as the field of measurement and statistics advances, other options to these difficult issues emerge. One obvious solution to the problem posed by measurement error is to use SEM to estimate the relationship between constructs (which can give estimates of error-free results given the right conditions), rather than using our traditional methods of assessing the relationship between measures. This eliminates the issue of overcorrection or undercorrection, which estimate of reliability to use, and so on. Given the easy access to SEM software, and a proliferation of SEM manuals and texts, it is more accessible to researchers now than ever before. Having said that, SEM is still a complex process and should not be undertaken without proper training and mentoring (of course, that is true of all statistical procedures).

Another emerging technology that can potentially address this issue is the use of Rasch modeling. Rasch measurement utilizes a fundamentally different approach to measurement than classical test theory, which many of us were trained in. Use of Rasch measurement provides not only more sophisticated, and probably accurate, measurement of constructs, but more sophisticated information on the reliability of items and individual scores. Even an introductory treatise on Rasch measurement is outside the limits of this chapter, but individuals interested in exploring more sophisticated measurement models are encouraged to refer to Bond and Fox (2001) for an excellent primer on Rasch measurement.

WHAT IF WE HAD ERROR-FREE MEASUREMENT?

To give a concrete example of how important this process might be as it applies to our fields of inquiry, I draw from a survey I and a couple graduate students completed of the educational psychology literature from 1998 to 1999 (Osborne,

2008b). This survey consisted of recording all effects from all quantitative studies published in the *Journal of Educational Psychology* during the years 1998 and 1999, as well as ancillary information such as reported reliabilities.

Studies from these years indicate a mean effect size (d) of 0.68, with a standard deviation of 0.37. When these effect sizes are converted into simple correlation coefficients via direct algebraic manipulation, $d = 0.68$ is equivalent to $r = .32$. Effect sizes 1 standard deviation below and above the mean equate to rs of .16 and .46, respectively.

From the same review of the literature, where reliabilities (Cronbach's alpha) are reported, the average reliability is $\alpha = .80$, with a standard deviation of 0.10.

Table 9.5 contains the results of what would be the result for the field of educational psychology in general if all studies in the field eliminated the negative effects of low reliability (and if we assume reported reliabilities are accurate), such as if all analyses used SEM or error-free measures. For example, while the average reported effect equates to a correlation coefficient of $r = .32$ (coefficient of determination of .10), if corrected for average reliability in the field ($\alpha = .80$) the better estimate of that effect is $r = .40$, (coefficient of determination of .16, a 60% increase in variance accounted for.) These simple numbers indicate that when reliability is low but still considered acceptable by many ($\alpha = .70$, 1 standard deviation below the average reported alpha, and a level

Table 9.5 An Example of Disattenuation of Effects From Educational Psychology Literature

	Small Effect ($r = .16$, $r^2 = .025$, $d = 0.32$)	Average Effect ($r = .32$, $r^2 = .10$, $d = 0.68$)	Large Effect ($r = .46$, $r^2 = .21$, $d = 1.04$)
Poor Reliability ($\alpha = .70$)	$r = .23$ $r^2 = .052$ $d = 0.47$	$r = .46$ $r^2 = .21$ $d = 1.04$	$r = .66$ $r^2 = .43$ $d = 1.76$
Average Reliability ($\alpha = .80$)	$r = .20$ $r^2 = .040$ $d = 0.41$	$r = .40$ $r^2 = .16$ $d = 0.87$	$r = .58$ $r^2 = .33$ $d = 1.42$
Above-Average Reliability ($\alpha = .90$)	$r = .18$ $r^2 = .032$ $d = 0.37$	$r = .36$ $r^2 = .13$ $d = 0.77$	$r = .51$ $r^2 = .26$ $d = 1.19$

decidedly *not* considered acceptable by me), the increase in variance accounted for can top 100%—in this case, our average effect of $r = .32$ is disattenuated to $r = .46$, (coefficient of determination of .21). At minimum, when reliabilities are good, 1 standard deviation above average ($\alpha = .90$), the gains in effect size range around 30%—still a substantial and potentially important increase as Figure 9.1 visually shows.

Figure 9.1   Effect Sizes and Measurement Error

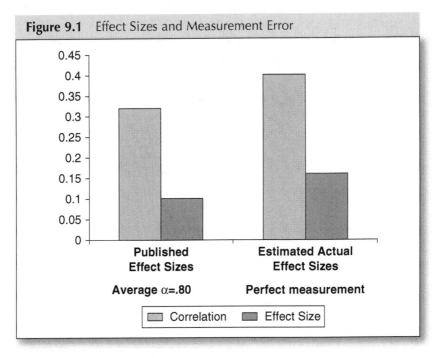

AN EXAMPLE FROM MY RESEARCH

I now return to the previously mentioned example, where I administered two closely related scales to high school students: the School Perceptions Questionnaire (SPQ) and the Identification With School questionnaire (IWS). Recall that internal consistency estimates were $\alpha = .88$ and .81, respectively, considered good by most researchers in the field. Recall also that after averaging the items to create composite scores and testing assumptions of simple correlation,[9] the correlation was calculated to be $r = .75$, which translates to a coefficient of determination (percentage variance accounted for) of .56. This is generally considered a relatively strong correlation for the social sciences and is expected from two measures of similar constructs. Using formula to estimate of the "true" relationship between the IV and DV, I estimated that the corrected correlation should be $r = .89$, but of course have no way of verifying that to be the case using this example.

However, we can simulate what perfect measurement might yield as a correlation between these two variables using AMOS structural equation modeling software to construct latent variables representing each of these scales. While structural equation modeling is a relatively advanced procedure, and getting into the intricacies of the analysis is beyond the scope of this chapter, for our purposes all you need to understand is that SEM can be used to estimate relationships between variables as though they were measured perfectly. As Figure 9.2 shows, the estimate, therefore, of the correlation under perfect correlation was $r = .90$ (coefficient of determination of .81), very close to that estimated our formula. Thus, we can have a good level of confidence that is what the true correlation should be if perfect measurement were possible.

And while some of you may be inclined to shrug and observe that correlations of .90 and .75 are both "pretty large," note that the effect sizes are dramatically different—0.56 with good but imperfect measurement and 0.81 with a simulation of perfect measurement. That means that with good but imperfect measurement, approximately one-third (30.87%) of the effect size was lost compared to the actual relationship in the population.

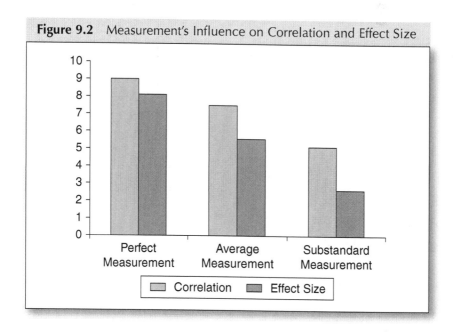

Figure 9.2   Measurement's Influence on Correlation and Effect Size

However, as $\alpha = .83$ (standard deviation of 0.10) is the *average* alpha reported in top educational psychology journals (Osborne, 2008b), it is not difficult to find studies published in well-respected journals with alphas that are substantially lower. In fact, it is not difficult to find alphas under .70 (1 standard deviation below the average alpha), and even 2 standard deviations or more below the mean (0.63), despite the fact that means that a substantial portion of the variance in measures are error!

Therefore, to simulate how unfortunate reliability levels can affect effect sizes, I took the same data and randomly substituted numbers for 20% of the items in each scale.[10] This simulated random responding had the effect of lowering the internal consistency of the scales to simulate poorer internal consistency. After this random substitution, the alphas were .64 for the SPQ and .59 for IWS.[11]

After inserting some random error variance and lowering the effective reliability of the measurement, the correlation for these two scales was still a respectable $r = .51$. Many of us would be delighted to see that magnitude correlation occur in our research. However, note that with a coefficient of determination of .26, the effect under poorer measurement levels (but still levels found in published journal articles) is underestimated by 67.90% (compared to perfect measurement as estimated through SEM). That is, more than two-thirds of the effect is lost to measurement error in studies reporting analyses based on measurement reliability of this level. Worse, as mentioned earlier, in more complex analyses like multiple regression, this underestimation of effect can have unpredictable effects on other variables in the analyses, leading to dramatic overprediction of those effects. In other words, researchers using measures with poor reliability risk not only Type II errors from underestimating particular effects, but also inflate the risk of Type I error for other effects in the same analysis. This should be considered an undesirable state of affairs in the 21st century, particularly when it is relatively simple to improve measurement in scales by increasing item numbers or through analysis by using modern methods like structural equation modeling.

Finally, as another test, I calculated a disattenuated correlation using the data with the reduced internal consistency estimates (.64, .59 that yielded $r = .51$). Put another way, if I, as a researcher came across a correlation of $r = .51$ in my data based on reliabilities of .64 and .59, would it be legitimate to use our formula to correct such poor reliabilities? A quick calculation using that formula yielded a disattenuated correlation of .83 (coefficient of determination of .69), much closer to the "true" correlation of .90 than the observed correlation, to be sure. Importantly, it appears that even in this situation, this simple method of disattenuation does a relatively good job of estimating the true relationship as modeled by SEM (a methodology that was not readily available at the time these corrections were being disseminated). Furthermore, I was gratified to see no evidence that this formula would overcorrect. If anything, when internal consistency estimates get relatively low, the formula provides a slightly conservative correction (leaving the coefficient of determination approximately 10 below where it should be).

DOES RELIABILITY INFLUENCE OTHER ANALYSES?

You may be wondering whether reliability can have the same deleterious effects on other types of analysis, like ANOVA or t-tests. Recent decades have brought these various procedures together under the heading of *general linear modeling,* both conceptually and mathematically. Because ANOVA-type analyses can be easily expressed in equations similar to that of regression equations, similar effects should result. The difference between ANOVA-type analyses and regression or correlation analyses is that categorical variables, such as sex and experimental condition, tend to be measured much more reliably than continuous variables such as the psychological scales I used in the previous example. Thus, in simple ANOVA analyses, it is usually only the dependent variable that has significant amounts of error variance, leaving the analysis on stronger ground with only one of the two variables containing increased error variance. This still reduces effect sizes.

In some simulations I ran preparing for this chapter, I often saw 15% to 20% reduction of effect sizes between the ANOVA analyses with average reliability and the ones with poor reliability. In this example below, we use the SPQ with original reliability (.88) and reduced reliability (.64).

This example looks at identification with academics (SPQ scores) as a function of whether the student withdrew from school.[12] Conceptually, those who stay in school (do not withdraw or drop out) should have higher scores in the SPQ than those who do. A simple ANOVA[13] performed on the SPQ with normal reliability ($\alpha = .88$) showed a strong difference between those who stayed in school (mean = 4.35 out of 5.00, with a $SD = 0.45$) and those who withdrew from school (mean = 3.50 out of 5.00, with a $SD = 0.61$). This effect was significant ($F_{(1, 166)} = 94.96, p < .0001, \eta^2 = .36$).[14] But when the dependent variable was the SPQ with poor reliability ($\alpha = .64$), the effect was still significant and in the same direction (Mean = 3.87 versus 3.22) but the effect size was reduced ($F_{(1, 166)} = 58.29, p < .0001, \eta^2 = .26$) by 27.78% (which is approximately what would be expected given that in the parallel analysis with two variables of poor reliability the effect size was reduced by about 54%—$r = .75$ versus $r = .51$). This effect of poor reliability is significant enough that in an analysis with reduced sample size (and hence, reduced power) researchers are more likely to experience a Type II error. This highlights the importance of paying attention to the quality of measurement in research.

THE ARGUMENT THAT POOR RELIABILITY IS NOT THAT IMPORTANT

I might be biased, but I hope I have persuaded you this is an issue worthy of attention. Other articles espouse the opposite view, just as some authors argue it is irresponsible to remove outliers or transform nonnormal data.

One example is a previous article by Schmitt (1996), wherein he argued that even relatively low alphas (e.g., .50) do not seriously attenuate validity coefficients, which are correlations. In his example, he cites the maximum validity coefficient under α as the square root of α (in this case, $\alpha = .50$ would yield a maximum validity coefficient of 0.71). Yet in making this argument, Schmitt and others have overlooked an important aspect of interpreting correlation coefficients—while 0.50 and 0.71 seem relatively close in size, if you examine their relative effect sizes—their coefficients of determination, which represents the percentage variance accounted for—you see that the effect size for $r = .50$ is 0.25, and for .71 is 0.50—double the effect size. But more importantly, by having an alpha of .50, and capping a reliability coefficient at .71, you therefore essentially give away 50% of the potential effect size for your research. In other words, you have now set the ceiling for the highest possible effect size you can report in your research at 0.50, rather than 1.00. This should be a serious concern for any researcher. Even Schmitt's own results showing examples of disattenuation of correlations show profound effects of poor reliability. In one example (Schmitt, 1996, table 4) two variables with α of .49 and .36, respectively, show an observed correlation of $r = .28$. Correcting for low reliability produced an estimated "true" correlation of 0.67. Again, it is only when one examines the coefficients of determination ($r^2 = .08$ and .45, respectively) where the true damage low reliability causes—in this case, the true effect size is reduced by 82.18%—or *the correct effect size is over five times larger*). I hope you are of the mind that in your research you are not happy to give away a majority of your effect sizes, instead desiring to accurately model what is actually occurring in the population.

CONCLUSIONS AND BEST PRACTICES

If the goal of research is to provide the best estimate of the true effect within a population, and we know that many of our statistical procedures assume perfectly reliable measurement, then we must assume that we are consistently underestimating population effect sizes, usually by a sizable amount. Using the field of educational psychology as an example, and using averages across 2 years of studies published in top-tier empirical journals, we can estimate that while the average reported effect size is equivalent to $r = .32$, (10% variance accounted for), once corrected for average reliability the average effect is equivalent to $r = .40$, (16% variance accounted for). If you take these numbers seriously, this means that many studies in the social sciences *underestimate* the population effects by about one-third.

So what would research look like in an ideal world? In the social sciences, measurement is challenging, but that does not mean it is impossible to do well. Researchers need to use measures and methods that produce reliable and valid data. So the first recommendation is to research the measures and methods you intend to use and confirm they are the best possible.

Next, all researchers should assess and report reliability so that consumers of research have the information necessary to interpret their results. Unfortunately, even in modern journals this does not always happen (Osborne, 2008b). Researchers should always make sure they estimate reliability on unidimensional measures only, and if using multidimensional measures (such as scales with multiple subscales) reliability should be calculated for each dimension separately to avoid underestimating reliability.

Finally, it is my belief from the examples presented in this chapter that authors should use methods that correct for imperfect measurement and report both original and disattenuated estimates. Furthermore, authors should explicitly explain what procedures were used in the process of disattenuation. Since latent variable modeling is more easily accessible these days, my recommendation would be for researchers to routinely use that technique if reliability of measurement is a concern (although SEM does require larger samples than your average t-test or multiple regression). Rasch or item response theory modeling is another option where possible, as are the formulae presented in this chapter.

FOR FURTHER ENRICHMENT

1. Download the spreadsheet from the book's website that allows you to explore correcting simple correlations for low reliability. Enter a correlation, and the two reliabilities for each of the two variables used in the correlation, and examine the effects of good or poor reliability on effect sizes (particularly the percentage variance accounted for).

2. Examine a good journal for your field. Can you, like me, easily find an article reporting results where alpha was .70 or lower? Find one of these articles, correct a correlation for low reliability using the information from the article (and the spreadsheet available from this book's website). How would the author's results have looked different if the variables were measured with perfect reliability? Send me an e-mail with what you find, and I may share it on the book's website.

NOTES

1. This chapter incorporates some aspects of a previously published article; see Osborne (2003).

2. Among those articles actually reporting internal consistency estimates, which may be a biased sample.

3. In past decades, when computing power was not as easily accessible, variants and derivative formulas such as the Kuder-Richardson (e.g., KR-20) indicators were used because in special situations (e.g., dichotomous correct/incorrect or yes/no scoring of tests) these formulae simplify calculation. These are unnecessary in the modern age of computing as KR-20 and alpha should produce identical results under those special conditions (Cortina, 1993; Cronbach, 1951).

4. But only when item standard deviations are equal using the Spearman-Brown split-half reliability formula, otherwise alpha underestimates reliability. There is another formula that takes into account standard deviations of items, which alpha

replicates more closely (Cortina, 1993). Regardless, this is an appropriate conceptual understanding of alpha, despite mathematical inconsistencies such as these.

5. Split-half reliability estimates suffer from serious drawbacks that can cause reliability to be seriously underestimated, which is partially alleviated through application of the Spearman-Brown correction, (Brown, 1910; Spearman, 1910).

6. Note again that many estimates of reliability, such as alpha, are lower-bound estimates that can lead to overcorrection. Thus, conservativeness is advised when correcting in this manner. Specifically, one of my advisors in graduate school advocated correcting reliability to .95, rather than 1.00 to reduce the probability of overcorrection when using structural equation modeling. In this case, I think a good idea is to add .05 or so to any reliability estimate prior to using it in a formula such as this to be conservative and limit overcorrection.

7. You did not expect the guy writing the book on data cleaning to skip that part, did you? All assumptions met.

8. Taking my advisor's admonition to avoid overcorrecting to heart, if I correct the reliability estimates by adding .05 to each the more conservative disattenuated correlation is estimated to be .84 (coefficient of determination = .70), which still represents a 25.03% increase in effect size. However, as you will see, the original calculation may not be an overcorrection.

9. You did not expect the guy writing the book on data cleaning to skip that part, did you? All assumptions met.

10. If you are interested in this particular esoteric point, please feel free to contact me. Essentially what I did was randomly selected 20% of each answers for each item and randomly substituted a whole number from 1 to 5, as both scales were 5-point Likert scales.

11. Believe it or not, I have seen comparable alphas reported in well-respected journals by well-respected scholars.

12. If you are interested in this topic, refer to a recent theoretical piece by myself and my colleague Brett Jones (Osborne & Jones, 2011) explaining how identification with academics is theoretically related to outcomes like dropping out of school. For purposes of this example, you have to trust that it should be.

13. Again, all assumptions met except perfect reliability.

14. Eta-squared is the effect size indicating percentage variance accounted for in ANOVA, analogous to the coefficient of determination or r^2 in correlation and regression.

REFERENCES

Aiken, L. S., & West, S. (1991). *Multiple regression: Testing and interpreting interactions* Thousand Oaks, CA: Sage.

Bohrnstedt, G. W. (1983). Measurement. In P. H. Rossi, J. D. Wright & A. B. Anderson (Eds.), *Handbook of survey research* (pp. 69–121). San Diego, CA: Academic Press.

Bond, T. G., & Fox, C. M. (2001). *Applying the Rasch model: Fundamental measurement in the human sciences.* Mahwah, NJ: Erlbaum.

Brown, W. (1910). Some experimental results in the correlation of mental abilities. *British Journal of Psychology, 3,* 296–322.

Cohen, J. (1968). Weighted kappa: Nominal scale agreement provision for scaled disagreement or partial credit. *Psychological Bulletin, 70*(4), 213–220.

Cohen, J., Cohen, P., West, S., & Aiken, L. S. (2002). *Applied multiple regression/ correlation analysis for the behavioral sciences.* Mahwah, NJ: Lawrence Erlbaum.

Cortina, J. (1993). What is coefficient alpha? An examination of theory and applications. *Journal of Applied Psychology, 78,* 98–104.

Cronbach, L. (1951). Coefficient alpha and the internal structure of tests. *Psychometrika, 16*(3), 297–334.

Nunnally, J. C., & Bernstein, I. (1994). *Psychometric theory* (3rd ed.). New York: McGraw-Hill.

Osborne, J. W. (1997). Identification with academics and academic success among community college students. *Community College Review, 25*(1), 59–67.

Osborne, J. W. (2003). Effect sizes and the disattenuation of correlation and regression coefficients: Lessons from educational psychology. *Practical Assessment, Research, and Evaluation, 8(11).* Retrieved from http://pareonline.net/getvn.asp?v=8&n=11

Osborne, J. W. (2008a). Is disattenuation of effects a best practice? In J. W. Osborne (Ed.), *Best practices in quantitative methods* (pp. 239–245). Thousand Oaks, CA: Sage.

Osborne, J. W. (2008b). Sweating the small stuff in educational psychology: How effect size and power reporting failed to change from 1969 to 1999, and what that means for the future of changing practices. *Educational Psychology, 28*(2), 1–10.

Osborne, J. W., & Jones, B. D. (2011). Identification with academics and motivation to achieve in school: How the structure of the self influences academic outcomes. *Educational Psychology Review, 23*(1), 131–158.

Pedhazur, E. J. (1997). *Multiple regression in behavioral research: Explanation and prediction.* Fort Worth, TX: Harcourt Brace College.

Schmitt, N. (1996). Uses and abuses of coefficient alpha. *Psychological Assessment, 8*(4), 350–353.

Spearman, C. (1910). Correlation calculated from faulty data. *British Journal of Psychology, 3,* 271–295.

Voelkl, K. E. (1996). Measuring students' identification with school. *Educational and Psychological Measurement, 56*(5), 760–770.

Voelkl, K. E. (1997). Identification with school. *American Journal of Education, 105*(3), 294–318.

ADVANCED TOPICS
IN DATA CLEANING

TEN

RANDOM RESPONDING, MOTIVATED MISRESPONDING, AND RESPONSE SETS

Debunking the Myth of the Motivated Participant

A sk your friends how they are doing today. Ever notice that some people tend to flip between extremes (e.g., "wonderful" or "horrible") while others seem to be more stable (e.g., "OK" or "fine") no matter what is going on? This is an example of one sort of response set, where individuals tend to vary in a narrow band around an average or vary at the extremes around the same average.[1]

WHAT IS A RESPONSE SET?

A response set is a strategy people use (consciously or otherwise) when responding to educational tests, questionnaires, or things like psychological tests (or even questions posed in casual conversation, per our example above). These response sets range on a continuum from unbiased retrieval, where individuals use direct, unbiased recall of factual information in memory to answer questions, to generative strategies, where individuals create responses not based on factual recall, due to inability or unwillingness to produce relevant information from memory (see Meier, 1994). Response sets have been discussed in the measurement and research methodology literature for more than 70 years now (Cronbach, 1942; Goodfellow, 1940; Lorge, 1937). Some researchers (Cronbach, 1950) argue that response sets are ubiquitous, found in almost every population on almost every type of test or assessment. In fact, early researchers identified response sets on assessments as diverse as the Strong Interest Inventory (Strong, 1927), tests of clerical aptitude, word meanings, temperament, and spelling, and judgments of proportion in color mixtures, seashore pitch (angle), and pleasantness of stimuli, (see summary in Cronbach, 1950, table 1).

Researchers (myself included) are guilty of too often assuming respondents exclusively use unbiased retrieval strategies when responding to questionnaires or tests, despite considerable evidence for the frequent use of the less desirable and more problematic generative strategies (Meier, 1994). Thus, the myth addressed in this chapter is the myth of the motivated participant, referring to the assumption many of us make that we can take subject responses at face value as accurate.

The goal of this chapter is to demonstrate why researchers should pay more attention to response sets, particularly the detrimental effects of random responding, which can substantially increase the probability of Type II errors.

COMMON TYPES OF RESPONSE SETS

Examples of common response sets discussed in the literature include the following.

Random responding is a response set in which individuals respond with little pattern or thought (Cronbach, 1950). This behavior adds substantial error variance to analyses, which completely negates the usefulness of responses. Meier (1994) and others suggest this may be motivated by lack of preparation, reactivity to observation, lack of motivation to cooperate with the testing, disinterest, or fatigue (Berry et al., 1992; Wise, 2006). Random responding is a particular focus of this chapter as it can mask the effects of interventions, biasing results toward null hypotheses, smaller effect sizes, and much larger confidence intervals than would be the case with valid data. As you might imagine from reading the previous chapters, random responding is a potentially significant threat to the power and validity of research in any science that relies on human responses.[2] Much of the research scientist's performance relies on the goodwill of research participants (students, teachers, participants in organizational interventions, minimally compensated volunteers, patients in health care research, and the like) with little incentive to expend effort in providing data to researchers. If we are not careful, participants with lower motivation to perform at their maximum level may increase the odds of Type II errors, masking real effects of our research through response sets such as random responding.

Malingering and dissimulation. Dissimulation refers to a response set in which respondents falsify answers in an attempt to be seen in a more negative or more positive light than honest answers would provide. Malingering is a response set where individuals falsify and exaggerate answers to appear weaker or more medically or psychologically symptomatic than honest answers would indicate, often motivated by a goal of receiving services they would not otherwise be entitled to (e.g., attention deficit or learning disabilities evaluation; see Kane, 2008; Rogers, 1997) or avoiding an outcome they might otherwise receive (such as a harsher prison sentence; see e.g., Ray, 2009; Rogers, 1997). These response sets are more common on psychological scales where the goal of the question is readily apparent, such as "Do you have suicidal thoughts?" (see Kuncel & Borneman, 2007). Clearly, this response set has substantial costs to society when individuals dissimulate or malinger, but researchers also should be vigilant for these response sets, as motivated responding such as this can dramatically skew research results.

Social desirability is related to malingering and dissimulation in that it involves altering responses in systematic ways to achieve a desired goal— in this case, to conform to social norms or to "look good" to the examiner (Nunnally & Bernstein, 1994). Many scales in psychological research have attempted to account for this long-discussed response set (Crowne & Marlowe, 1964), yet it remains a real and troubling aspect of research in the social sciences that may not have a clear answer, but can have clear affects for important research (e.g., surveys of risky behavior, compliance in medical trials).

Other response styles, such as acquiescence and criticality, are response patterns wherein individuals are more likely to agree with (acquiescence) or disagree with (criticality) questionnaire items in general, regardless of the nature of the item (e.g., Messick, 1991; Murphy & Davidshofer, 1988).

Response styles peculiar to educational testing also are discussed in the literature. While the response styles above can be present in educational data, other biases peculiar to tests of academic mastery (often multiple choice) include: (a) response bias for particular columns (e.g., A or D) on multiple choice items, (b) bias for or against guessing when uncertain of the correct answer, and (c) rapid guessing (Bovaird, 2003), which is a form of random responding (discussed earlier). As mentioned previously, random responding (rapid guessing) is undesirable as it introduces substantial error into the data, which can suppress the ability for researchers to detect real differences between groups, change over time, or the effect(s) of interventions.

Summary. We rely on quantitative research to inform and evaluate many types of innovations, from health care and medicine to consumer research and education. Often this research holds high stakes and financial implications for society as a whole. Some interventions involve tremendous financial and time investment (e.g., instructional technology, community outreach agencies), and some might even be harmful if assessed validly, and therefore can be costly to individuals in terms of frustration, lost opportunities, or actual harm. Thus, it is important for researchers to gather the best available data on interventions to evaluate their efficacy. Yet research must rely on the good faith and motivation of participants (e.g., students, teachers, administrators, parents) to put effort into data gathering for which they may find neither enjoyment nor immediate benefit. This leaves us in a quandary of relying on research to make important decisions, yet often having flawed data. This highlights the importance of all data cleaning (including examining data for response bias) in order to draw the best possible inferences. This chapter, and our example, focuses on educational research, but the lesson should generalize to many areas of scientific research.

IS RANDOM RESPONDING TRULY RANDOM?

An important issue is whether we can be confident that what we call random responding truly is random, as opposed to some other factor affecting responses. In one study attempting to address this issue, Wise (2006) reported that answers identified as random responding on a four-choice multiple choice test (by virtue of inappropriately short response times on computer-based tests) were only correct 25.5% of the time, which is what one would expect for truly random responses in this situation. On the same test, answers not identified as random responding (i.e., having appropriate response times) were correct 72.0% of the time.[3] Further, this issue does not appear to be rare or isolated behavior. In Wise's (2006) sample of university sophomores, 26% of students were identified as having engaged in random responding, and Berry and colleagues (1992) reported the incidence of randomly responding on the MMPI-2 to be 60% in college students, 32% in the general adult population, and 53% amongst applicants to a police training program. In this case, responses identified as random were more likely to be near the end of this lengthy assessment, indicating these responses were likely random due to fatigue or lack of motivation.

DETECTING RANDOM RESPONDING IN YOUR RESEARCH

There is a large and well-developed literature on how to detect many different types of response sets that goes far beyond the scope of this chapter to summarize. Examples include addition of particular types of items to detect social desirability, altering instructions to respondents in particular ways, creating equally desirable items worded positively and negatively, and for more methodologically sophisticated researchers, using item response theory (IRT) to explicitly estimate a guessing (random response) parameter. Meier (1994) (see also Rogers, 1997) contains a summary of some of the more common issues and recommendations around response set detection and avoidance. However, I focus here on random responding, one of the most damaging common response sets (from an inference perspective).

Creation of a Simple Random Responding Scale

For researchers not familiar with IRT methodology, it is still possible to be highly effective in detecting random responding on multiple choice educational tests (and often on psychological tests using Likert-type response scales as well). In general, a simple random responding scale involves creating items in such a way that 100% or 0% of the respondent population should respond in a particular way, leaving responses that deviate from that expected response suspect. This may be done in several ways, depending on the type of scale in question. For a multiple choice educational test, one method (most appropriate when students are using a separate answer sheet, such as a machine-scored answer sheet, used in this study, and described next) is to have one or more choices that are illegitimate responses.[4]

A variation of this is to have questions scattered throughout the test that 100% of respondents should answer in a particular way if they are reading the questions (Beach, 1989). These can be content that should not be missed (e.g., $2 + 2 =$ ___), behavioral/attitudinal questions (e.g., I weave the fabric for all my clothes), nonsense items (e.g., February has 30 days) or targeted multiple choice test items such as: How do you spell *forensics*? (a) forensics, (b) forn-sicks, (c) phorensicks, (d) forensix.

Item Response Theory

One application of IRT has implications for identifying random respond-ers using the theory to create person-fit indices (Meijer, 2003). The idea behind this approach is to quantitatively group individuals by their pattern of responding and then use these groupings to identify individuals who deviate from an expected pattern of responding. This could lead to inference of groups using particular response sets, such as random responding. Also, it is possible to estimate a guessing parameter and then account for it in analyses, as men-tioned above.

I do not have the space to include a thorough discussion of IRT in this chapter. Interested readers should consult references such as Edelen and Reeve (2007) (see also Hambleton, Swaminathan, & Rogers, 1991; Wilson, 2005). However, IRT does have some drawbacks for many researchers, in that it gen-erally requires large (e.g., $N \geq 500$) samples, significant training and resources, and finally, while it does identify individuals who do not fit with the general response pattern, it does not necessarily show what the response set, if any, is. Thus, although useful in many instances, we cannot use it for our example.

Rasch Measurement Approaches

Rasch measurement models are another class of modern measurement tools with applications to identifying response sets. Briefly, Rasch analyses produce two fit indices of particular interest to response sets and random responding: infit and outfit, both of which measure sum of squared standard-ized residuals for individuals. Large outfit mean squares can indicate an issue that deserves exploration, including haphazard or random responding. Again, the challenge is interpreting the cause (response set or missing knowledge, for example, in an educational test) of the substantial infit/outfit values. We use this application of Rasch as a check on the validity of our measure of random responding below. Again, a thorough discussion of this approach is beyond the scope of this chapter, but interested readers can explore Bond and Fox (2001) or Smith and Smith (2004).

No matter the method, it is generally desirable for researchers to include mechanisms for identifying random responding in their research, as random responding from research participants seems relatively commonplace and can be a substantial threat to the validity of research results.

DOES RANDOM RESPONDING CAUSE SERIOUS PROBLEMS WITH RESEARCH?

To stimulate discussion and to encourage researchers to examine their data for this issue, I present an example from my own research with a colleague, Margaret Blanchard. In the course of this project, we saw how a small number of individuals engaging in random responding obscured the effects of a relatively robust educational intervention, decreasing our ability to detect the real effects of an educational intervention until the random responding was dealt with.

From what you know about random responding thus far, let us suggest that in the data to come we should see the following.

1. Students who engaged in random responding should perform significantly worse than students not engaged in random responding.

2. When random responders are removed from analyses, the effects of educational interventions should be clearer; that is, stronger and more likely to be detected.

EXAMPLE OF THE EFFECTS OF RANDOM RESPONDING

The example data presented in this chapter are borrowed from another study (Blanchard et al., 2010) that compared the effects of two instructional methods on student learning and retention.[5] As the details of the intervention and instructional methods are irrelevant here, we will call the instructional methods *method 1* and *method 2*. In this study, middle school science students completed a unit on forensic analysis, developed specifically to compare the effects two teaching methods. Prior to the unit, a pretest was administered, and following, an identical posttest was administered to assess the effects of the instructional methods. The hypothesis was that method 1 would produce stronger growth in student test scores than method 2. In all, 560 middle school students completed both tests and were thus eligible for inclusion in this study.

Identifying Random Responding

The test contained 37 multiple choice questions assessing mastery of the unit material. Most questions had four answer options (A to D), but several toward the end (question numbers 29, 31, 32, 35, 36, 37) had either two (true/ false) or three (A to C) answer options. All answers were entered on standard machine-readable answer sheets for scoring. These answer sheets had *five* answer options (A to E). On a traditional test the only way to identify random responders (or student error) would be to find an answer of E where no item included E as a legitimate answer. In this data set, that was a low frequency event, occurring in only 2% of student tests.

To identify random responders we used a variation of a simple random responding scale composed of legitimate test questions with fewer than four answer choices. With a calculated 91% chance of detecting random responding (see below), and substantial differences in performance between students identified as random responders and non–random responders, this method is preferable to having no method of detecting random responding.

Because six of the 37 items did not conform to the four-answer option question format, illegitimate answers were defined as entering a C or D on questions 29, 31, or 32, or a D on questions 35, 36, or 37. This is a variation of what Beach (1989) discussed as a random response scale, wherein test authors embed several items within a scale or test that all respondents who read and understand the question can only answer one way, such as: How many hours are there in a day? (a) 22 (b) 23 (c) 24 (d) 25. According to Beach, the probability of detecting a random responder through this method is:

$$p = 1 - (1/x)^n$$

where p is the probability of detecting a random responder, x is the number of possible answers in each question, and n is the number of questions in the random responding subscale. In this case, as there were three items with three possible answers and three items with two possible answers (i.e., three items had one illegitimate answer and three items had two illegitimate answers, with an average of 1.5 illegitimate answers across all six items). With $x = 1.5$, and $n = 6$, we had a probability of accurately detecting random responders (accuracy of classification) $p = .91$. Unidentified random responders would serve to bias our results toward no effect of random responding. Therefore, if this method missed a substantial number of random responders, we should show little or no significant effect of random responding. As described below, it appears that we correctly identified the majority.

In this sample, 40.0% of students were identified as engaging in random responding on the pretest, 29.5% on the posttest. Overall, of the original 560 students in the sample, 279 (49.8%) entered no illegitimate answers on either pretest or posttest, while 108 (19.3%) were identified as random responders *both* pretest and posttest. A dummy variable indicating random responding status was created, with random responders assigned a 1 and non–random responders assigned a 0.

As Expected, Random Responders Score Lower Than Others

I used repeated measures ANOVA to examine whether students identified as random responders performed differently than students answering accurately. The results showed a striking difference as a function of random responding status (RRS). Combined, all students showed a significant change in test scores over time ($F_{(1, 383)} = 38.96$, $p < .0001$, partial $\eta^2 = .09$), with pretest scores averaging 12.55 and posttest scores averaging 14.03. Random responders averaged significantly lower scores than non–random responders ($F_{(1, 383)} = 177.48$, $p < .0001$, partial $\eta^2 = .32$; means $= 10.27$ vs. 16. 31, respectively), supporting the hypothesis that method 1 would produce stronger growth in test scores. Finally, there was an interaction with random responding and a change in test scores ($F_{(1, 383)} = 34.47$, $p < .0001$, partial $\eta^2 = .08$).[6] The means for this interaction are presented in Figure 10.1.

As Figure 10.1 shows, random responders scored significantly lower than non–random responders, and random responders showed no significant growth from pretest to posttest, while non–random responders showed higher mean scores and stronger growth over time. This supports the hypothesis, in that random responders not only scored lower, on average, than non–random

Figure 10.1 Differences Between Random and Non-Random
Responders

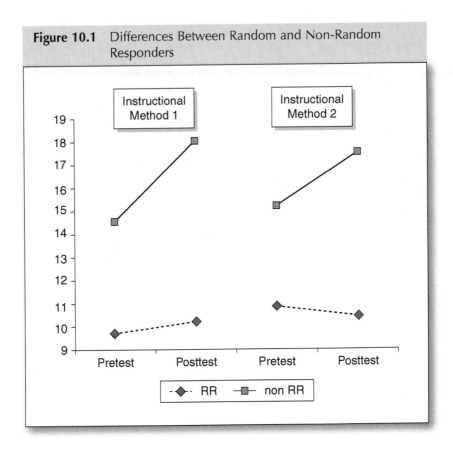

responders, but also that the change in test scores over time was significantly affected by RRS. For random responders there was no substantial change in test scores over time, as might be expected. For non–random responders, there was substantial growth in test scores over time, as might be expected of students who learned something from an instructional unit and whose test scores reflected their mastery of the topic.

Does Removing Random Responders Improve Statistical Inference?

With all random responders in the analysis, there was significant main effect of growth from pretest (mean = 12.91) to posttest (mean = 15.07; $F_{(1, 558)}$ = 127.27, $p < .0001$, partial $\eta^2 = .19$). A significant but weak main effect of instructional method indicated that students taught through method 2 generally outscored those taught through method 1 (means = 14.53 and 13.45, respectively; $F_{(1, 558)}$ = 7.65, $p < .006$, partial η^2 = .01). The important effect, the interaction between time and instructional method, was not significant ($F_{(1, 558)}$ < 0.10) indicating no difference in student growth over time as a function of instructional method. If Dr. Blanchard and I had ended our analyses here, we would have concluded there is no evidence for any benefit of one instructional method over another.

However, when random responders were removed, results indicated a significant and substantial change over time in student test scores (mean scores grew from 14.78 to 17.75; $F_{(1, 277)}$ = 101.43, $p < .0001$, partial η^2 = .27; note that this is *a 42% increase in effect size over the previous analysis*). Also, in contrast to the last analysis, there was a significant interaction between time and instructional method ($F_{(1, 277)}$ = 4.38, $p < .04$, partial η^2 = .02), as Figure 10.2 shows. Consistent with predictions from the original study, students taught through method 1 showed significantly stronger growth than students taught through method 2.

Figure 10.2 Differences Between Instructional Methods

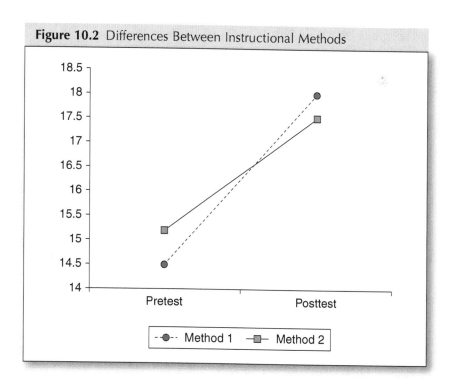

ARE RANDOM RESPONDERS
TRULY RANDOM RESPONDERS?

Our initial attempt to identify random responders through simple design of test questions toward the end of the test is simple and something all researchers can do. Some skeptics reviewing our work wondered whether these truly were individuals who were randomly responding or they were just poorly performing students. Admittedly, our use of a random responding scale does not employ the powerful, modern measurement technologies available (e.g., IRT, Rasch).

To examine this question, I subjected the same data to Rasch analysis, using outfit mean square scores as an indicator of random responding (students with large outfit scores should be the same ones identified as random responders). The goal here was to see whether students we identified as random responders also would be identified as a student having an unexpected response pattern, and whether those with unexpected response patterns tend to score significantly lower than those without these patterns.

To answer the first question, we performed a binary logistic regression analysis, predicting random responding status (0 = not random responding, 1 = having a random response) from outfit mean square (where scores significantly above 1.0 can indicate unexpected response patterns). As expected, the odds that those with higher outfit mean squares would be identified also as a random responder were significantly and substantially higher (odds ratio = 241.73, $p < .0001$). This means that the odds of being labeled a random responder increased just over 241 times for each increase of 1.0 for outfit mean square.[7]

To test the second question, we examined the correlation between outfit mean square and overall test score. As expected, those with higher outfit mean squares had significantly lower test scores ($r_{(560)} = -.53$, coefficient of determination = 28.09%) than those with more expected patterns of responding.

SUMMARY

These analyses provide convergent evidence that those students we initially identified as engaging in random responding also were identified as having unexpected response patterns by Rasch analyses. Further, these findings confirm that those students who were identified as engaging in random responding tend to score much lower on the study's knowledge test than those not engaging in random responding.

BEST PRACTICES REGARDING RANDOM RESPONDING

In many branches of science, change in subject responses is an important method of comparing the efficacy of interventions or methods. Even under ideal conditions, students or respondents may not be motivated or able to provide accurate, high-quality data. In education, students whose performance does not reflect ability or mastery of learning objectives add error to the data and reduce the validity of the test's scores (Cronbach, 1950), diminishing a researcher's ability to detect or compare effects of instructional interventions or methods. In other fields, participants who are fatigued or distracted may engage in random responding on any type of survey, again necessitating researchers examine and clean their data prior to analysis or risk Type II errors.

Although there is a long tradition of research on response sets in social sciences research, few studies in modern times seem to attend to this issue. In fact, classic measurement texts (e.g., Nunnally & Bernstein, 1994) rarely give the topic more than cursory attention, generally presenting random responding as nuisance or random error variance, not worth addressing actively.[8] Quite the contrary, this is an issue of importance for both practical and conceptual reasons. First, the random error this sort of response set can introduce, as you can see, has the potential to substantially reduce power to detect group differences or change over time. It is therefore important to consider preparing for this issue when constructing data gathering instruments, and examining data for evidence of random responding should be an integral part of initial data cleaning. But perhaps even more importantly, this is a special case of heterogeneous groups (introduced in Chapter 3). Similar to the cola preferences study example in Chapter 3, in this real-world example there are two groups: students who attempted to accurately assess their learning and those who did not. In general, education researchers performing this sort of analysis are interested in generalizing the results of their intervention to those students who are actually attempting to learn and complete the assessments successfully. From a sampling perspective, this sort of data cleaning also makes sense.

MAGNITUDE OF THE PROBLEM

In this sample, a substantial number (up to 40.0%) of middle school students engaged in random responding (and estimates in other populations are similar in magnitude; e.g., Berry et al., 1992). While this might surprise researchers at first glance, given the low stakes of the test and no apparent motivation to succeed, it is not surprising. As can be seen from the average test scores, the test used in this research was designed to be challenging, which has been shown to increase response biases such as random responding (Cronbach, 1950; Wise, 2006; Wise & Kong, 2005).[9] This reinforces the importance of including screening for response set as a routine part of data cleaning.

Researchers need to consider that not all respondents participating in their research are equally motivated to perform at their peak, given the lack of significant incentives for compliance and consequences for failure to perform as requested. Researchers should incorporate methods to detect these issues in their data. This recommendation is particularly valuable where important policy or pedagogical decisions are involved, such as large-scale standardized national and international tests (NAEP, TIMSS), which have substantial effects on policy and outcomes for constituencies, but for which individual students may not be significantly motivated.

FOR FURTHER ENRICHMENT

1. Think about how you could include a measure (a question, an item, a scale) that would help you determine if any of your subjects are not responding thoughtfully to your measures. Create a plan to do so to examine the quality of the data you might be collecting. What actions could you take to examine this issue in your own research?

2. Examine the data set presented on the book's website. Can you identify the participants engaging in random responding? What happens to the results when they are eliminated from the analysis?

NOTES

1. Parts of this chapter were adapted from Osborne and Blanchard (2011).
2. I also know some dogs and cats that are pretty lazy, so perhaps it is not a phenomenon confined to human respondents. I leave this to others to explore.

3. Wise used computer-based testing, allowing him to look at individual items rather than students' total test scores. While computer-based testing can eliminate some aspects of random responding, such as choosing illegitimate answers, it does not eliminate random selection of items or rapid guessing.

4. One option, used in this particular data set included having 20 questions with four choices: A to D, with other questions scattered throughout the test, and particularly near the end, with items that contain only three (A to C) or two (A to B) legitimate answers. Students or respondents choosing illegitimate answers one or more times can be assumed to be randomly responding, as our results show.

5. Note that these analyses should in no way be construed as a test of these hypotheses, nor should the results be interpreted substantively to infer which teaching method is superior. Those interested in the substantive results of the study should consult Blanchard and colleagues (2010).

6. The three-way interaction between RRS × method × time was not significant, indicating that this difference was not dependent on instructional method.

7. We also examined results for the standardized outfit statistic, which is essentially a z score of the outfit mean squares. Similar results were obtained.

8. The exception to this exists in some literature around assessment of mental health and personality disorders, wherein random responding, poor effort, malingering, and exaggeration (all different types of response bias) detection can signal certain types of mental disorders (Clark, Gironda, & Young, 2003; Iverson, 2006).

9. This is due to the fact that response bias on multiple choice tests is, by definition, found in errors, not correct answers. Thus, easier tests and higher-scoring students are less likely to demonstrate response bias.

REFERENCES

Beach, D. A. (1989). Identifying the random responder. *Journal of Psychology, 123*(1), 101–103.

Berry, D. T. R., Wetter, M. W., Baer, R. A., Larsen, L., Clark, C., & Monroe, K. (1992). MMPI-2 random responding indices: Validation using self-report methodology. *Psychological Assessment, 4*(3). 340–345.

Blanchard, M. R., Southerland, S. A., Osborne, J. W., Sampson, V. D., Annetta, L. A., & Granger, E. M. (2010). Is inquiry possible in light of accountability?: A quantitative comparison of the relative effectiveness of guided inquiry and verification laboratory instruction. *Science Education, 94*(4), 577–616.

Bond, T. G., & Fox, C. M. (2001). *Applying the Rasch model: Fundamental measurement in the human sciences.* Mahwah, NJ: Erlbaum.

Bovaird, J. A. (2003). *New applications in testing: Using response time to increase the construct validity of a latent trait estimate* (Doctoral dissertation). Retrieved from Dissertation Abstracts International (UMI No. 3082643).

Clark, M. E., Gironda, R. J., & Young, R. W. (2003). Detection of back random responding: Effectiveness of MMPI-2 and personality assessment inventory validity indices. *Psychological Assessment, 15*(2), 223–234.

Cronbach, L. J. (1942). Studies of acquiescence as a factor in the true-false test. *Journal of Educational Psychology, 33*(6), 401–415.

Cronbach, L. J. (1950). Further evidence on response sets and test design. *Educational and Psychological Measurement, 10*, 3–31.

Crowne, D., & Marlowe, D. (1964). *The approval motive.* New York: Wiley.

Edelen, M. O., & Reeve, B. B. (2007). Applying item response theory (IRT) modeling to questionnaire development, evaluation, and refinement. *Quality of Life Research, 16* (Supp. 1), 5–18.

Goodfellow, L. D. (1940). The human element in probability. *The Journal of General Psychology, 33*, 201–205.

Hambleton, R. K., Swaminathan, H., & Rogers, H. J. (1991). *Fundamentals of item response theory.* Thousand Oaks, CA: Sage.

Iverson, G. L. (2006). Ethical issues associated with the assessment of exaggeration, poor effort, and malingering. *Applied Neuropsychology, 13*(2), 77–90.

Kane, S. T. (2008). Minimizing malingering and poor effort in the LD/ADHD Evaluation Process. *ADHD Report, 16*(5), 5–9.

Kuncel, N. R., & Borneman, M. J. (2007). Toward a new method of detecting deliberately faked personality tests: The use of idiosyncratic item responses. *International Journal of Selection & Assessment, 15*(2), 220–231.

Lorge, I. (1937). Gen-like: Halo or reality? *Psychological Bulletin, 34*, 545–546.

Meier, S. T. (1994). *The chronic crisis in psychological measurement and assessment: A historical survey.* San Diego, CA: Academic Press.

Meijer, R. R. (2003). Diagnosing item score patterns on a test using item response theory-based person-fit statistics. *Psychological Methods, 8*(1), 72–87.

Messick, S. (1991). Psychology and methodology of response styles. In R. E. Snow & D. E. Wiley (Eds.), *Improving inquiry in social science* (pp. 161–200). Hillsdale, NJ: Erlbaum.

Murphy, K. R., & Davidshofer, C. O. (1988). *Psychological testing.* Englewood Cliffs, NJ: Prentice Hall.

Nunnally, J. C., & Bernstein, I. (1994). *Psychometric theory* (3rd ed.). New York: McGraw-Hill.

Osborne, J. W., & Blanchard, M. R. (2011). Random responding from participants is a threat to the validity of social science research results. *Frontiers in Psychology, 2*, 12. doi: 10.3389/fpsyg.2010.00220

Ray, C. L. (2009). The importance of using malingering screeners in forensic practice. *Journal of Forensic Psychology Practice, 9*(2), 138–146.

Rogers, R. (1997). Introduction. In R. Rogers (Ed.), *Clinical assessment of malingering and deception* (pp. 1–22). New York: Guilford.

Smith, E. V., & Smith, R. M. (2004). *Introduction to Rasch measurement.* Maple Grove, MN: JAM Press.

Strong, E. K. J. (1927). A vocational interest test. *Educational Record, 8*, 107–121.

Wilson, M. (2005). *Constructing measures: An item response modeling approach.* Mahwah, NJ: Lawrence Erlbaum.

Wise, S. L. (2006). An investigation of the differential effort received by items on a low-stakes computer-based test. *Applied Measurement in Education, 19*(2), 95–114.

Wise, S. L., & Kong, X. (2005). Response time effort: A new measure of examinee motivation in computer-based tests. *Applied Measurement in Education, 18*(2), 163–183.

ELEVEN

WHY DICHOTOMIZING CONTINUOUS VARIABLES IS RARELY A GOOD PRACTICE

Debunking the Myth of Categorization

There is a very long tradition in many different sciences of splitting people into easily analyzed groups. Health sciences researchers split people into sick and healthy, or obese and normal weight, despite the fact that people vary on a continuum from very healthy to very ill or from very thin to very heavy. In the social sciences we categorize people as low income or not, successful or not, old and young, depressed or not, and so on, again despite most variables being continuous in nature. In fact we can even argue about whether states such as dropping out of school, being a tobacco user, being male or female, or even being dead are categorical or continuous.

The traditional myth has been that it is easier for readers to understand analyses that compare one group to another rather than relationships between variables. In general, I

When is low self-esteem not low self-esteem? The case of the misinformed advisor.

As I mentioned in Chapter 3, when I was in graduate school my advisor and I were exploring self-esteem effects in college undergraduate samples. In one project my advisor directed me to split students into "high self-esteem" and "low self-esteem" groups and do a 2×2 ANOVA (self-esteem by experimental condition). Yet individuals tend to rate their global self-esteem relatively high. This is probably a good thing, as we generally want people to feel good about themselves, but when you have a variable (like global self-esteem) that theoretically ranges from 1 to 4 but has a median of 3.14, one must wonder what it means to split a variable like this at the median. Was it really capturing low self-esteem and high self-esteem? Or were we studying very high self-esteem as compared to moderately high self-esteem but misrepresenting the results?

disagree, provided we as researchers do a good job clearly communicating research results.

When I studied epidemiology (after years of graduate school in psychology) I resisted the tendency to want to group people into two categories. When studying cardiovascular epidemiology, we were taught to group people into high blood pressure or normal blood pressure groups and analyze their risk of heart attack. It was certainly interesting to see that individuals above a certain threshold had increased odds of experiencing a heart attack relative to individuals below that threshold, but I never felt comfortable splitting a continuous variable such as blood pressure into two categories.

Let us say we define anyone with a diastolic pressure (that is the second number in the traditional 120/75-type of blood pressure measurement) more than 80 as having "high blood pressure" and anyone at less than 80 as "normal blood pressure." We are essentially saying that someone with a diastolic blood pressure (DBP) of 81 is in a completely different category than someone with one of 79, despite the fact that in reality those are probably not meaningfully different pressures and the risks of heart attack for these two individuals are probably similar. Further, we are saying that someone with a BDP of 81 is the same as someone with a DBP of 120, or that someone with a DBP of 79 is the same as someone with DBP of 50. I doubt many doctors or epidemiologists would agree with either of those statements, however. In all likelihood, the difference in risk of experiencing a heart attack in this scenario is at least as large *within each group* as between the two groups. So why not simply do a correlation between DBP and age of heart attack or use logistic regression to predict incidence of heart attack based on DBP as a continuous variable? Just like it does not make sense to say that all people less than 65 years of age are the same, and all people over 65 are the same, it often does not make sense to group people based on continuous variables. We are potentially giving away a lot of useful information, and definitely creating a lot of error variance.

My goal in this chapter is to debunk several myths relating to splitting continuous variables into groups (such as dichotomization or median-splitting): that this makes effects more easily understood by readers, more powerful in terms of effect size, or more robust in terms of measurement. Instead, I intend to persuade you that this relatively common practice is really undermining your ability to detect effects (i.e., increasing the odds of Type II errors), drastically increasing error variance, and causing misestimation (generally underestimation) of true effects. Oh, and I finally want to tell my former advisor that she was just plain wrong, at least about this issue, and demonstrate in detail why.

WHAT IS DICHOTOMIZATION AND WHY DOES IT EXIST?

Let us start with a definition. Dichotomization is the practice of splitting individuals measured on a continuous (or ordinal) scale into two groups, often through a median split or use of another cutoff point. A median split is a common methodological procedure (MacCallum, Zhang, Preacher, & Rucker, 2002) that groups objects or individuals by whether they fall above or below the median. Dichotomization can use other cutoff points, (Cohen, 1983), but the median is often preferred as it technically represents the exact middle of a distribution (i.e., 50% of the scores will fall above and 50% will fall below regardless of the shape of the distribution). Other indicators of centrality (e.g., mean) are more strongly influenced by nonnormality and outliers, which could result in relatively uneven groups if used to split a sample.

Dichotomization and median-splits are a special case of *k-group* splits with which researchers convert a continuously measured variable into a variable represented by *k* number of groups. For example, some researchers (and governmental agencies) tend to use tertiles (grouping into three groups based on where the 33.33rd and the 66.67th percentiles fall, such as low-, medium-, and high-income groups), quartiles (grouping into four groups, usually at the 25th, 50th, and 75th percentiles), deciles (grouping into 10 groups of relatively equal size or span), and so forth. In all cases, the commonality is that the researcher is converting a continuous variable into a categorical variable, which can cause significant loss of information and increase error variance (Knüppel & Hermsen, 2010). I demonstrate that point a little later.

The origins of this practice are difficult to trace. Relatively few articles have been written about the procedure itself, compared to the hundreds of thousands of times it has been used in peer-reviewed journal articles. My assumption is that the technique is probably rooted in the late 19th century and early 20th century, when scholars were constructing inferential statistical tests such as Student's t-test and the Pearson product-moment correlation (Pearson, 1901; Student, 1908), or was borrowed from early epidemiology and health sciences, where groups were often split into two (as discussed above) for easier computation of odds ratios and relative risk. Prior to the wide availability of statistical computing software, some of these calculations, particularly for procedures with continuous variables, were onerous and difficult (Cohen, 1983). Furthermore, in many branches of science there were traditions of using analyses requiring categorical independent variables—e.g., analysis of variance (ANOVA) or odds ratios (ORs). Therefore, a tradition of simplifying computations through dichotomization developed (for example, refer to Blomqvist, 1951). Early statisticians (at least in the social sciences) were generally well aware that they were compromising quality and power for convenience. For example, Peters and Van Voorhis (1940) explicitly pointed out that computing correlations using dichotomous variables gives away large amounts of their effect sizes (particularly if the groups are unequal, as highlighted in Cohen, 1983). This important point seems to have been lost over the years as the acceptance of this methodology continued. Subsequent generations of scholars were trained in the tradition of quantitative analysis (and I am not sure epidemiologists and health sciences researchers acknowledge the issue to this day), perhaps without questioning whether there are better ways to conduct analyses. By the early 1970s, as researchers had more access to statistical computing, researchers began calling for the end to this practice, reminding scientists of the forgotten costs of this procedure (i.e., substantial misestimation of effects), and calling for the widespread use of regression techniques as an alternative to this practice (Humphreys & Fleishman, 1974).

As I have noted in previous chapters, traditions and mythologies in statistics seem to be tenacious once established, and the one advisor I refer to here, although an extremely smart woman, had difficulty getting beyond her own training and tradition to see the potential downsides of such practices. Likewise, the professors teaching the epidemiology courses I took thought it a silly idea to use continuous variables in their analyses. They do not appear to be alone (Fitzsimons, 2008), though I hope readers of this book will be among the growing number of researchers to understand the drawbacks of this practice.

HOW WIDESPREAD IS THIS PRACTICE?

In the year that I write this chapter (2011), dichotomization in the particular form of median split methodology can be found referenced in more than 340,000 articles catalogued by Google Scholar, spanning such important topics as the following.

- Alzheimer's Disease
- HIV Interventions
- Diabetes
- Personality and Mortality Due to Cardiovascular Disease

- Androgyny
- Problem Solving
- Facial Recognition
- Acculturation to New Situations
- Spatial Learning in Female Meadow Voles
- Therapy for Bipolar Disorder
- Leadership
- Gene Expression and Cancer Treatment
- Empathy
- Humor and Coping With Stress
- Environmental Knowledge
- Meal Variety and Caloric Intake
- Aggressive Behavior
- Acculturation to Latino Culture and Cancer Risk
- Memory and Gene Expression
- Maternal Anxiety and Fetal Outcomes
- Postmenopausal Estradiol Treatment and Intellectual Functioning
- Social Support and Coping With Pain
- Internet Purchasing Behavior
- False Memories
- Depression in Asylum Seekers
- Entrepreneurial Behavior
- Burnout
- Unconscious Decision Making
- Goal Orientation and Motivational Beliefs
- Condom Usage in Adolescent Populations
- Maternal Responsiveness and Infant Attachment
- Body Image
- Brain Growth in Children With Autism
- Disability Due to Pain
- Attitudes Toward Female Business Executives
- Service Quality Expectations
- Glaucoma
- Effectiveness of Physical Therapy on Osteoarthritis of the Knee
- Loneliness and Herpes Latency
- The Subjective Effects of Alcohol Consumption
- Creativity
- Impulsive Buying Behavior[1]

Authors have been vocal about the deleterious effects of dichotomization (Cohen, 1983) and similar techniques in fields such as psychology/social science (MacCallum et al., 2002), medical research (Royston, Altman, & Sauerbrei, 2006), pharmaceutical research (Fedorov, Mannino, & Zhang, 2009), stock market forecasting (Lien & Balakrishnan, 2005), and consumer research (Fitzsimons, 2008). Despite these recent efforts, the practice persists to this day as a common occurrence (e.g., DeCoster, Iselin, & Gallucci, 2009). For example, MacCallum and colleagues (2002) found that 11.5% of articles in two highly respected psychology journals contained analyses that had at least one continuous variable converted to dichotomous.

Not only are scientists still using the procedure, researchers are still arguing for their use. For example, Westfall argues that in certain applications, dichotomization can improve power in biopharmaceutical research (Westfall, 2011),[2] and others argue it can enhance ease of interpretation for readers in criminology and psychiatric research (Farrington & Loeber, 2000).[3] I think evidence is on the side of letting dichotomization slip into the history books as an anachronistic practice, due to all the drawbacks of this practice that this chapter demonstrates.

WHY DO RESEARCHERS USE DICHOTOMIZATION?

Attempting to understand why smart, sophisticated researchers publishing in good journals continue to use this practice (and perhaps why reviewers and editors continue to allow it), DeCoster and colleagues (2009) surveyed more than a hundred authors of recent articles in respected journals who used this practice to attempt to understand the reasoning behind these dichotomization decisions. Some of the myths surrounding the continued use of dichotomization seem to include three general categories of proposed benefits: distributions of the continuous variables or improved measurement, ease of analysis or interpretation, and prior precedent within the field (see also Fitzsimons, 2008).

ARE ANALYSES WITH DICHOTOMOUS VARIABLES EASIER TO INTERPRET?

Some researchers (such as my former advisor) seem to be under the impression that certain types of analyses are much more easily interpretable by nontechnical audiences if dichotomous variables are used. So, for example, this argument holds that it is more confusing for a reader to ponder a correlational relationship such as: "As socioeconomic status increases, student achievement test scores tend to increase." Instead, this argument posits that this type of finding is more easily received as "students with high socioeconomic status tend to score higher on achievement tests than low-SES students." Leaving aside the notion that Type II errors are more likely in the latter case (reducing rather than enhancing the clarity of the literature), most consumers of research I have talked to[4] seem equally able to digest both types of finding if presented clearly. Some particular authors (Farrington & Loeber, 2000) seem to think that logistic regression (which uses a regression-type analysis to predict a dichotomous or multigroup outcome variable) are more easily interpretable with dichotomous predictors (but see the strong dissenting opinion by Fitzsimons, 2008). This idea is again rooted in tradition and origins of the technique, where the earliest epidemiologists such as John Snow (1855) made simple hand calculations of 2×2 matrices (e.g., did or did not drink water from the Broad Street Pump and did or did not contract cholera) calculating odds ratios.

Indeed, in modern epidemiology it is often this simple 2×2 analysis that leads to important investigations. But as with other historical analyses, such as certain types of correlations or internal consistency estimates, they are not superior to more complex analyses, merely easier to calculate. Thus, I argue it is as easy for a reader to read, "Individuals drinking more frequently from the Broad Street pump have odds of contracting cholera that are 1.25 times that of those drinking less frequently" as it is to read, "the odds of contracting cholera for those having drank from the Broad Street well were 3.20 times that of those who had never drank from that well."

ARE ANALYSES WITH DICHOTOMOUS VARIABLES EASIER TO COMPUTE?

To be sure, sometimes dichotomization creates simplicity in formulae, leaving researchers easier computations (Cohen, 1983). Yet this argument is a bit silly in the 21st century when we have cell phones in our pockets with more power than some of the mainframe computers on which I first ran statistical analyses years ago. Most statistical software provides analyses for either categorical or continuous variables with just a few mouse clicks or a few lines of code. In my opinion, this is not a rationale for dichotomization.

ARE DICHOTOMOUS VARIABLES MORE RELIABLE?

The most common reasons for performing dichotomization include: (a) refining crude or unreliable measurement, and (b) dealing with irregular or non-normal distributions, or the presence of outliers (DeCoster et al., 2009). Let us take each of these related arguments in order.

Dichotomization Improves Reliability of Measurement

The myth here is founded on the argument that measurement becomes more reliable under dichotomization because: (a) all members of each group have identical scores, and (b) measurement is probably more replicable lumping people into two groups (i.e., it is more likely that a person in a "high depression" or "low depression" group will be in that same group at a following measurement, whereas it is unlikely that a second administration of a depression inventory would produce an identical score). This argument is misguided on several counts.

It is true that reliable measurement is important to research and that one hallmark of reliable measurement is repeatedly assigning the same score to an individual (assuming the individual's underlying trait has not changed). However this argument assumes that being assigned to a different group (e.g., first being assigned to the depressed group and then to the nondepressed group) is equivalent in importance to receiving a different score on whatever inventory is being used (e.g., 38 versus 39). This is an obvious misstatement. There is a meaningful difference between being assigned to one group versus the other, whereas there may not be a meaningful difference between a score of 38 and 39 on a depression inventory. Following this logic, the ultimate reliability would be achieved from putting everyone in a single group, assigning everyone the same score. But clearly that is not a desirable strategy from a scientific or statistical point of view *unreliable* in fact, this would create the maximally measurement.

The reason we care about reliable measurement is that more reliable measurement means *less error variance* in the analysis. To the extent that measurement is unreliable, we have increased error variance, which undermines our ability to detect effects and causes in underestimation of effect sizes. So let us think this process through. If we perform a median or mean split, more of the sample lies very close to the cutoff point than far away from it. If we have less than perfect measurement (and we almost always do), it is likely we have a good number of subjects moving across the cutoff score to the other category due to minor fluctuations. When a variable is kept continuous, these minor fluctuations are largely ignorable (e.g., a grade point average moving from 2.95 to 3.01 is not a big deal, but if 3.0 is the cutoff for admission to a university, that minor fluctuation has a large effect). Yet under dichotomization, differences between being in one group or the other have large implications, and group membership for a large portion of the sample may be influenced by random fluctuation around the cutoff score. So categorization may not increase replicability, perhaps undermining one of the original arguments for using this procedure.

Let us also look at the issue of error variance, which is quantified by the residual, or the difference between expected (predicted) scores and actual scores. In ANOVA-type analyses, we can look at the difference between individual scores and group averages. In regression-type analyses, we can similarly look at the difference between a predicted score and an actual score. It simply does not make sense to argue that dichotomization (e.g., assigning everyone below the median a score of 1 and everyone above the median a 2) would reduce error, as we now have vast differences between individual scores and the group mean, whereas each individual would be much closer to their predicted score in a regression equation.

Let me demonstrate this with a concrete example. Starting with two highly correlated variables from the Education Longitudinal Study of 2002 (Ingels et al., 2004), 10th grade math achievement test score (BYTXMIRR) and 12th grade math achievement test score (F1TXM1IR), we can explore the effects of dichotomization. Both variables are initially normally distributed, as Figure 11.1 and 11.2 shows (both skew close to 0.00). Furthermore, the two variables, as one might expect, are very strongly correlated ($r_{(13,394)}$ = .89, $p < .0001$, with 10th grade math scores accounting for 79.7% of the variance in 12th grade math scores). In other words, students who score higher on 10th grade math assessments are likely to score higher on 12th grade math assessments.

As you can see in Figure 11.3 on page 241, there is not a tremendous amount of error variance in this analysis—only 20.3% of the variance is unaccounted for, and the residuals are relatively small, as Figure 11.4 on page 241 shows. The average (unstandardized or raw) residual is 3.73, with a standard deviation of 4.70 (recall these variables range from 12.52 to 69.72 for 10th grade, and 15.20 to 82.54 for 12th grade). If dichotomization truly does improve reliability of measurement, the size of the residuals should diminish after splitting students into "low

Figure 11.1

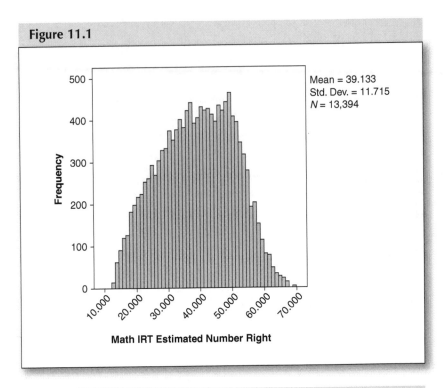

Figure 11.2

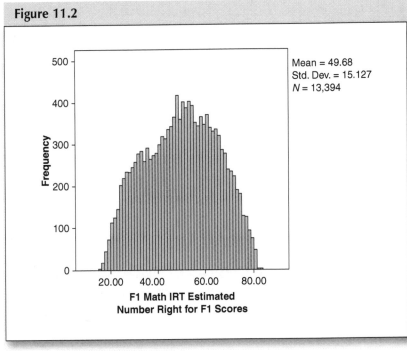

Figure 11.3   10th and 12th Grade Math Achievement Test Scores, *r* =. 89

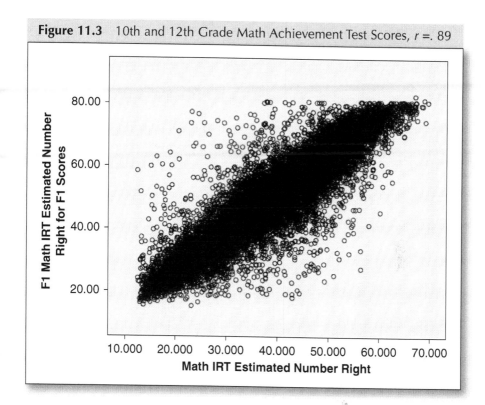

Figure 11.4   Residuals from the Correlation of Math Achievement Test Scores

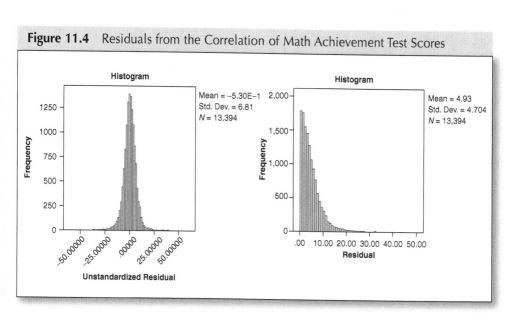

Figure 11.5   Scatterplot Following Dichotomization

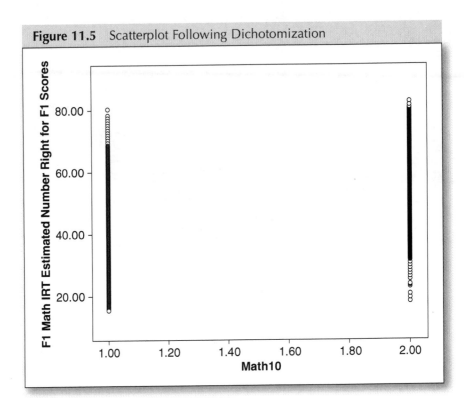

performers" and "high performers." To test this, I performed a median split on the 10th grade variable and an ANOVA with grade achievement as the dependent variable. As you can see in Figure 11.5, when 10th graders are dichotomized into low and high, the dispersion of the data at each group is now much larger than the dispersion around any given point in Figure 11.3.

Once dichotomized, we come to the same conclusion: low math performers in 10th grade tend to score lower in 12th grade than high math performers: average scores = 38.45 (SD = 10.56) and 60.91 (SD = 9.69), respectively, $F_{(113, 387)}$ = 16433.22, $p < .0001$, $\eta^2 = .55$. And in fact, there is still a strong effect present, with the dichotomous 10th grade math performance variable accounting for 55% of the variance in 12th grade math performance. This is a 30.99% reduction in effect size, and the residuals (presented in Figure 11.6) show an equal increase. The average residual is now 8.26, with a standard deviation of 5.87. Thus, this simple dichotomization increased the average size of the residuals 221.45%.

Figure 11.6   Residuals Following Dichotomization

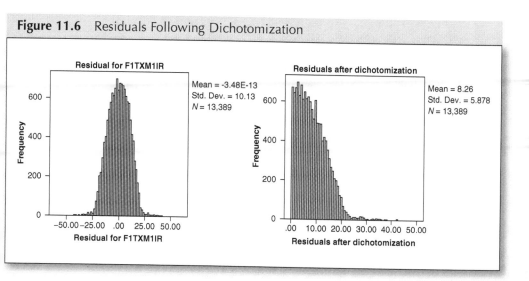

Remember that this is an unusually strong relationship, and most researchers do not deal with effect sizes this large. Imagine how more modest effects would fare. How many researchers would still find significant effects giving away one-third of their effect sizes?

The other argument, that measurement is more reliable because of the reliability of repeated categorization, also is shown to be false in this analysis. Again, even with this tremendously strong correlation between the two administrations of the math test, 13.3% of the students change classification from low to high or from high to low between 10th and 12th grade.[5] Does this mean that more than 1,700 students in this sample got appreciably more or less adept at math? Probably not. This changing of categories is most often caused by minor variation in performance near the median, where most students are, rather than by students who radically change performance levels. And again, this effect would be theoretically more pronounced with less perfect measurement.

By taking the absolute value of the distance of each individual from the median (BYTXMIRR − 39.63) and comparing distances between people who switched classification from low to high math-achiever or the opposite direction, it is clear that this is exactly what is happening. The average distance for people switching classification was 3.91 points ($SD = 3.57$), whereas for those who maintained their classification consistently, the average distance was

10.72 ($SD = 6.27$; significant effect $F_{(113, 387)} = 1992.48$, $p < .0001$, $\eta^2 = .13$). This example supports some important conclusions about dichotomization.

First, even with very high relationships between variables and excellent measurement properties, categorization reduces effect sizes dramatically. This does not seem to be consistent with improved reliability, as some proponents of this technique have argued. Second, approximately one in seven in this sample switched from high to low achievement categories between 10th and 12th grade. Thus, dichotomization does not seem to improve reliability of measurement. Errors (residuals) are appreciably larger under dichotomization. And finally, those who move categories are those closest to the median, therefore creating the appearance of large differences in performance when in fact these changes are due to relatively *small changes* consistent with random fluctuation rather than meaningful improvement or decline.

Dichotomization Deals With Nonnormality or Outliers

My immediate response, as you might imagine, is to encourage use of a data transformation to deal with variables that are not normally distributed, as discussed in Chapter 8. Further, my inclination regarding outliers is to examine the potential cause of them and fix them where appropriate. Other options, as examined in the Chapter 7 on extreme scores, are probably more desirable than merely ignoring the fact and dichotomizing.

To explore this issue we will revisit data from Chapter 8 on university size and average faculty salary. Recall the data were from 1,161 institutions in the United States collected on the size of the institution (number of faculty) and average faculty salary by the American Association of University Professors in 2005. As Figure 11.7 shows, the variable number of faculty is highly skewed (skew = 2.58, kurtosis = 8.09), while faculty salary (associate professors) was more normally distributed to begin with, with a skew = 0.36 and kurtosis = 0.12. Recall also that an initial correlation between the two variables of $r_{(1,161)} = .49$, $p < .0001$ (coefficient of determination or percentage variance accounted for of 24.0%) was improved to $r_{(1,161)} = .66$, $p < .0001$ (coefficient of determination or percentage variance accounted for 0.44, or an 81.50% increase). Likewise, the average residual was 48.49 ($SD = 38.92$) before this transformation and 42.94 ($SD = 33.46$) after.

Instead of performing this data transformation, let us imagine we dichotomized the number of faculty variable through median split (this variable

Figure 11.7

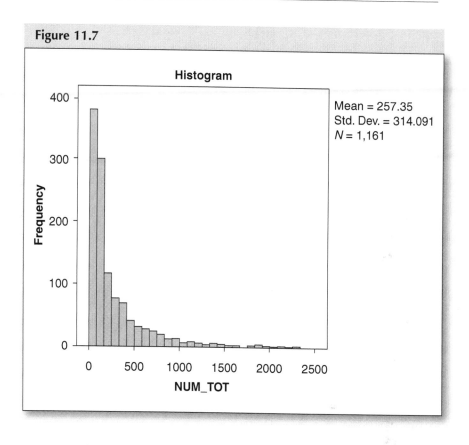

Histogram

Mean = 257.35
Std. Dev. = 314.091
N = 1,161

ranged from 7 to 2,261, with a median of 132.0 and a mean of 257.35). Following dichotomization, the correlation is indeed somewhat improved over the untransformed data $r_{(1,161)} = .57, p < .0001$ (coefficient of determination or percentage variance accounted for of 33.0%). But rather than demonstrate the potential of this method, this analysis highlights the weakness. Recall that following a good normalizing Box-Cox transformation, the effect size was one-third *stronger* than dichotomization (coefficient of determination = 44%). Similarly, the residuals are closer in magnitude to the untransformed data than the appropriately transformed data (average residual was 46.88, $SD = 35.11$). Thus, I would suggest that even in the case of extremely nonnormal data such as this variable, appropriate transformation yields is still a better practice (in this case, 33.33% stronger effect size over dichotomized data). Similarly, appropriately dealing with outliers will be a more satisfactory solution than dichotomization. Finally, there is some evidence that other procedures that are nonparametric, such as logistic regression, similarly suffer reduced effect sizes from dichotomization (Farrington & Loeber, 2000).

OTHER DRAWBACKS OF DICHOTOMIZATION

Curvilinearity and Interactions Will Be Masked or Undetectable

Sometimes variables have nonlinear relationships. As I often tell my students, interactions and nonlinear relationships are often among the more interesting results we can find. It seems unrealistic to expect all things in nature to be perfectly linearly related. However, conversion of variables to dichotomous effectively eliminates the opportunity to look for curvilinear relationships. Most statistical software packages include simple ways to model nonlinear relationships (and in those that do not easily support this type of analysis, you can easily incorporate exponential terms in regression equations to test for curvilinearity). Thus, it seems a shame to lose this possibility (and more accurate representation of the true nature of the effect) through artificially dichotomizing a continuous variable. (See also Farewell, Tom, & Royston, 2004; Maxwell & Delaney, 1993.)

The Variable Is by Nature Categorical

To be sure, there probably are instances where individuals cluster together, creating the illusion of categorical groups (MacCallum et al., 2002). If a variable is truly categorical, why is it being measured continuously? What the researcher probably means is that the sample or population is not evenly distributed across the entire range of the variable. But then, is dichotomization an appropriate response to this phenomenon? I tend not to think so. And even where individuals clearly cluster into well-defined and separated groups, care must be taken to accurately categorize. This may involve more than two groups, split at points not necessarily represented by the median, and so on. My decades of experience tell me this will be an unusual event. But it is possible.

Spurious Statistical Significance

Type I errors might be encouraged by the use of dichotomized covariates that fail to adequately remove the effects of the variable had it been left continuous (Maxwell & Delaney, 1993). Along the same lines, prediction equations or models can be significantly biased when artificial dichotomization is used (Hin, Lau, Rogers, & Chang, 1999), as can the goodness of fit of predictive modeling (Lien & Balakrishnan, 2005). Finally, for those interested in the nuances of logistic regression: dichotomization can inappropriately inflate a variable's effect size by altering the nature of an increment of 1.0.

Logistic regression calculates an odds ratio as the change in odds as a function of a change of 1.0 in the independent variable. Thus, if you have a variable such as percentage correct on a test as an independent variable, with perhaps 50 increments of 1.0, you can get highly significant effects that look very small (odds ratio of, say, 1.05). Changing this variable to z scores changes the interpretation from an increment of 1.0 percentage points to 1.0 standard deviations, and it can change the odds ratio. Note that this is only an apparent increase in effect size that results from redefining what an increment of 1.0 means. Similarly, dichotomizing changes the interpretation yet again. Where there were potentially 50, or 6 increments accounting for the effect, now there is only 1: above the mean versus below the mean. At this point, the odds ratio may be substantially larger, inappropriately because of the dichotomization, making this variable look substantially more important than when it was continuous or z-scored. But this is an illusion. The actual variance being accounted for should drop.

In Table 11.1 I present some simple examples from the Education Longitudinal Study of 2002. I used logistic regression to predict whether a student graduated from high school or dropped out prior to completion as a function of 10th grade reading achievement test score. Reading achievement ranges from 10.20 to 49.09, with a standard deviation of 9.69. Thus, left as is, the original variable has almost 40 increments of 1.0 to account for the effect of graduating. As the table shows, reading is a significant predictor of graduation and dropout. For every increase of 1.0 in reading, the odds of being retained through graduation are 1.082 that of those who scored one point lower. The analysis reports accounting for about 10.2% of the variance in this outcome. As one might expect, converting reading scores to z scores has no effect on the variance accounted for, which is identical. However, because we have redefined the number of increments of 1.0 (in this case, about four in the observed range), each increment of 1 standard deviation leads to an increase in the odds of graduating of 2.152. Note that this seems to be an inflation of effect size but is defensible as it keeps the original variable intact, accounts for the same

Table 11.1 Illusory Effects of Dichotomization on Logistic Regression

Model	Nagelkerke Pseudo-r^2	Odds Ratio	95% CI Odds Ratio
Reading Continuous	.102	1.082*	1.076–1.088
Reading z-Scored	.102	2.152*	2.037–2.273
Reading Dichotomized	.076	3.795*	3.389–4.248
Reading Extreme Groups	.169	9.246*	7.425–11.513

Note. * p < .0001. N = 15,982, N = 6,293 for extreme groups analysis

amount of variance, and when performed on *all* continuous variables, allows for direct comparisons across predictors.

The third line in the table shows how dichotomization (mean split) can inappropriately inflate the apparent effect size. In this case, the odds ratio inflates to 3.795, however the variance accounted for dropped substantially. This represents an inappropriate inflation of apparent effect size.

Furthermore, as discussed previously, extreme groups analysis can inappropriately increase apparent effect size through eliminating individuals in the center of the distribution. In this case, choosing students ± 1.0 standard deviations from the mean *only* eliminates a majority of the sample but inappropriately inflates both variance accounted for and apparent odds ratio. This is inappropriate because the comparison eliminates the majority of the sample, making it nonrepresentative, and changes the definition of the comparison from the original (1 point or 1 standard deviation increase) to represent a comparison between those substantially below the mean only to those substantially above the mean.

Inhibiting Accurate Meta-analysis of Results

Widespread dichotomization has implications for researchers as the methodology of meta-analysis becomes more widely used. As Hunter and Schmidt (1990) correctly point out, dichotomization has the potential to significantly bias the results of the analysis (compared to what analyses with the original data would have shown).

Extreme Groups Analysis

One special case of dichotomization is extreme groups analysis, where researchers purposefully take groups only from the extremes of the distribution. In this way, researchers artificially inflate effect sizes (Preacher, Rucker, Mac-Callum, & Nicewander, 2005). This is the opposite of the restricted range issue discussed in Chapter 3, though it carries similar risks: misestimation. Specifically, if you are examining variables that have broad ranges in the population but only select extreme samples, you as a researcher are artificially creating an effect where there might not be one. Absent a very strong rationale for doing this, this practice seems to me like a dangerous way to dramatically inflate Type I error rates and purposefully misrepresent the population parameters.

This is *not* the same thing as examining extreme groups (such as very low performing or very high performing students) in an attempt to understand issues unique to those groups. Those analyses examine groups of interest with hopes of learning lessons from them, and they attempt to accurately model what is happening within a particular subgroup. Extreme groups analysis, on the other hand, seeks to illegitimately create or enhance an effect where one might not exist by comparing individuals who reside at the extremes of a distribution—and therefore who are by definition *not representative of the majority of the population* the researcher wishes to speak to.

For an example, taking the relationship between university size and faculty salaries, I dichotomized university size to represent those institutions below the 10th percentile (with 44 or fewer faculty) and above the 90th percentile (with 658 or more faculty). This extreme groups analysis yielded a correlation of $r_{(212)} = .84$, $p < .0001$, coefficient of determination = 70.7% variance accounted for. This is a substantial misestimation of the effect, which was originally 24%, 33% with dichotomization of the highly skewed variable, and 44% with an appropriately transformed variable. While it is often interesting and desirable to explore those at the margins of distributions (e.g., very small universities, for example), this particular version of dichotomization of extreme groups analysis does not have a place in legitimate research.

FOR FURTHER ENRICHMENT

1. Download the data set from the book's website. Compare an analysis with continuous variables and dichotomized variables. How do interpretations and effect sizes suffer when continuous variables are illegitimately dichotomized?

2. Look through the best journals in your field and see if you can find an example in which an author dichotomized a continuous variable. What was the justification for doing so? Do you agree it was a legitimate analytic strategy?

3. Using one of your own (or your advisor's) data sets, explore how dichotomization can alter or damage power and effect sizes.

NOTES

1. This is, sadly, only a brief summary of the 340,000 articles I found that include median split methodology. This does not include other dichotomization techniques that may not involve median splitting, or other techniques for converting continuous variables to categorical e.g., converting to four groups.

2. I am not sure dichotomization can *legitimately* improve power in any line of research, given the inflation of error variance. But later in this chapter I show how *inappropriate* applications of this methodology (such as extreme groups analysis) can *illegitimately* inflate effect sizes and power.

3. It may not surprise you to learn that I disagree. Farrington makes the point that in logistic regression dichotomous variables are more interpretable. Having written on best practices in logistic regression, I believe that even nontechnical audiences can appreciate and understand odds ratios based on continuous variables if presented appropriately. For example, researchers can convert continuous variables to z scores, thus changing the interpretation of the odds ratio to the change in odds as the predictor changes *1 standard deviation* rather than one point. Furthermore, this application of z-scoring allows continuous variables to be directly compared for effect size, whereas without doing this they are not directly comparable. This does not seem a barrier to interpretability. Furthermore, when dichotomization of control variables occurs, biased odds ratios can result (Chen, Cohen, & Chen, 2007) as the effects of these covariates are not completely removed from the analysis due to dichotomization. All in all, a very weak argument, in my opinion, that promotes the use of a very poor practice.

4. I have a long history of working with nonresearchers like teachers, policymakers, and health care professionals. They all seem to digest results generated by continuous variables easily.

5. Not surprisingly, an equal number of students moved from high-performing to low-performing categories as moved the other way: 890 moved from the low to high group, while 886 moved the other way. This is consistent with random fluctuation around a fixed point rather than some other purposeful change in performance.

REFERENCES

Blomqvist, N. (1951). Some tests based on dichotomization. *The Annals of Mathematical Statistics, 22*(3), 362–371.

Chen, H., Cohen, P., & Chen, S. (2007). Biased odds ratios from dichotomization of age. *Statistics in Medicine, 26*(18), 3487–3497.

Cohen, J. (1983). The cost of dichotomization. *Applied Psychological Measurement, 7*(3), 249–253.

DeCoster, J., Iselin, A., & Gallucci, M. (2009). A conceptual and empirical examination of justifications for dichotomization. *Psychological Methods, 14*(4), 349–366.

Farewell, V., Tom, B., & Royston, P. (2004). The impact of dichotomization on the efficiency of testing for an interaction effect in exponential family models. *Journal of the American Statistical Association, 99*(467), 822–831.

Farrington, D. P., & Loeber, R. (2000). Some benefits of dichotomization in psychiatric and criminological research. *Criminal Behaviour and Mental Health, 10*(2), 100–122. doi: 10.1002/cbm.349

Fedorov, V., Mannino, F., & Zhang, R. (2009). Consequences of dichotomization. *Pharmaceutical Statistics, 8*(1), 50–61.

Fitzsimons, G. (2008). Death to dichotomizing: Editorial. *Journal of Consumer Research, 35*(1), 5–8.

Hin, L. Y., Lau, T. K., Rogers, M. S., & Chang, A. M. Z. (1999). Dichotomization of continuous measurements using generalized additive modelling—application in predicting intrapartum Caesarean delivery. *Statistics in Medicine, 18*(9), 1101–1110.

Humphreys, L., & Fleishman, A. (1974). Pseudo-orthogonal and other analysis of variance designs involving individual-differences variables. *Journal of Educational Psychology, 66*(4), 464–472.

Hunter, J., & Schmidt, F. (1990). Dichotomization of continuous variables: The implications for meta-analysis. *Journal of Applied Psychology, 75*(3), 334–349.

Ingels, S., Pratt, D., Rogers, J., Siegel, P., Stutts, E., & Owings, J. (2004). *Education Longitudinal Study of 2002: Base year data file user's manual* (NCES 2004-405). Washington, DC: U.S. Department of Education, National Center for Education Statistics.

Knüppel, L., & Hermsen, O. (2010). Median split, k-group split, and optimality in continuous populations. *AStA Advances in Statistical Analysis, 94*(1), 53–74.

Lien, D., & Balakrishnan, N. (2005). On regression analysis with data cleaning via trimming, Winsorization, and dichotomization. *Communications in Statistics-Simulation and Computation, 34*(4), 839–849.

MacCallum, R., Zhang, S., Preacher, K., & Rucker, D. (2002). On the practice of dichotomization of quantitative variables. *Psychological Methods, 7*(1), 19–40.

Maxwell, S., & Delaney, H. (1993). Bivariate median splits and spurious statistical significance. *Psychological Bulletin, 113*(1), 181–190.

Pearson, K. (1901). Mathematical contribution to the theory of evolution. VII: On the correlation of characters not quantitatively measurable. *Philosophical Transactions of the Royal Society of London, Series A 195*, 1–47.

Peters, C., & Van Voorhis, W. (1940). *Statistical procedures and their mathematical bases.* New York: McGraw-Hill.

Preacher, K., Rucker, D., MacCallum, R., & Nicewander, W. (2005). Use of the extreme groups approach: A critical reexamination and new recommendations. *Psychological Methods, 10*(2), 178–192.

Royston, P., Altman, D., & Sauerbrei, W. (2006). Dichotomizing continuous predictors in multiple regression: A bad idea. *Statistics in Medicine, 25*(1), 127–141.

Snow, J. (1855). *On the mode of communication of cholera.* London: John Churchill.

Student. (1908). The probable error of a mean. *Biometrika, 6*(1), 1–25.

Westfall, P. (2011). Improving power by dichotomizing (even under normality). *Statistics in Biopharmaceutical Research, 3*(2), 353–362.

✣ TWELVE ✣

THE SPECIAL CHALLENGE OF CLEANING REPEATED MEASURES DATA

Lots of Pits in Which to Fall

As I wrote the other chapters and worked with students in various statistics classes, it occurred to me that some data cleaning issues are particular to repeated measures analyses but are not always obvious. In this chapter I briefly outline some of the issues and potential ways to deal with them. This is an area I hope to expand on at a later time.

TREAT ALL TIME POINTS EQUALLY

Repeated measures analyses are peculiar creatures: powerful at detecting changes over time, but riddled with difficult assumptions that are rarely met in practice. In many statistical packages, such as SPSS, repeated measures analyses can compensate for failing the assumption of *sphericity*[1] by altering the statistics to eliminate that assumption. If you are using a software package that does not automatically compute alternative statistics for dealing with assumptions of sphericity, you might be inclined to perform a transformation to equalize variance across time points.

One rule I find helpful is to *treat all time points equally*. In other words, they are all the same variable, just measured at different points in time. They must *all* be treated equally.

The implications of not treating all time points equally is that you might end up creating strong differences across time points when in fact there were none. Performing a transformation on one time point and ignoring others is a fantastic way to get large effect sizes in repeated measures analysis, but the effects are not reflective of anything other than an analysis error.

An illustration of this point is presented in Figure 12.1. For this figure I randomly generated four variables with 100 data points in each variable. All distributions were to have a mean of 10.0 and a standard deviation of 1.0 (although you can see, with relatively modest data sets they deviate slightly from those statistics). Imagine these are four repeated measures. They are, in actuality, not significantly different. When subjected to a repeated measures ANOVA, the four repeated measures have $F_{(3, 297)} < 1.00$, $p < .56$, with a partial eta-squared of .007. However, if I decide the third data point is a little more skewed than I like, and apply a square root transformation ($\lambda = 0.50$ in Box-Cox transforms, which you should be familiar with by this point), I end up with a large effect of $F_{(3, 297)} = 2476.24$, $p < .0001$, partial eta-squared of .96.

As you can see in Figure 12.2, by transforming just one subset of all observations, I just created a huge error. But, if I had transformed all four time points in

Figure 12.1   Examples of Distributions With Mean of 10.0 and Standard Deviation of 1.0

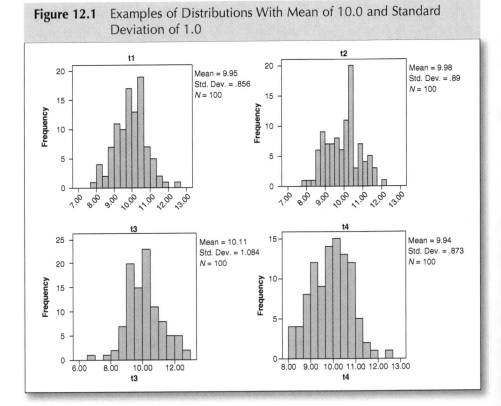

Figure 12.2   Not Treating All Time Points Equally Creates Type I Errors

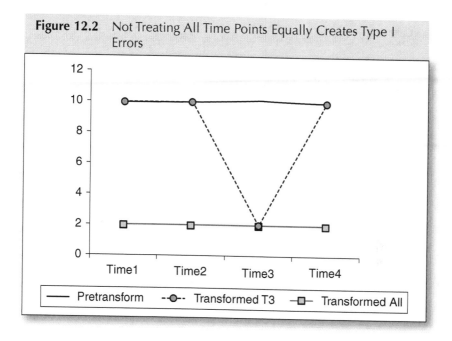

the identical fashion, I would have come to the correct, original conclusion that there was no difference over time: $F_{(3, 297)} = < 1.0$, $p < .71$, eta-squared $= .005$.

Taking the example of applying a transformation, one of the practices I endorse is anchoring the variable at 1.0. Yet if you subtract a different number from each time point so that all time points are anchored at 1.0, you may just have erased your differences across groups in a quest to improve normality!

Taking a similar example, in Figure 12.3 you see four distributions with means of about 5, 8, 11, and 14, all with standard deviations of about 1.0 (again, randomly generated data). These data should result in a very large effect size, and indeed a simple repeated measures shows this to be the case $F_{(3, 297)} = 1581.73$, $p < .0001$, eta-squared $= .94$. Yet if I were to follow the guidelines for best practices in transformation, anchoring each time point at 1.0 and then applying a transformation (such as our old friend the square root transform, $\lambda = 0.50$), my very strong effect has now disappeared. After anchoring at 1.0 and transforming each time point, the results are $F_{(3, 297)} = < 1.00$, $p < .78$, eta-squared $= .004$.

Should you decide it is important to impose a data transformation on repeated measures data, it is important to figure out the minimum value of *any* time point and anchor that time point at 1.0. You would subtract the same

Figure 12.3   Anchoring All Time Points at 1.0 Produces Type II Errors

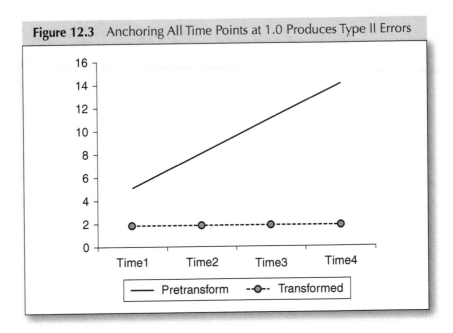

amount from every other score in every other repeated measure. This will not anchor all time points at 1.0, but will bring many of them close, and will be consistent with the rule of treating all time points equally.

Thus, knowing this rule of thumb, taking appropriate anchoring strategy of subtracting 1.61 from all data points (2.61 is the minimum value overall within the four time points), I can apply a simple transformation (again, square root or $\lambda = 0.50$). While it might not look like the change over time is as substantial as prior to transformation, the results are similarly strong: $F_{(3, 297)} = 1363.39$, $p < .0001$, eta-squared $= .93$.

Likewise, it might be tempting to use a different λ on each time point to optimally transform each one to normality. Doing that, however, violates the rule of treating all time points equally. If you decide to transform one time point with $\lambda = 1.75$, you must do the same for all other time points.

The tricky part in dealing with repeated measures data is that it is not always the case that all points in time are equally nonnormal. In some examples I have seen, it is possible that of four repeated measures, only one is significantly nonnormal, and applying a transformation that normalizes the one time point causes significant nonnormality in the other three. In repeated measures, it is an art to arrive at the best decision for all time points. It might be the case that you must leave data from one time point nonnormal in order to keep the others normally distributed. Or it might be the case that you must choose a more mild transformation that does the most good for some points while doing the least harm for other time points. Again, the key is to decide what is best for all repeated measures and treat them all equally.

WHAT TO DO WITH EXTREME SCORES?

Given the discussion in Chapter 7, you might be under the impression that if you have an extreme score it should be removed. The problem with this in a repeated measures framework (particularly repeated measures ANOVA) is that person would be removed from the entire analysis if they have missing data at one time point. So by removing an outlier from one time point, you essentially remove that person from the entire analysis, which may be undesirable, particularly in small-sample situations.

As mentioned in Chapter 7, an extreme score might occur for many reasons, and that is no different in repeated measures analyses. It is possible the score is a legitimate one. It is possible that it was a data entry error, caused by carelessness on the part of the participant, sample contamination, and so forth. You, the researcher, must determine whether you can fix the extreme score through correcting a mistake in data entry, contacting the person to verify the value of the observation, or through inference. If not, you should determine the costs and benefits of keeping the individual in the data set.

Truncation is a possible solution in cases in which it is not possible to correct the error and where it is not desirable to remove the individual completely from the analysis. Extremely low or high scores can be corrected to be equivalent to the next most extreme score, which maintains the ordinal order of the data without some of the drawbacks of having such an extreme score. This technique involves altering the actual data you are analyzing, and so should be performed with caution. And researchers should always report having done this, with a justification for keeping the individual in the data set under these altered conditions.

Another potential strategy might be to delete the data point and attempt to use appropriate missing data techniques to impute a more appropriate score. Again, this is only defensible in cases where it is obvious that the extreme value is illegitimate and it is important to keep the individual in the data set.

In this case, multiple imputation or strong imputation from closely correlated variables would be most appropriate.

Examination of standardized residuals is valuable to data cleaning with repeated measures as with other analyses. It is always possible that analyses can be biased by the inclusion of an individual who appears relatively extreme compared to others at a particular time point.

Finally, one can use modern methods of analyses to explore repeated measures. Some modern methodologies, such as hierarchical linear modeling (Raudenbush & Bryk, 2002) do not require complete data at all time points, and thus can manage these situations effectively.

MISSING DATA

Recalling that traditional repeated measures analyses require complete data, missing values on one time point can cause an individual to be removed from the entire analysis. However, appropriate intervention with missing data can prevent the biases that might be introduced by complete case analysis of repeated measures.

One of the advantages of missing data analysis in repeated measures designs is that the researcher often has very closely correlated data (data from the same person at different time points) in order to impute reasonable scores. This is often a case of strong single imputation, and can be very effective in multiple imputation frameworks as well. I would encourage researchers employing repeated measures designs to utilize imputation to deal with missingness (or to use hierarchical linear modeling, which again does not require complete data at all time points for all participants).

SUMMARY

I hope these brief thoughts are of value to those of you wanting to perform due diligence on your data cleaning in repeated measures contexts. I hope to elaborate and provide examples in future versions of this chapter. In the meantime, remember the prime directive: treat all time points identically. And keep participants with missing data in the data set via imputation or use of alternative analysis strategies (where appropriate).

NOTES

1. Sphericity is an assumption in repeated measures that relates to equality of variance across time points. It is rarely met in practice without transformation.

REFERENCES

Raudenbush, S. W., & Bryk, A. S. (2002). *Hierarchical linear models: Applications and data analysis methods* (Vol. 1). Thousand Oaks, CA: Sage.

⚜ THIRTEEN ⚜

NOW THAT THE MYTHS ARE DEBUNKED . . .

Visions of Rational Quantitative Methodology for the 21st Century

Throughout this book I have led you on an exploration of some of the important issues researchers need to consider (a) before beginning data collection and (b) after data collection but before analysis of the data. These are not all the issues and decisions that a good, ethical researcher will face, but they represent some of the most common ones (in my opinion).

We have explored 10 different myths that statisticians and quantitative researchers seem to hold (as evidenced by their actions and publications). My hope is that by this point you are convinced of the following.

1. It is important to plan for data analysis by carefully considering how many participants you might need to achieve your goals. I hope this saves you from wasted effort collecting too much data and saves you from the frustration of collecting insufficient data to adequately test your hypotheses.

2. It is vitally important to consider how you will collect your sample of data, and how that will meet your original goals for the study. I hope I have convinced you to carefully consider defining your population and the need to carefully craft your sampling plan so that your results will speak to the issues and population(s) to which you originally wanted to speak.

3. It is important to understand the sampling framework of any large secondary data sets you plan to use, and it is important to account for that information in planning your analyses. If you are exploring large national or

international data sets, weights and design effects will be your constant companions—if you want your analyses to be generalizable and accurate.

4. Assumptions are important and should be tested (and met) prior to interpreting the substantive results of any analysis you might perform. Most of the analyses you are likely to perform in the 21st century are *not robust* to violations of assumptions, particularly the complex multivariate analyses we tend to enjoy using these days. Even when procedures are robust to violations, your results are more likely to be accurate and replicable if they are met.

5. Data screening is important and relatively easy. I hope I have convinced you by this point that careful screening of your data can pay large dividends in terms of the goodness of your results. Contrary to common belief, it is not a waste of time. What *is* a waste of time is spending a great deal of resources collecting data, only to have the results be misestimated, leading to erroneous conclusions that could have been prevented by simple data cleaning.

6. Missing data can not only be useful as an object of analysis itself, but can add value and accuracy to analyses if dealt with appropriately. Statistical software *rarely* deals with missing data appropriately by default, but it is not terribly difficult to deal with appropriately if you know how.

7. It is important to examine your data for extreme or influential data points. Your results *will not be more accurate or replicable* if you leave extreme scores in your analysis. There are simple ways to deal with extreme scores based on why you think they are extreme, and sometimes extreme data points can lead your research in unexpected and important directions.

8. Results are more accurate and replicable if assumptions of normality are met. Though using Box-Cox transformations, many difficult variables can be successfully normalized. It is worthwhile to take a few minutes to normalize variables prior to conducting your hypothesis testing.

9. Reliability matters. The better your reliability, the more accurate and generalizable your results. We often accept poor reliability for our measures when modern analyses (such as structural equation modeling) can accurately model relationships even with unruly variables.

10. Not all data points are equally representative of the population to which you wish to speak. Not all subjects give you high-quality data, and failure to distinguish between those giving high-quality data and low-quality

data can dramatically undermine the odds of having replicable, accurate results.

11. Dichotomizing continuous variables is almost always a bad idea, and almost always leads to misestimation of effects. You should be particularly skeptical of logistic regression analyses that incorporate dichotomized continuous variables, as authors may be trying to inappropriately inflate the perceived importance of a variable.

12. If you are engaging in repeated measures analyses, it is critically important that you be very thoughtful about data cleaning, as the identical procedures must be performed on each repeated measure or you can cause errors in your analyses.

As I say in Chapter 1, none of this is all that revolutionary, and almost none of this information is new (although I do hope it is presented in such a way that you are thinking in new ways about these old issues). We, as scientists, may have become seduced by the power and ease of statistical computing in the latter half of the 20th century, and we need to all remain thoughtful and careful about what it is we do. It does not take a lot of effort to implement these simple planning and data cleaning steps into your routine, yet it might help you contribute more productively to the scientific literature. I hope I have demonstrated the value of considering each of these practices as important prior to the point at which you are testing your hypotheses and drawing conclusions.

It is possible you might disagree with me after reading some of my suggestions. I am under no illusion that I have all the answers for all circumstances. Like many of you reading this, I am always open to improving my ideas, particularly where I am attempting to describe best practices. If you think I have gotten something wrong, and you can demonstrate it empirically, I welcome your feedback and empirical demonstration. If I agree with you, I will feature your correction or exception on the website for this book, incorporate it into the next revision of this book, and prominently acknowledge your contribution to the literature. Or I may invite you to coauthor an article exploring the issue. As I mention in Chapter 1, my e-mail address is: jasonwosborne@gmail.com, and I welcome your comments and suggestions.

Statistical analysis and quantitative research is a vast field that is constantly evolving. We must remain humble and open to learning new ideas and techniques, remembering that our goal is not self-aggrandizement but rather improvement of the human condition for current and future generations.

Toward this end, I call on journal editors and peer reviewers to begin mandating authors address these basic issues of research quality in every article, detailing the results of tests of important assumptions, data screening and cleaning steps undertaken (and results), enumerating missing data and describing how they were dealt with, and so forth. If our goal is quality and replicability of research findings, and if you believe I have convincingly demonstrated the value of these steps in achieving that goal, then it is time to become more prescriptive in submission guidelines. Note that most of these issues can be dealt with in a few brief sentences, so there is little implication for journal space or article length.

I also would ask scholarly conferences who aspire to present high-quality research to consider requiring proposals to include brief descriptions of actions taken regarding these issues. Researchers consistently performing these simple steps are more likely to have useful, replicable, accurate results to share.

SUBJECT INDEX

Aggregation errors, 46–48, 49 (figure)
Alpha, 192–193, 194, 201
Analysis of variance.
   See ANOVA analyses
ANOVA analyses, 3–5, 90
   effect of extreme scores on, 161–165
   identification of extreme scores,
     152–153
   null effect in, 78–79
   reliability influencing, 205–206
   research on, 5–8
A posteriori power, 20, 21–22
Appropriately modeled (AM)
   software, 77
A priori power, 20, 34
Arcsine transformation, 174–175
Assumptions, testing, 8
Available case analysis, 117

Bell-shaped curve, 87
Best practices, 10–11
   in accounting for complex sampling,
     74–76
   missing or incomplete
     data, 130–131
   power and, 20–22
   random responding, 225
   reliability, 207–208
Bias, sampling, 54–56, 146
Binary logistic regression,
   77–78, 79 (table)
Bivariate extreme scores, 151,
   159–160
Box-Cox transformations, 171, 174,
   175–176, 181–184, 262
   application and efficacy of, 176–181
Bureau of Justice Statistics, 72

Categorical gorups
   of variables, 246
Categories of missingness,
   109–110
Ceiling effect, 59–60, 92–93
Centers for Disease Control and
   Prevention (CDC), 72
Cluster sampling, 73
Complex sampling
   best practices in accounting for,
     74–76
   importance of, 72–74
   types of studies using, 72
   weighted data in, 75, 76–80
Composite scores, 121–122
Consent procedures, 54–56
Consistency, internal, 192
Cook's distance, 160
Correlation
   coefficients, 31–33
   effect of extreme scores
     on, 156–161
   partial, 195–196, 197 (table)
   reliability and simple, 193–195
Cronbach's alpha, 192–193,
   194, 201
Curvilinearity, 246

Data, weighted, 75, 76–81
Databases, publicly
   available, 71–72
Data cleaning
   assessment of research in,
     5–8, 8–10
   best practices and, 10–11
   fixing sampling problems with,
     33–34

⑤SAGE research methods online

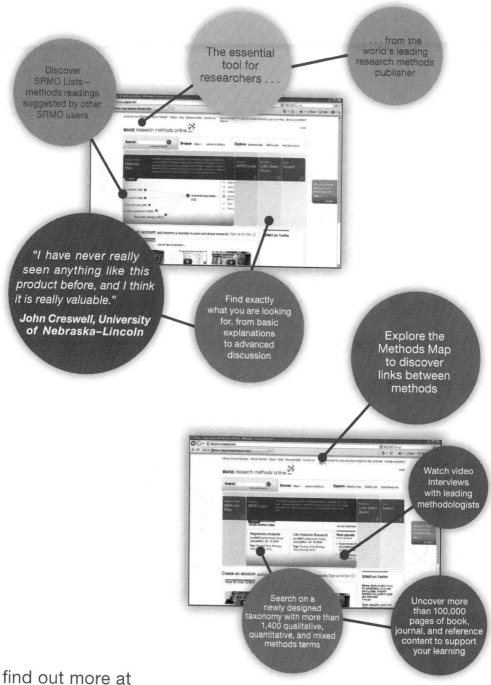

Discover SRMO Lists—methods readings suggested by other SRMO users

The essential tool for researchers . . .

. . . from the world's leading research methods publisher

"I have never really seen anything like this product before, and I think it is really valuable."

John Creswell, University of Nebraska–Lincoln

Find exactly what you are looking for, from basic explanations to advanced discussion

Explore the Methods Map to discover links between methods

Watch video interviews with leading methodologists

Search on a newly designed taxonomy with more than 1,400 qualitative, quantitative, and mixed methods terms

Uncover more than 100,000 pages of book, journal, and reference content to support your learning

find out more at
www.srmo.sagepub.com

Made in the USA
Lexington, KY
19 March 2018